PR
457
C35

Chandler

A dream of order.

71-663

A DREAM OF ORDER

A Dream of Order

The Medieval Ideal in
Nineteenth-Century English Literature

ALICE CHANDLER

UNIVERSITY OF NEBRASKA PRESS · LINCOLN

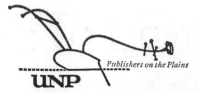

Publishers on the Plains

Copyright © 1970 by the University of Nebraska Press
All Rights Reserved
International Standard Book Number 0–8032–0704–2
Library of Congress Catalog Card Number 69–10413

First printing: May 1970
Second printing: June 1971

Manufactured in the United States of America

To the memory of my father

Contents

ACKNOWLEDGMENTS   ix

INTRODUCTION   1

1   Origins of Medievalism: Scott   12

2   Historical Background: Cobbett   52

3   Broadening the Vision: The Lake Poets and Some Contemporaries   83

4   Faith and Order: Carlyle   122

5   Medievalism in Action: Young England and Disraeli   152

6   Art and Society: Ruskin and Morris   184

7   The Failure of the Vision: Adams   231

BIBLIOGRAPHY   249

INDEX   265

Acknowledgments

I should like to express my gratitude to Professors Jerome Hamilton Buckley, Kent Hieatt, Emery Neff, Marshall Suther, and William Wieler, all of whom helped me in the earlier stages of this book. My thanks go, too, to my friends and family for their long patience and encouragement.

ALICE CHANDLER

The City College of New York

A DREAM OF ORDER

Introduction

THE MEDIEVAL REVIVAL was a complex and yet coherent movement. Like the Romantic movement, which helped foster it and which it partly shaped, it is hard to define and delimit, and yet it was always a recognizable entity and unmistakable tradition. Although medievalism involved varying and sometimes contradictory ideas and programs, its basic aims remained very similar throughout an existence that stretched from the Renaissance into modern times and that embraced England, the Continent, and even America. Its manifestations can be traced in art and architecture, literature and philosophy, economics and sociology, politics and religion. At the height of the revival scarcely an aspect of life remained untouched by medievalist influence. The very beds people slept in were apt to be Gothic. But behind all these varying expressions of a medievalizing imagination lay a single, central desire—to feel at home in an ordered yet organically vital universe. The more the world changed, and the period of the medieval revival was an era of ever accelerating social transformation, the more the partly historical but basically mythical Middle Ages that had become a tradition in literature served to remind men of a Golden Age. The Middle Ages were idealized as a period of faith, order, joy, munificence, and creativity. Feudalism was seen as fatherhood, and the medieval world—to adopt Carlyle's phrase—was thought to be "godlike and my Father's." The Middle Ages became a metaphor both for a specific social order and, somewhat more vaguely, for a metaphysically harmonious world view.

As a social and political ideal the Middle Ages were usually invoked as a corrective to the evils of the present. The various phases of the medieval revival can usually be correlated with contemporary changes or revolutions in the structure of society, whose faults suggested the need for a counterbalancing appeal to the past. The earliest medievalism of the Elizabethan period arose in response to the rapid shifts in politics and religion that characterized the sixteenth century. Writers of the period used the Middle Ages to provide authority for these changes— to show that the Protestant Reformation was really an outgrowth of the historic English church and that the Tudors were really the legitimate claimants to the medieval monarchy. The Elizabethans differed from their successors in their approaches to the past, since they used the Middle Ages to support change rather than challenge it. By the seventeenth century, however, medievalism had taken what would become a more familiar turn and was used to oppose the current tendencies. The depredations of Cromwell's soldiers during the Civil War, their destruction of churches, monasteries, and ancient buildings, enhanced the value of the past. Societies were formed to study and preserve the ancient monuments whose importance was suddenly real- ized now that they were disappearing, and the discarded customs of the past were made objects of interest and veneration. An even more significant influence on seventeenth-century medievalism was the "Glorious Revolution" of 1688, which limited the power of the monarchy. Peaceful as it was, this revolution bred two new attitudes toward the Middle Ages: first, a Whiggish celebration of the antiquity of British freedom; and second, and ultimately more influential, a Tory regret for the rejected feudal past.

During the eighteenth century, as social and economic changes accelerated, the Middle Ages became increasingly idealized. By the end of the century the rise of industrialism had created a very obvious nostalgia for the past. But even earlier in the century the apparent destruction of the yeoman class, traditionally seen as the backbone of England's greatness, had helped to create a newly resolute medievalism, characterized by a longing for ancient customs and traditions. William Cobbett, himself a yeoman born, is the archexemplar of the period, and his regret for a pastoral, more prosperous, smock-frocked England captures the spirit of the age.

The idea that the common man had been materially better off in medieval times continued in the next century when writers began to criticize the condition of factory workers. Throughout the nineteenth century medievalists expressed horror over the degraded and impoverished condition of the industrial proletariat, working an eighty-four-hour week in lint-choked factories and living in sickness-breeding, filthy hovels. They believed that by comparison to the modern wage slave, even a thirteenth-century serf was fortunate. But the medievalism of the period also sounds a deeper note of dismay. It is not just the hunger, the disease, the exploitation of the worker that begin to appear in medievalist writers, but a sense of the loss of connection within society itself. In contrast to the alienated and divisive atmosphere of an increasingly urbanized and industrialized society, the Middle Ages were seen as familial and patriarchal. The feudal structure was said to give each man his place in society and, despite many tyrannous and cruel exceptions among its leaders, to have provided men with responsible masters. Within small units, too—the home, the farm, the craftsman's workshop—medievalists also saw a lost sense of closeness. Farmer and laborer, apprentice, journeyman, and master were all said to have been linked together in the past by reciprocal ties now shattered by the social atomism of laissez faire economics. One of the leitmotifs of late eighteenth-century and early nineteenth-century medievalist writing is the complaint that farmers and field hands no longer dine together and that the farmers now give their employees money rather than food—a financial rather than a familial nexus.

The idea of connection as one of the elements belonging to the world that has been lost repeats and intensifies itself throughout the nineteenth century. Robert Southey uses it over and over again in his comparison between medieval times and modern, and Carlyle finds the lack of human ties one of the most appalling symptoms of contemporary life. In one of his most shocking passages in *Past and Present*, he symbolizes this alienation and the human destruction it causes by telling the story of the Irish widow who, after being rejected in her applications for help, proves her membership in humanity by infecting seventeen of her neighbors with typhus. Disraeli summed up the

3

feelings of his generation when he wrote of the "two nations—the rich and the poor."

Nowhere are the differences between a competitive and unorganized rather than a communal and regulated economic system shown more succinctly than in the works of Karl Marx, who traces the existence of a debased and deracinated proletariat to the ending of the feudal system. Although he also writes of his opposition to the medieval revival and to the Middle Ages themselves, this passage from *The Communist Manifesto* is a perfect statement of what medievalism stood for in Victorian times:

> The bourgeoisie, wherever it has got the upper hand, has put an end to all feudal, patriarchal, idyllic relations. It has pitilessly torn asunder the motley feudal ties that bound man to his *natural superiors*, and has left remaining no other nexus between man and man than naked self-interest, than callous *cash-payment*. It has drowned the most heavenly ecstasies of religious fervour, of chivalrous enthusiasm, of philistine sentimentalism, in the icy water of egotistical calculation. It has resolved personal worth into exchange value, and in place of the numerous indefeasible chartered freedoms, has set up that single unconscionable freedom—Free Trade.

Although nineteenth-century medievalists were sympathetic to the sufferings of the poor, they were also fearful of that very revolution which Marx predicted was inevitable. Medievalism was a response to the ever growing problems arising from the Industrial Revolution, but it was also a reaction to the shock waves of the French Revolution and to the threat of violent rebellion that hung over the whole post-Napoleonic period. While all the writers in the medieval tradition pitied the worker, they were also afraid of him. Regretting the separation of classes, they nevertheless regarded the poor as an alien and dangerous race. The word *Jacquerie* crops up many times in the writings of such authors as Scott, Southey, and Wordsworth and always evokes a negative reaction. Most "new feudalists" believed that the poor must be given compassionate leadership because they needed it and also because they would engage in uncontrollably destructive rioting without it. This ambivalence toward the poor makes the compound epithet Tory-Radical an apt one for the writers here considered. Forward-looking in economics, with a view of the state that foreshadowed the paternalism of the twentieth century, they were unable to accept even the partial democracy of the 1832 and 1867 Reform Bills.

These seeming contradictions in medievalist thought were grounded, however, upon a consistent view of human nature. With few exceptions, medievalist writers shared a pessimistic attitude toward man. They saw him as a fallible, selfish creature, dominated by emotion rather than reason, and prone to weakness, error, and greed. They believed that society controlled man's selfishness by forcing him to accede to the social contract and that tradition reduced his fallibility by making experience his guide. A return to the Middle Ages thus became a way of reorganizing man into a closely knit and organic social structure that could engage his emotions and loyalties with a wealth of traditions and customs. Transformed from a mode of criticism into a program of action, the medievalism of the mid-nineteenth century demanded a renewed commitment from the "natural leaders" of society. The upper classes and the Church were asked to bestir themselves once again and to restore that great chain of feudalism in which each of the estates of the realm owed reciprocal allegiance to the others. Only under such guidance, they believed, could the disintegration of society be checked and the rule of order revived.

As it manifested itself among the wealthy and well-born, the program of Victorian medievalism was characterized by its antiutilitarian bias, particularly in economics. The laissez faire doctrine that the utilitarians espoused was based on the theory that individual selfishness —"looking out for Number One," as Dickens termed it—was the mainspring of the social mechanism. The economy flourished when those who had money enjoyed it and when those who wished to acquire money competed for it. Any interference in the clockwork operation of profit and loss was only a sentimental hindrance to prosperity. In contrast to this relatively new conception of political economy, ultimately grounded in eighteenth-century rationalism, medievalists adhered to the time-honored theory of conditional wealth. Handed down from the Middle Ages, and Biblical in origin, it sought to overcome man's innate selfishness by stating that rights entailed responsibilities and that the possession of wealth or rank implied the fulfillment of corresponding duties. This glorification of *noblesse oblige*, as opposed to self-interest, fitted easily with such widespread Victorian ideas as sacrifice and renunciation. It was particularly appealing to the youthful aristocrats of the Young England party, who, influenced by the novels of Scott, attempted to transform antiutilitarian medievalism into practical political activity. But the general idea that those who have power must use it to serve the less fortunate colors the whole medieval movement and can be found most explicitly during the Victorian period in the works of Carlyle, Disraeli, and Ruskin. Although the aristocrats they refer to are usually those of the land, the new Captains of Industry are also enjoined to accept their responsibilities and to institute a neo-feudal paternalism in their factories.

The activities of the Church, too, were influenced by medievalism. If the first estate, or the nobility, was expected by medievalist writers to devote itself to what Ruskin called *largesse*, the second estate, or clergy, was also expected to fulfill a social function. The whole of the nineteenth century was filled with debates over the role of the Church and a constant outcry over its inadequacy. One of the forms this criticism took was a comparison between medieval and modern religious institutions. The medieval Catholic church was praised for performing a valuable social purpose in uniting all men in worship and using its wealth to give alms and succor to the poor. The modern Anglican church was attacked for neglecting its duties and becoming more a fashionable establishment than a meaningful social organization. The same drive that moved toward a revitalization of the upper classes in terms of their supposed role in the Middle Ages also led to a demand for renewal on the part of the Church.

As the lot of the poor started to improve toward the end of the century, and as various national and municipal organizations began to fill in the vacuum left by the decline of the manor and parish as administrative units, medievalism changed its focus. Its emphasis was not on the deprivation or alienation of the masses, although these themes continued to be important, but on the quality of life in a mechanical society. Comparing the lot of the medieval workman with that of his modern counterpart, Ruskin argued that the artisan of the Middle Ages was both happier and freer. He was not simply the tool of a tool—an automaton operating a machine or executing another's commands—but a creative agent, able to find joy in his work. It was for this reason, Ruskin and Morris thought, that medieval art was so much greater than modern, for it was the product of a society closer to nature—one that allowed man to record, in permanently beautiful forms, his perception of a harmonious universe.

The association of such ideas as nature, harmony, creativity, and joy with medievalism points up the other major aspect of the medieval revival, its attempt to create a coherent world view. As we have seen, medievalism was a response to historic change and to the problems raised by the various revolutions and transformations of the eighteenth and nineteenth centuries. But medievalism was also simultaneously a part of that vast intellectual and emotional response to change which we somewhat fuzzily denominate Romanticism. As such it had links to the renaissance of interest in nature, primitivism, and the supernatural and to the increasing valuation placed upon the organic, the joyous, and the creative. Just as medievalism was very much a part of the desire to give man a sense of social and political belonging, so it was also an attempt, in the decline of any transcendental order, to naturalize man in the universe and make him feel related to it. It was opposed to the Newtonian and Lockean view of the universe as a vast machine in which man was a subordinate mechanism moved by pleasure and pain. As part of the Romantic contradiction of these concepts, medievalism substituted a picture of man as a dynamic and generous creature, capable of loyal feeling and heroic action. Far from being isolated from nature, medieval man was seen as part of it, and his chivalry mirrored its benevolence. In its hostility to a mechanistic metaphysics, medievalism as a philosophical movement thus paralleled its opposition to machinery on economic and social grounds. Both aspects of medievalism—the

7

political and the metaphysical—saw materialism and mechanization as inimical to the human. The return to the Middle Ages was conceived of as a homecoming.

For all its eventual breadth and depth, medievalism as an expression of man's need to create at least the myth of a coherent universe often seemed to have quite trivial origins. In poetry and antiquarianism it began as a restatement of the mutability theme, a lament for lost times that was often tinged by a vague supernaturalism. Ruined churches by moonlight and forsaken graveyards and tombstones were among its most frequent elements; hence most medievalist verse of the eighteenth century was termed "Graveyard Poetry." The Gothic novel, too, which initiated a medieval revival in fiction, was also dependent upon melancholy and supernaturalism and often designed to create a sense of terror. Even the medievally inspired pseudo-Gothic architecture of the period shows the same *ubi sunt* motif and the same desire to titillate the emotions.

In all these aspects early medievalism sometimes seems rather a sham, certainly a rather banal exercise of the imagination. And yet these attempts to create a sense of the remote, forgotten past and to arouse a sense of horror, or at least of wonder, were far from insignificant, for they allowed the reader to experience in his imagination a world beyond the real. Medievalism forced man to imagine a totally different society instead of merely aquiescing in his own. From this vicariously medieval world of heightened action and feeling he could then return to question his own conventional existence and the mechanistic assumptions on which it was based. His role-playing in the past had expanded his perspective for judging the present. It is no accident that the villains of eighteenth-century Gothic fiction and the nineteenth-century medievalist novel are often calculating rationalists, for rationalism and calculation—like utilitarianism and laissez faire—were precisely the forces that opposed the emotionally based approach to life that the medievalists were seeking.

In its allegiance with nature, too, medievalism shows its connection with the deepest currents of the Romantic search for meaning. Although originally condemned in the early eighteenth century as barbaric and restrictive, medieval architecture and, by extension, medieval life were soon linked with nature. The very irregularity, asymmetry, and plenitude of Gothic architecture came to be a sign of its organic structure and thus of its closeness to nature. Toward the end of the eighteenth century medieval people became associated with the natural and thereby with the heroic, the vital, and the creative. As earlier people living in a less artificial period, they were thought to be closer to their feelings and freer and more unconstrained than modern man. In contrast to the classic, which was measured, rational, and calm, the medieval came to represent boundless energy and aspiration. The Gothic arch, for instance, was associated with both these ideas. It was said to be an imitation of the interlaced branches of a forest and was thus natural in shape. It also pointed skyward and hence emblematized aspiration. It seemed to show the medieval artist embracing nature and expressing his inner freedom in the architectural forms he chose. Again, the correspondences to the socio-historical aspects of medievalism are clear : the admiration of natural forms parallels the regret for the loss of a pastoral England, while the concept of aspiration echoes the late eighteenth-century belief in medieval freedom.

In the nineteenth century the various emotional needs fulfilled by medievalism became complex indeed. Writers of both the Anglo-Catholic and Roman Catholic revivals invoked the spirit of medieval times to inspire a renewal of religious feeling at the same time that they appealed to the structure of the medieval church to restore its social responsibilities. Both in England and on the Continent, the rituals and ornaments of medieval Catholicism were reintroduced in the hope that they would serve to stimulate a medieval intensity of belief. Once again man was using medieval myth or metaphor to establish a connection between himself and the universe.

While the Tractarians and others were making this attempt through formal religion, other writers were trying to achieve a renewal of faith through a more secular appeal to the medieval spirit. Carlyle, for example, shattered by eighteenth-century Scottish rationalism, with its purely clockwork view of the Creation, sought first in the German medievalists and then in his own English medieval background for a basis to renew his faith. Ruskin, too, for all his moments of despair, shows the use of the Middle Ages as a symbol not just of an ordered society but of an ordered and meaningful, basically fatherly, cosmos.

The fundamental assumption behind Ruskin's medievalism that the paternalistic and benevolent structure of society in the Middle Ages echoed the paternalistic and benevolent structure of nature returns us once again to the unifying theme of the entire medieval revival: that by reanimating the spirit of the medieval past man could find himself a home. But while the adoption of the medievalist social and economic programs did help to accomplish the transition from pure laissez faire capitalism to various modern forms of the protective or welfare state, the metaphysical attempt to find in medievalism the guide to an understandable and approachable universe failed completely. Nowhere is the failure made clearer than in Henry Adams's *Mont-Saint-Michel and Chartres*, in some ways the loveliest and saddest of all medievalist works. Using the Virgin Mary and St. Thomas Aquinas as his symbols, Adams shows that neither love, nor freedom, nor order can be at the heart of the universe, however much man may wish them to be there. What was a living faith for the Middle Ages can be only the memory of a myth for contemporary man. Not surprisingly, the book ends with the triumph of the machine—the symbol of purposeless power and the antithesis of human hopes.

Any evaluation of the medieval movement as a whole must take into account both its aspects—its use as a social and political ideal and its symbolic value as a metaphor of belief. It must also take into account all kinds of peripheral manifestations of the interest in the Middle Ages: its dependency on historical writings, its influence in art and decoration, its manifestations in popular fiction and poetry, and its inevitable attraction for parodists. Whatever else medievalism accomplished, it changed the face of England and, to a lesser degree, of America and the Continent, too, leaving to this day in churches and colleges, public buildings and railroad stations, a visual record of its predominance. I have tried in the opening sections of each chapter to give some sense of the scope of the medieval revival by surveying its varying manifestations both in England and on the Continent. In this way I have hoped to place the medieval revival in its larger intellectual matrix. I have also tried to show how the individual writers under consideration fit into a continuing medievalist tradition. But my major attempt has been to trace the growth and meaning of the medievalist ideal through a detailed study of the books that proclaimed it.

Because the medievalist movement was so widespread and pervasive, its impact is difficult to evaluate. We can trace its influence from Sir Walter Scott to the Young England movement and thence to the social legislation of the Disraeli administration; or we can follow it through the works of Carlyle, Ruskin and Morris to the socialism of Clement Attlee and the British Labour party. But the aftereffects of medievalism were not caused by medievalism alone. The paternalistic legislation of the latter part of the nineteenth century and, of course, of the whole twentieth century, was an inevitable response to the problems of a complex industrial society which could no longer survive without guidance. Medievalism was influential because it fitted in with the dominant pattern of the age. It provided the most relevant answer that the past could offer to the problems of a new society. Thus, while we may admire the medievalists for their philanthropy or criticize them for their patronizing and fearful attitude toward the common man, we must always consider their ideas as part of a larger social movement still being acted out today.

We must also think of the larger pattern in considering medievalism as a search for faith and order. Medievalism had ultimately to fail, not because it did not see far enough, but because it asked too much. Neither modern science nor contemporary social developments gave man any grounds for believing that he was at home in the universe. Medievalism was one of the last great outflarings of the religious spirit, of man's need to believe that he belonged. But as Henry Adams said, faith alone could support the Gothic arch. In contrast to the certainties of the Middle Ages, modern life seemed to offer only broken lines and meaningless energies.

I

Origins of Medievalism: Scott

IT WAS a nineteenth-century commonplace that the medieval revival had begun with Sir Walter Scott, but the commonplace was only half true. Quite as much as Scott's poems and novels had created much of the medievalism that followed, they were themselves the product of more than two centuries' investigation of the feudal past. Starting as far back as the Elizabethan era, when England was still in some ways a medieval state, the study of the Middle Ages had continued to develop throughout the seventeenth and eighteenth centuries. Scott brought this interest to a focus by creating a completely believable medieval world, which he portrayed so vividly and attractively that many of his readers took it for historical truth rather than historical fiction. For almost a century after Scott began to write, Englishmen not only read and reread his novels but tried to recreate them in reality by building houses with battlements and churches with flying buttresses. By late Victorian times there was hardly a city in England without some brand-new Gothic edifice. More significantly, the Middle Ages became idealized and in the works of writers such as Southey, Carlyle, and Ruskin, to name but a few, were used as a standard by which to measure and modify current-day life. Neither Scott nor the later medievalists would have been able to popularize the Middle Ages, however, were it not for the era in which they wrote. Medievalism was a philosophy rather than a fad because it satisfied the nation's needs. It brought to an increasingly urbanized, industrialized, and atomistic society, the vision of a more stable and harmonious social order, substituting the paternal benevolence of manor and guild for the harshness of city and factory and offering the clear air and open fields of the medieval past in place of the blackening skies of England.

In a sense, the Middle Ages had never died, even in Scott's time. Although the enclosure acts had crisscrossed the English countryside with hedgerows and dotted it with flocks of sheep, Chaucer's plowman would have found England's rural life very familiar. The tools and produce of agriculture had scarcely changed for centuries; the old country customs and festivals were only slowly dying out; and the whir of the spinning wheel had just begun to grow silent. By the 1790s farmers no longer ate side by side with their workmen, but the abandonment of the old feudal relationship still caused comment. Medieval art forms had remained alive, too, except in the city, where popular tradition had become rootless and denatured. In the country and at such places as Oxford, the Gothic tradition of building survived right through the neoclassical period. The old tales of Bevis of Hampton and Guy of Warwick, long condemned by cultivated critics as "barbaric," kept their place at the rural fireside until their "simple grandeur" was rediscovered; and the same pattern held true for folk songs and ballads.

But while the populace would have been astonished to discover it was being medieval, more sophisticated minds had been investigating the Middle Ages practically from the moment that they ended. Some of this early historicism was motivated by a purely antiquarian concern for a vanished and vanishing era, but much of it was propagandistic, using the medieval past as an authority to support the Tudor throne and the Anglican church. Even before the reign of Elizabeth, such historians as Edward Hall were looking back at the Middle Ages for lessons in statecraft, while ecclesiastical writers made use of the existence of a medieval English church to bolster their arguments for separation from Rome. John Foxe, for instance, prefaced an edition of the Anglo-Saxon gospels with the statement that the new Anglican church was "no new reformation of things lately begun, but rather a reduction of the Church to the pristine state of old conformity." [1]

[1] Quoted in René Wellek, *The Rise of English Literary History* (Chapel Hill, N. C.: University of North Carolina Press, 1941), p. 17.

Other churchmen based similar arguments on different pre-Conquest writings. Archbishop Parker, in particular, founder of the Society of Antiquaries and a mighty collector of books, published such works as Aelfric's epistles and Asser's *Life of Alfred* to justify the Anglican establishment.

Since all this work presupposed a reading knowledge of Anglo-Saxon, lectureships in that language were established at Oxford and Cambridge during the seventeenth century, was stimulating the publication of many Old English texts. The poetry of Caedmon and portions of the Anglo-Saxon psalter, chronicles, and Heptateuch, all appeared between 1640 and 1692, as did an Anglo-Saxon dictionary and grammar. The most outstanding of these linguistic studies was George Hickes's *Linguarum Veterum Septentrionalium Thesaurus Grammatico-Criticus et Archaeologicus* (1705), a work that has never been wholly superseded. Middle English, too, came in for study in the eighteenth century, as did the language and literature of other medieval and primitive peoples. Although specialized in themselves, these studies often had literary repercussions. Thomas Gray, for example, was stimulated by the increased knowledge about earlier civilizations to write imitations of all sorts of primitive poetry, including Norse, Provençal, Welsh, and medieval Spanish—a striking instance of the interrelationship of scholarship and literature.

Collections of documents also helped build up knowledge about the Middle Ages. John Leland, who was commissioned king's antiquary by Henry VIII, spent many years gathering records, manuscripts, and other relics from the colleges, monasteries, and cathedrals that his master was despoiling. Work such as his was also done in the sixteenth and seventeenth centuries by William Camden, Sir Robert Cotton, Archbishop Ussher, and Isaac Casaubon. Thomas Rymer's *Foedera* (1704–35), which presented documents covering six centuries of English foreign affairs, started providing source material for medieval history at about the same time that Robert Harley, earl of Oxford, began collecting what was to become the famed Harleian Miscellany of more than 400,000 books and manuscripts. All through the eighteenth century the newly developed interest in the past stimulated a concern

14

for its records. Old parchments and vellum sheets and volumes found their way into the hands of private bibliophiles and antiquarians and then often filtered into the larger, more public collections. Such materials led to a greatly increased understanding of the Middle Ages. They also led to the reissuing of many works and records long lost from public view. By the end of the eighteenth century the existence of these documents had made possible a historiography of the Middle Ages that was still wildly inaccurate and biased at times but far in advance of the near ignorance and prejudice that had preceded it. Joseph Strutt, Robert Henry, and Sharon Turner were the foremost representatives of what amounted to a new historical school, and their impact on Scott and other later medievalists should not be underestimated.

Moreover, scholarship began to be organized. The London Society of Antiquaries was re-established in 1707 for the purpose of studying all memorials of English culture prior to the reign of James I. It was soon followed by societies in Peterborough, Doncaster, Stamford, and Worcester, whose members zealously, though unmethodically, collected information on ancient buildings, customs, and literature; helped preserve crumbling edifices; and collected fragments of the stained glass which was being destroyed by the enlightened taste of a generation that preferred bright and cheery churches. Assuredly, the activities of these amateurs were often naïve and inaccurate, on a par, as has been said, with the craze for "Giant Fungi and Greek Inscriptions." But their researches did pave the way for their better-equipped successors in the Roxburghe, Bannatyne, Camden, and Early English Text societies.

Owing to these societies, early medieval researches tended to be the property of gentleman antiquaries rather than scholars and were emotional rather than technical in intent. If the first wave of medievalism had begun during the Tudor period when a rising nationalism had stimulated an interest in England's heritage, the second wave seems traceable to the post-Cromwellian period when the end of the Civil War revealed the destruction of many monuments. Anthony à Wood, for instance, wrote of his regret for the depredations that Cromwell's armies had wrought in tearing down the towers of Oxford and daubing paint over the frescoes and ornaments in the Merton College choir. Together with his friend William Dugdale, whose *Antiquities of Warwickshire* (1656) had inspired Wood's own studies of the Oxford countryside, he initiated a concern for local history. Such histories continued to have vogue well into the nineteenth century and became almost a genre in themselves, usually marked by a pervasive melancholy. As Wood wrote upon viewing a pre-Norman abbey, "The place hath yet some ruins to shew, and to instruct the pensive beholder with an exemplary frailty."[2] His sentiment was echoed by another antiquary, Thomas Gent, who wrote that the "awful Ruins" of Kirkstall Abbey in Yorkshire "were enough to strike the most harden'd Heart into the softest and most serious Reflexion."[3] This concern for the past also led to a fortunate concern for its physical relics. The eighteenth century reveals many instances of buildings saved from destruction by zealous antiquaries. The ruins of Waverley Abbey were rescued just in time from a Farnham farmer who was demolishing them for paving stones.

The urge to save and to collect also manifested itself in literature. The more ancient and historically famous documents and literary works were, as we have seen, increasingly collected after the Tudor period, but as the eighteenth century wore on this interest in reclaiming lost works of literature extended itself to more popular works such as ballads. Scottish poetry was anthologized in Allan Ramsay's famous collection, *Evergreen*, in 1724, while the preceding year saw the appearance of a *Collection of Old Ballads*, generally ascribed to Ambrose Philips. Welsh poetry was directly translated for the first time in Evan Evan's *Some Specimens of the Poetry of the Ancient Welsh Bards* (1764). The best known of these anthologies, however, was Bishop Percy's *Reliques of Ancient English Poetry* (1765), which was vastly influential both in England and abroad, where it stimulated Continental collections of early verse and helped develop an interest in folk culture.

[2] Quoted in B. Sprague Allen, *Tides in English Taste (1619–1800)*, 2 vols. (Cambridge, Mass.: Harvard University Press, 1937), II, 51.

[3] Thomas Gent, *Antient and Modern History of the Loyal Town of Rippon* (York, 1733), p. 26 (second pagination).

What Percy had to say about medieval poetry is almost as important as the actual poetry he collected since it contributed to the idealization of chivalry that recurred in various forms for at least a century. He wrote that

> that fondness for going in quest of adventures, that spirit of challenging to single combat, that respectful complaisance shown to the fair sex . . . are all of Gothic origin, and may be traced to the earliest times among all the Northern nations. These existed long before the feudal ages, though they were called forth and strengthened in a peculiar manner under that constitution, and at length arrived to their full maturity in the times of the Crusades, so replete with romantic adventures.[4]

Percy's attitude is even more forcefully expressed in Richard Hurd's *Letters on Chivalry and Romance* (1760). Hurd's writings are particularly significant since they exhibit an underlying change in attitude toward the Middle Ages. Although medievalism had always to contend with anti-Catholicism as an adverse influence, the latter half of the eighteenth century saw this hostility gradually diminish. Instead of being viewed as periods of superstition, medieval times became linked with "nature" and thus with a desirable simplicity. As Hurd wrote in a passage that seems to mark the ending of an exclusively neoclassic ideal, Homer would have preferred the Middle Ages to his own times *"for the improved gallantry of the feudal times and the superior solemnity of their superstitions."*[5] This idea was echoed in *The History of English Poetry* (1774–81) by Thomas Warton, who claimed that medieval manners had "the same common merit with the pictures in Homer, that of being founded in truth and reality."[6]

Such a concern for the relics and values of the past had an influence on art as well as on these scholarly endeavors. How this concern,

[4] Thomas Percy, *Reliques of Ancient English Poetry*, 3 vols. (London, 1857), III, 3.

[5] Richard Hurd, *Hurd's Letters on Chivalry and Romance*, ed. Edith J. Morley (London: Henry Frowde, 1911), p. 108.

[6] Thomas Warton, *The History of English Poetry* (London, 1870), p. 34.

as applied to architecture, led first to the building of sham ruins and then to the construction and preservation of Gothic mansions and public buildings will be seen in a later chapter; for no consideration of eighteenth- and nineteenth-century medievalism can ignore the visual impact of the Gothic Revival in architecture. But the use of the Middle Ages as an ideal depended mainly upon a literary tradition of medievalism which developed during the middle of the eighteenth century as an outgrowth of earlier medieval scholarship. All kinds of influences —the nostalgia of the gentleman antiquaries, the scholarship of the historians, the primitivism of the folklorists—contributed to the growth of this literary medievalism, which made itself felt in all genres: poetry, fiction, and, to a lesser extent, drama. This literary medievalism, which gradually became more realistic, helped in its turn to build up a generally accepted sense of what the Middle Ages had been like and established the past as an imaginative entity with a life of its own. The existence of this imagined world, as George Herbert Mead has pointed out, provided a new area for romantic role-playing. By stepping back into this imagined past, the reader could extend his sense of self, vicariously live another life, and return to the present with a broader perspective on reality. At first this stepping backward was rather tentative. (Only in the nineteenth century would the confrontation between past and present become dramatic, with the imaginative time-traveler returning from the Middle Ages to castigate contemporary society.) In the eighteenth century, when medievalism first began to influence belles-lettres, no such confrontations seemed necessary. The journey into the past was then simply a projection of wishes—melancholy or heroic at will.

Although some eighteenth-century poetry, such as Thomas Chatterton's Rowley poems or James Macpherson's Ossian directly reproduced —or attempted to reproduce—medieval verse itself, most eighteenth-century poets were content simply with evoking or re-creating the past. An examination of eighteenth-century poetry shows, as in the work of contemporary antiquarians, a predominant sense of melancholy. The past was seen as fragile and its monuments as emblems of mortality. Such concerns are especially prominent in the works of the "Graveyard

Poets," whose obsessive concern with time past and death omnipresent led them to concentrate on those aspects of the Middle Ages which emphasized mortality. Such phrases as "the cloister's silent gloom," "hoary mouldered walls," "low-browed misty vaults," "gloomy aisles," and "tatter'd coats of arms" became clichés, all serving to remind the reader that the "paths of glory lead but to the grave." At least fifty well-known eighteenth-century authors can be named who employed such funereal imagery, of whom Pope, Thomson, Blair, Young, Rogers, Akenside, Gray, Shenstone, Smart, Goldsmith, Blake, Cowper, and Burns are but the most famous. Far from being painful, however, such medieval meditations were among what Mark Akenside called, "The Pleasures of Imagination":

> To muse at last amid the ghastly gloom,
> Of graves and hoary vaults, and cloister'd cells;
> To walk with spectres through the midnight shade.[7]

The fearfulness of the past, as well as its fragility, delighted the eighteenth-century poet. Echoing the continuing, though diminishing, fear of Roman Catholicism—its "general darkness" and its "bigot power"—poets used the imagery of medievalism, particularly that of monasticism, to create a sense of terror. Akenside's "The Pleasures of Imagination," though extolling the virtues of cloistral melancholy, also warns against "the poisonous charms / Of baleful superstition" and the "monkish horrors" of the past.[8] In a similar and highly fashionable poem, James Beattie writes of

> ... ghosts that to the charnel dungeon throng
> And drag a length of clanking chain and wail
> Till silenc'd by the owl's terrific song.[9]

While such terror-imagery had a fascination of its own, it was

[7] Mark Akenside and James Beattie, *The Poetical Works of Akenside and Beattie, with a Memoir of Each* (Boston: Houghton Mifflin, 188–), p. 132.
[8] *Ibid.*, pp. 132–133.
[9] *Ibid.*, p. 20.

seldom separated in poetry from the *ubi sunt* motif, or the theme of passing time. The use of medieval elements to emphasize mutability is clearly shown in these lines from David Mallet, though a dozen similar instances might easily be cited:

> Behind me rises huge a reverend pile
> Sole on his blasted heath, a place of tombs,
> Waste, desolate, where Ruin dreary dwells.
> Brooding o'er sightless sculls and crumbling bones,
> Ghastful he sits, and eyes with stedfast glare
> (Sad trophies of his power, where ivy twines
> Its fatal green around) the falling roof,
> The time-shook arch, the column gray with moss,
>   The leaning arch, the sculptured stone defac'd.[10]

The sense of horror was even more fully evoked in the Gothic novels that became popular in the latter half of the eighteenth century, partially eclipsing the vogue for Graveyard poems. In these works, too, the Middle Ages were used to evoke a sense of fear, though the use of such emotions was actually quite complex. In one kind of Gothic novel, the element of terror was simply part of a general atmosphere of wonder and supernaturalism. The huge helmet and mailed fist in Horace Walpole's *The Castle of Otranto* (1765), like the soon-to-be-familiar bleeding statues, mysterious portraits, horrid cloisters, and subterranean passages, seem mainly designed to create a tremor of excitement. This excitement is made more immediate by the fact that Walpole's allegedly medieval heroes and heroines are temperamentally eighteenth-century gentlemen and ladies with whom his readers can identify, thus giving themselves the opportunity for some vicariously thrilling role-playing. Although even in *Otranto* this role-playing confronts the reader with the darker and wilder aspects of existence, it is mainly in another kind of Gothic novel—the novel of sensibility— that the confrontation with the past becomes important. *The Mysteries*

[10] Quoted in Patricia Meyer Spacks, *The Insistence of Horror: Aspects of the Supernatural in Eighteenth-Century Poetry* (Cambridge, Mass.: Harvard University Press, 1962), p. 156.

of Udolpho (1794) is a classic example of the use of the medieval past
to suggest new levels of experience. In this novel by Ann Radcliffe,
the heroine is raised in the gentle landscape of the Garonne, where she
and her father can enjoy those hours of "pensive tenderness" when the
final "tints of light die away; . . . [and] the stars one by one, tremble
through ether, and are reflected on the dark mirror of the waters."[11]
But she is soon forced to go to the wilder, ruder, and more fearful
atmosphere of an ancient Italian castle, where her response to her
environment is perforce more active. Here she is exposed not only
to the sinister machinations of the villain but to a host of other dis-
quieting experiences, from the barbarity of marauding banditti to the
terrors of a mysterious portrait. Although Emily eventually returns
to "the blessed bowers" of La Vallee, she does so only after she—and
the reader—have explored, through medieval imagery, the irrational
terrors of the mind.

Mrs. Radcliffe does make some attempt in *The Mysteries of Udolpho*
to re-create the various stages of developing civilization—the outlaw
bands, the bucolic peasantry, the medieval baron, the rational eighteenth-century gentleman—but she is not really interested, as later
medievalizing writers would be, in creating social contrasts. Nor does
any of the purely Gothic fiction that persisted as a genre well into the
nineteenth century make any attempt to convey the actual nature and
texture of the past. While indebted to the Gothic tale of terror or
sensibility, the historical novel must thus be traced to other sources.
It probably originates in such volumes as Thomas Leland's *Longsword,
Earl of Salisbury* (1762)—"a tale of Chivalry, Love, and Religion"—
and Clara Reeve's *The Old English Baron* (1777). Although both
these works are hopelessly inaccurate as studies of the Middle Ages—
Clara Reeve's castles have shutters on the windows—they at least
strive toward historicism. Leland's *Longsword* is supposedly based
on a medieval chronicle, perhaps Roger of Wendover's thirteenth-
century *Flores Historiarum*, while Mrs. Reeve's claims that she relied
on Paul de Rapin-Thayras's *History of England* for *The Old English*

[11] Ann Radcliffe, *The Mysteries of Udolpho* (London and New York: J. M.
Dent and E. P. Dutton, 1931), pp. 4–5.

Baron. Both writers also present the same view of chivalry that Richard Hurd and Bishop Percy had been suggesting and that would become a significant element in the medievalism of Scott and his followers. Clara Reeve quotes Percy in the introduction to one of her works. She writes that the old historical songs "inspired the enthusiasm of glory" and should thus be praised rather than ridiculed.[12]

As Leland's and Mrs. Reeve's novels show, the interest in the medieval past was persistent. The sense of nationalism which had led Tudor and seventeenth-century historians to investigate the Middle Ages continued to inspire writers in the eighteenth century as well. Akenside, for example, confidently invoked past monarchs in support of England's greatness:

> O Alfred, father of the English name,
> O valiant Edward, first in civil fame,
> O William, height of public virtue pure,
> Bend from your radiant seats a joyful eye,
> Behold the sum of all your labours nigh,
> Your plans of law complete, your ends of rule secure.[13]

And even the usually antifeudal William Shenstone, hearing of a "rumoured tax upon luxury," wrote an elegy on the character of the ancient Britons in which he praised their heroic simplicity and love of freedom. It is from this new association of the past with noble grandeur and the simple virtues, rather than from any of the other expressions of a reviving interest in the Middle Ages, that nineteenth-century medievalism chiefly evolved. None of the previously developed approaches to the Middle Ages disappeared utterly. The medieval past, as it appeared in literature continued to be used as a vehicle of mingled terror and nostalgia and as an avenue for antiquarian research. But the use of the Middle Ages as an ideal, the major subject of this study, should probably be dated back to the eighteenth-century

[12] Clara Reeve, *The Progress of Romance and the History of Charoba, Queen of Egypt*, Colchester edition, 1785, reproduced with a bibliographical note by Esther M. McGill (New York: Facsimile Text Society, 1930), pp. 33, 38.
[13] Akenside and Beattie, *Poetical Works*, p. 303.

identification of the Middle Ages with nature and, as a consequence, with freedom and hardihood, too.

This identification of the medieval, or the Gothic, with the natural and the free represented an important reversal of earlier attitudes. Even while the antiquarians and poets of the late seventeenth and early eighteenth centuries were exploring their medieval subject-matter, the word *gothic* had retained a largely unpleasant connotation of tyranny and restriction. Duelling was a "gothic crime," feudalism and super-stition were "a Gothic chain," and a tight-laced corset was a "gothic ligament." [14] Gradually, as more was learned about medieval history and particularly about medieval architecture, these prejudices waned. The irregularity of medieval buildings was seen as evidence of freedom rather than barbarity, and the pointed shape of the Gothic arch became identified with the natural forms of interbranching trees and the aspiration of men's hearts toward God. The same forces that were leading to expressionism rather than formalism in the arts and to a preference for the picturesque rather than the symmetrical led—along with antiquarianism, Graveyard Poetry, and Gothic fiction—to the rehabilitation of the Middle Ages. All these movements were, in fact, part of the growing concern with "nature," which was perhaps the basic characteristic of the new Romanticism.

Whatever the causes of this complex movement, the connection between medievalism and naturalism or, more accurately between medievalism and primitivism—the cult of simpler peoples—had been clearly made by the middle of the eighteenth century. A characteristic poem of the period is Akenside's "Ode to the Country Gentlemen of England" (1758), which links the nation's greatness with her former simplicity and heroism:

> Whither is England's ancient spirit fled?
> Where are those valiant tenants of her shore,
> Who from the warrior bow the strong dart sped,
> Or with firm hand the rapid pole-axe bore?

[14] Arthur O. Lovejoy, "The First Gothic Revival and the Return to Nature," in *Modern Language Notes*, XLVII (1932), 419.

> Freeman and Soldier was their common name,
> Who late with reapers to the furrow came,
> Now in the front of battle charg'd the foe;
> Who taught the steer the wintry plough to endure,
> Now in full councils check'd encroaching power,
> And gave the guardian Laws their majesty to know.[15]

The association of medievalism and primitivism can be seen even earlier in James Thomson's *Liberty* (1730). While still hostile to some aspects of the later Middle Ages, Thomson sees the early Anglo-Saxons —those "careless sons of nature"—as the founders and creators of English liberty. Anticipating a long tradition of pride in Anglo-Saxon origins, he writes that

> . . . the fierce race
> Poured in a fresh invigorating stream,
> Blood, where an unquelled mighty spirit glowed
>
> . . . .
>
> Nor were the surly gifts of war their all
> Wisdom was likewise theirs, indulgent laws,
> The calm gradations of art-nursing peace.
> And matchless orders, the deep basis still
> On which ascends my British reign. Untamed
> To the refining subtleties of slaves,
> They brought that happy government along
> Formed by that freedom which, with secret voice,
> Impartial nature teaches all her sons.[16]

According to Thomson it is this spirit of freedom, clearly associated with both nature and the Middle Ages, that triumphed in the glories of 1688 and the "matchless Constitution" then achieved.

Serious historians also subscribed to these libertarian views of the Middle Ages. The radical Mrs. Catherine Macaulay prefaced her

---

[15] Akenside and Beattie, *Poetical Works*, p. 364.

[16] James Thomson, *The Complete Poetical Works of James Thomson*, ed. J. Logie Robertson (London and New York: Oxford University Press, 1908), pp. 375–377.

History of England (1763–83) with Thomson's *Ode*, and her history has been called "a very unpoetical ode to the same cause." [17] However, her idealization of the Anglo-Saxon political system was moderate compared to that of the historian T. H. B. Oldfield, who believed that a completely democratic parliament—similar to a New England town meeting—existed among the English even before King Alfred's time. Such ideas also appear in the pioneering historical works of Gilbert Stuart, and they reappear much later on, during the nineteenth century, in the works of the so-called Germanic school of historians, who sought to trace the origins of English liberties in the primitive Teutonic tribes.

By the late eighteenth century, then, medievalism had become allied with what were to become the deepest intellectual currents of the Romantic age: its concern with time and its interest in nature, liberty, and primitivism. To one extent or other, all these modes of looking at the past, as well as purely gothic and antiquarian elements, occur in Scott's poems and novels; for Scott's reading and experiences were almost a capsule summary of all preceding medievalism. However, other ideas and influences were present, too, since Scott was very receptive to his own times. Combining eighteenth-century concern for the freedom of the past with nineteenth-century interest in its security and order, he turned the Middle Ages into a mythical kingdom whose laws and customs could legislate for the present.

II

Scott's scholarship began at home, for he learned much about the past from his childhood exposure to the lingering medieval tradition. In the Scotland of his youth, where ancient fortifications still dominated the landscape, many aspects of feudal land tenure still prevailed. Scottish peasants paid their rent with services as well as money—with *arriages* or ploughings, *bounages* or reapings, *carriages* or carting. Wordsworth's Highland reaper, singing of "old unhappy

[17] Thomas Preston Peardon, *The Transition in English Historical Writing, 1760–1830* (New York: Columbia University Press, 1933), p. 80.

far-off things, / And battles long ago," could have been a real figure in his archaic world.

Coming from a family imbued with local pride, Scott was aware from boyhood of his country's history. In his grandfather's house he heard "the old songs and tales which then formed the amusement of a retired country family." His grandmother, for whom the Border traditions were still vivid, told him "many a tale of Watt of Harden, Wight Willie of Aikwood, James Telfer of the fair Dodhead, and other heroes—merry men all, of the persuasion and calling of Robin Hood and Little John." And he learned, especially from his mother, ballads from even earlier periods of history. Hearing him declaim the pseudo ballad of "Hardyknute" from one of Allan Ramsay's collections of early Scotch verse, a clergyman declared that "one may as well speak in the mouth of a cannon as where that child is." [18] He was also passionately fond of the Gothic novel.

Scott himself dates for us the shift between the unconscious medievalism that was part of his family life and the conscious medievalism that shaped his maturity. He tells us how at the age of thirteen he first became acquainted with Bishop Percy's *Reliques:*

> But above all, I then first became acquainted with Bishop Percy's Reliques of Ancient Poetry. As I had been from infancy devoted to legendary lore of this nature, and only reluctantly withdrew my attention, from the scarcity of materials and the rudeness of those which I possessed, it may be imagined, but cannot be described, with what delight I saw pieces of the same kind which had amused my childhood, and still continued in secret the Delilahs of my imagination, considered as the subject of sober research, grave commentary, and apt illustration, by an editor who showed his poetical genius was capable of emulating the best qualities of what his pious labor preserved. [19]

Scott reacted to Percy's collection in the same way that many other

[18] John Gibson Lockhart, *Memoirs of the Life of Sir Walter Scott*, Cambridge Edition, 5 vols. (Boston and New York: Houghton Mifflin, 1902), I, 15.
[19] *Ibid.*, pp. 31–32.

late eighteenth-century writers, both English and Continental, did. Like Johann Gottfried Herder, who had been inspired by the *Reliques* to collect Lithuanian folk songs, Scott began gathering native Scottish materials. In fact, his youthful interest in ballads was so keen that at sixteen he wrote that he had a "longer acquaintance" with ballads than with any other form of learning, and that "his industry in this way [was] something marvellous."[20] At seventeen, when he joined a local debating group, he won the title of Duns Scotus for his researches in Anglo-Saxon, Norse, and early Scottish literature. At eighteen he lectured on the origin of the feudal system. By 1792, the year he came of age, Scott was making the first of seven successive "raids," as he called them, into Liddesdale—forays that helped provide him with material for his *Minstrelsy of the Scottish Border* (1802–1803). For this annotated collection of ballads, Scott had the co-operation of many contemporary medieval scholars, and he continued and augmented these friendships by his later membership in the Roxburghe and Bannatyne societies.

The relationship of Scott's medievalism to the scholarship of the medieval revival is easily seen by examining the notes he provided for many of his works. They show, first of all, a wide knowledge of the primary sources—particularly the poems and chronicles—that had been reprinted during the seventeenth and eighteenth centuries. It is hard to tell what editions he relied on for Froissart's *Chronicles*, Commines' *Memoirs*, Chaucer's *Canterbury Tales*, or Barbour's *Bruce*. But many of them probably date from the same period that produced the collections of materials on which he so often relied: George Ellis's *Specimens of Early English Poets* (1790) and *Specimens of Early English Romances in Meter* (1805), and Joseph Ritson's *Robin Hood* (1795) and *Ancient English Metrical Romances* (1802). He was also indebted to the revived interest in family and county history that was helping to develop a real knowledge of the life of the past. The notes merely to *The Lay of the Last Minstrel* and *The Lady of the Lake* list as sources histories of the Douglas, Sutherland, St. Clair, and Scott

[20] Sir Walter Scott, *The Letters of Sir Walter Scott*, ed. H. J. C. Grierson, 12 vols. (London: Constable, 1932), I, 4, 7.

families and studies of Cumberland, Westmoreland, Perthshire, and the Western Islands. His secondary sources, too, show an awareness of new materials. In *Ivanhoe*, for example, he gives as his chief authorities: Joseph Strutt, an expert social historian for his time; Robert Henry, the best of the late eighteenth-century medieval historians; and Sharon Turner, author of the monumental *History of the Anglo-Saxons*.

Like Scott's historical knowledge, the philosophical basis of his medievalism must have come from many untraceable sources. Much of it, especially its paternalism and sense of *noblesse oblige*, should probably be credited to a Scottish and familial heritage that included the gallantry of the "Forty-five" and the heroism of the Border. There is, indeed, a very close relationship between his Scottish historical novels and his medieval ones. The fantastic fidelities of the clan that mark such Scottish novels as *Waverley* and *Rob Roy* find their medievally costumed counterparts in such works as *Ivanhoe* and *Quentin Durward* and are inextricably mixed in a Scottish medieval novel such as *The Fair Maid of Perth*. But to the extent that sources can be found for medievalism as a social philosophy in Scott, Goethe's drama *Götz von Berlichingen*, which Scott very freely translated in 1799, stands out as a major influence. John Lockhart may well have exaggerated in his biography of Scott when he saw it as the basis for all of that writer's later work on the Middle Ages.[21] But the work was certainly influential enough upon Scott and sufficiently important in itself to merit consideration.

Published in 1771, Goethe's drama was in many ways a declaration of the superiority of medieval to modern times or, more accurately, of a chivalric to a commercial society. Goethe shows in the play that he is well aware of the limitations of the Middle Ages—their turbulence and their brutality—and is by no means sentimental enough to wish them to return. But, like many later medievalists, he fears that certain values of the human spirit have died with feudalism. Götz's final speech—"The age of frankness and freedom is past—that of treachery begins. The worthless will gain the upperhand by cunning, and the

[21] Lockhart, *Memoirs of Scott*, I, 275.

noble will fall into their net"[22]—sounds the keynote for the nine-teenth-century's contempt for its own materialism. It anticipates the famous lament for the past that Edmund Burke was to make a genera-tion later in his *Reflections on the Revolution in France:* "But the age of chivalry is gone. That of sophisters, oeconomists, and calculators, has succeeded; and the glory of Europe is extinguished for ever."[23]

The paternalism of Goethe's medievalism may also have affected Scott's viewpoint. Goethe writes in *Götz von Berlichingen* of lords who were truly the fathers of their people and has one of his characters recall that when

> the landgrave of Hanau made a grand hunting party, the princes and free feudatories enjoyed themselves under the open heaven, and the vassals were as happy as they; it was no selfish masquerade instituted for his own private pleasure or vanity—To see the great round-headed peasant lads and the pretty brown girls, the sturdy hinds, and the respectable ancients, all as happy as if they rejoiced in the pleasures of their master, which he shared with them under God's free sky.[24]

It is hoped that in the future "many such will rule together . . . to whom reverence to the emperor, peace, friendship with their neigh-bours, and the love of their vassals shall be the best and dearest family treasure."[25]

Götz himself, in spite of his errors, is the ideal feudal leader. He is gentle with his followers, who characterize him as a man hated by princes but loved by the oppressed. His paternal sense of responsibility shows itself in all his feudal relations—his love for his squire, his concern for his peasants, his generosity even to his enemies. Götz loves his people, however, because he pities their weakness, not because he respects their strength. He fears that like children they will

[22] Sir Walter Scott, *Poetical Works*, 12 vols. (Edinburgh, 1833–1834), XII, 561.
[23] Edmund Burke, *The Complete Works of Edmund Burke*, 16 vols. (London, 1803–1827), V, 149.
[24] Scott, *Poetical Works*, XII, 523–524.
[25] *Ibid.*, p. 524.

become unruly unless they are watched and led; only they are older than children and therefore more dangerous. In scenes imitative of the Jack Cade episodes in *Henry VI*, Goethe shows what happens when this childish mob goes mad. He has Götz, who sympathizes with the people's legitimate demands, try to lead them in an attempt to curb their excesses and then become their opponent when they fall to burning and plundering.

Goethe's ideals, then, are aristocratic, which is to say, feudal and paternal. The knights and princes are to act as guardians of the poor—creators of an Arcadia in which the peasant can enjoy the comforts of pastoral security, while for a few proud and high-born spirits are reserved the delights of freedom and magnanimity.

Scott's intuitive sympathies with Goethe's view can be seen in the introduction to his translation. He touches upon just the right points: Götz's pride and paternalism, the peasants' weakness and need. Much in Scott's own background might have taught him these values without Goethe. (His attitude toward the duke of Buccleuch, on the one hand, and his servant Tom Purdie, on the other, is a perfect instance of feudal deference to a lord and condescension to a vassal.) But it seems reasonable to assume that Goethe's play helped crystallize a young man's half-articulated beliefs and create the sense of the value of medieval society which is apparent even in his earliest narrative poems.

III

Like all Scott's works, the poems and novels set in the Middle Ages are built upon strong social contrasts. Coleridge was probably the first to discern this underlying dramatic conflict. In a comment made in 1820, he explained that the contest in Scott's novels is between "two great moving principles of social humanity; religious adherence to the past ... the desire and admiration of the permanent ... and the passion for increase of knowledge, instincts of *progression* and *free agency*."[26] Although Coleridge's dictum has retained critical

[26] Samuel Taylor Coleridge, *Miscellaneous Criticism*, ed. Thomas Middleton Raysor (London: Constable, 1936), pp. 341–342.

acceptance for more than a century, it has been developed and modified by recent writers, who see the basic conflict, not as between past and present, but as between the individual and society, law and lawlessness, heroism and chivalry. Central to all these interpretations, whatever the terminology, is the recognition that all Scott's novels, both Scottish and medieval, deal with societies in transition. They are not only set in the past (with the exception of *St. Ronan's Well*) but deal with a past that is passing away. There are thus four periods of time which the reader must consider in studying the Waverley Novels: the period that is coming to an end as the novel begins, the actual time of the novel, the new stage of civilization that is making itself felt, and the era in which Scott is writing. Unlike later medievalists, Scott almost never explicitly contrasts his own times with the historic past. But he does make oblique comments on his age by contrasting the different cultural levels that coexist within his story.

Although Scott was too much of a realist to resist change rigidly, his medieval novels do reveal a bias toward the remotest past—that is, toward the values and customs that are already dying out as the novel begins. In *Ivanhoe*, he regrets the end of Saxon society; in *Quentin Durward*, of French chivalry; in *Anne of Geierstein*, of the Lancastrian nobility. While these three novels show substitute values developing, other works seem to equate transition with decay. *The Talisman*, for example, shows the Crusaders' camp literally and symbolically decaying with sickness and corruption, and *Count Robert of Paris* parodies a medieval aristocracy that has grown cynical and effete. Scott knows that historical change is not to be resisted, but his preference for archaic social structures echoes the primitivism of his medievalist predecessors. Set in earlier, more romantic ages to begin with, Scott's novels reveal a longing for an anterior society viewed as generous, heroic, and loyal.

Scott's primitivism, however, is firmly limited. While he admires the heroic and chivalric past, his belief in freedom is balanced by his concern for order. Both the Scottish and the medieval novels consistently reject violence and lawlessness—both the violence of those who have remained too far in the past and the lawlessness of those who are moving too recklessly toward the future. In the Scottish novels such violence comes either from outlaw figures, such as Donald McBain in *Waverley*, or from hypercivilized disbelievers, such as George Stanton, the dissolute, deceiving Englishman of *The Heart of Midlothian*. In the medieval novels, too, the threats are either from those too brutal or too selfish to accept the social covenant—the bestial William de la Marck and his animalistic band in *Quentin Durward*, or the faithless, Machiavellian schemer Conrade de Montserrat in *The Talisman*. Bracketed between these extremes of violence and selfish calculation are the noble characters that Scott portrays, whose personal honor, belief in freedom, and chivalric altruism preserve the best of the old order within a framework of change.

The main elements of Scott's medieval vision can already be discerned in such narrative poems as *The Lay of the Last Minstrel* (1805) and *The Lady of the Lake* (1810). They show in their structure Scott's double nostalgia both for the actual past and for a still remoter period of time. The aged minstrel who narrates *The Lay* and the Harp of the North, which supposedly inspires *The Lady of the Lake*, are already historic in themselves, but their songs deal with an even earlier era. The aged minstrel, after some hesitation, obliterates the postmedieval present in his imaginings of a chivalric past:

> The present scene, the future lot,
> His toils, his wants, were all forgot;
> Cold diffidence and age's frost
> In the full tide of song were lost.[27]

Similarly, the already mouldering Harp of the North wakes in a crasser day to sing of former times when beauty reigned and knightly values flourished.

Although both poems take place in the sixteenth century, the world that Scott presents in them is still palpably medieval. *The Lay of the Last Minstrel*, in particular, with its goblin page and wizard Michael Scott, contains many of the Gothic mechanisms that Scott had inherited

[27] Scott, *Poetical Works*, VI, 48.

from such eighteenth-century favorites as Horace Walpole, Clara Reeve, and Ann Radcliffe and that he would continue to use in his novels. It also, as the "fair Melrose" passage testifies, is indebted to the Graveyard Poetry of the preceding century and its imagery of ruins and tombstones. But behind the superficial gothicism of the poem lies a society which is sufficiently backward for its century to constitute a feudal community. The native characters that Scott portrays both in *The Lady of the Lake* and *The Lay of the Last Minstrel* are what have been called "hard primitives"—that is, simpler peoples more distinguished by rough heroism and nobility than by a softer Rousseauean innocence. Scott describes them as living in a state "partly pastoral and partly warlike, and combining habits of constant depredations with the influence of a rude spirit of chivalry" (VI, 37).

Scott differs from earlier writers, however, in emphasizing the interdependence as well as the independence of medieval society. He sees the castle as the center of communal life:

> Knight and page, and household squire
> Loiter'd through the lofty hall
> Or crowded round the ample fire.

(VI, 49–50)

And he shows how at feast times all classes came together joyously:

> Steward and squire with heedful haste,
> Marshall'd the rank of every guest;
> Pages, with ready blade were there
> The mighty meal to carve and share.

(VI, 191)

This commingling of classes involved a communal sense of responsibility. The knights and squires were expected to repay their lord by snatching up their swords and Jedwood axes whenever the castle was threatened. But even the peasant was caught up in the reciprocity of feudal relations. In wartime he and his family could take refuge in the castle, provided he joined the feudal community in defending it.

33

Fidelity and honor are the chief virtues in this interconnected medieval world. The harshness of the outlaws in *The Lady of the Lake* is redeemed by their dutiful observance of the laws of hospitality and the sacred value they attach to their word. Scott is careful in this poem to give full due to James V, the representative of the coming centralized monarchy. But it is the noble Douglas, faithful and honorable even in exile, who is the true hero of the story. Guardian of King James's youth, he represents the best of a passing world—its heroism, its freedom, its generosity. A man apart, he stays aloof from the violence of Roderick Dhu, the irrationality of the mob, and the cold, subtle policy of King James's court. He is a forerunner of the exiled heroes of Scott's later medieval novels—Ivanhoe and King Richard in *Ivanhoe*, Quentin Durward in the novel of that name, Arthur Phillipson in *Anne of Geierstein*, and Hereward the Varangian in *Count Robert of Paris*—all of them patterns of virtue in a changing world.

Implicit in the characterization of individuals such as Douglas is the concept of order. Although unjustly treated by the king, he will endure rather than revolt. And when an unruly mob rises in his behalf, it was "With grief the noble Douglas saw / The Commons rise against the law" (VII, 249). He is a hero for Scott because his devotion is ultimately to his country rather than to himself.

The idea of order is further explored in the poem *Harold the Dauntless* (1817), in which an outlaw Viking marauder finally submits to the will of society. But the concept is most carefully developed in *Ivanhoe* (1820), Scott's fullest attempt to interpret medieval society in accordance with his social philosophy and the novel which most affected nineteenth-century attitudes toward the Middle Ages. Scott works in that novel with a wide range of cultural levels: from Urfrieda, the demented Saxon hag, who calls upon Wotan and Zernebock for vengeance, to Brian-de-Bois-Guilbert, who has so far outgrown chivalry and Christianity as to think honor and religion mere superstitions. As in all his works, Scott repudiates the extreme primitive. He rejects the savage Urfrieda, who prefers dishonor to death, just as he rejects the violent Front-le-Boeuf and his bestial allies. But if he condemns those who are too animalistic to accept the bonds of society, he is even more hostile to those who are too selfish to live by its rules. The wily King John and the unbelieving Brian-de-Bois-Guilbert are both presented as villains. John is untrustworthy and Bois-Guilbert is specifically stated to be false in his oaths, faithless to women, hypocritical in his religion. He is unwilling to fulfill his feudal responsibilities to the weak and oppressed and thinks only of his own freedom and ambition. In all this the Templar is a typical Gothic villain—something like Mrs. Radcliffe's Montoni. But to Scott he represents the decay of the medieval ideal and would be a potentially corrosive force in any age.

Between these two threatening extremes of brutality and sophistication, Scott portrays members of almost every medieval social class—serf, freeman, and yeoman; thane, noble, and king—and unobtrusively suggests what their relations should be to each other. At the bottom of the social scale are Cedric's serfs, Wamba and Gurth. Wamba shows the feudal relationship between master and man in its purest form. The jester is protected by Cedric—sheltered under his roof, fed at his table—in return for doing what he can: seasoning Cedric's meals with his jokes and helping Gurth herd the swine. Too irresponsible to make his own way in the world, he can nonetheless be as loyal and wise as the Fool in *King Lear*. It is he, after all, who disguises himself as a monk so that he can enter Cedric's cell and take his place in the dungeon and at the stake. The dialogue between master and man, in which Wamba tries to persuade his lord to let him do this, shows Scott's vision of the way feudalism should have worked: the serf willing to die for his master, the master willing to die for the man he considered his sovereign:

> "Leave thee in my stead!" said Cedric, astonished at the proposal; "why they would hang thee, my poor knave."
>
> "E'en let them do as they are permitted," said Wamba; "I trust—no disparagement to your birth—that the son of Witless may hang in a chain with as much gravity as the chain hung upon his ancestor the alderman."
>
> "Well, Wamba," answered Cedric, "for one thing I will grant thy

request. And that is, if thou wilt make the exchange of garments with Lord Athelstane instead of me."

"No, by St. Dunstan," answered Wamba; "there were little reason in that. Good right there is, that the son of Witless should suffer to save the son of Hereward; but little wisdom there were in his dying for the benefit of one whose fathers were strangers to his." [28]

Needless to say, Scott is too kind to allow poor Wamba to perish. His reward is an embrace from his grateful master and the assurance of a place at Cedric's hearth. Freedom, however, is not granted him, for he is not suited to it and does not want it. "The serf," says Wamba contentedly, "sits by the hall-fire when the freeman must forth to the field of battle. . . . Better a fool at a feast than a wise man at a fray" (XVII, 154).

Gurth is a very different character. He exemplifies the recurrent hard primitivism that Scott always associates with the idea of liberty. Notice the vocabulary that describes his dress and bearing. He is characterized as "stern, savage, and wild." His clothing is associated with the earliest stages of society, "being a close jacket with sleeves, composed of the tanned skin of some animal" (XVI, 8). Around his neck is twisted a brass collar, the symbol of the servitude that galls him in spite of his loyalty to Cedric. Too good a man to be faithless, he is nonetheless sullen about the service he renders. When Cedric unjustly punishes him for helping the banished Ivanhoe, he runs away.

Although he demands his freedom, Gurth is no villain who denies the social covenant. His flight lasts only as long as Cedric is safe. Then, like Wamba, he works to rescue his master. Because he is capable of it, his reward is freedom. "'THEOW and ESNE,'" Cedric declares, "'Art thou no longer . . . FOLKFREE and SACLESS art thou in town and from town, in the forest as in the field. A hide of land I give thee in my steads of Walbrugham, from me and mine to thee and thine for aye and for ever; and God's malison on his head who this gainsays!'" (XVII, 153). For this generosity Cedric is rewarded by hearing the

[28] Sir Walter Scott, *Waverley Novels*, 48 vols. (Edinburgh, 1829–1833), XVII, 38–39.

delighted Gurth cry out that his strength and his loyalty are doubled by his freedom and that he is still Cedric's true defender.

Freedom, then, which Scott always values, carries a concomitant of responsibility. Mere license—or freedom injurious to society—is always condemned, whether exercised by a brute like Front-le-Boeuf or a subtle nihilist like the Templar. But the degree of freedom is tempered by the degree of responsibility. For Gurth it is enough that as a serf he obeys his master's best interests and that as a freeman he tends to a plot of soil. His master Cedric is the leader of the people, however, and has a more complex task to carry out. He illustrates many of the medieval virtues that Scott found praiseworthy. He is a giver of feasts, who welcomes all to share in his plenty, even the caftaned Jew. Quick-tempered and slow-thinking, he is nevertheless staunch and loyal to what he believes to be his nation's best interest. Although Scott emphasizes the rudeness of Cedric's surroundings and the heartiness of his manners, he clearly prefers such bluntness to the finicky etiquette of the Normans, which masks selfishness, treachery, and cruelty. Scott has practically nothing favorable to say about the Normans in *Ivanhoe*. At the beginning of the book, they are described as feudal oppressors, a characterization immediately justified by their uncivil behavior to Gurth and Wamba. But even among themselves they are not much better. The dishonor and violence of Maurice de Bracy's carrying off Rowena to the Castle at Torquilstone is matched by the political perfidiousness of John's henchmen. Prince John's schemes against his brother are based on the co-operation of a group of "lawless resolutes" who place "their hopes of harvest in civil commotion." But his band of nobles and hangers-on desert him at the threat of Richard's return. Scott points out that the very barons who stood for their rights at Runnymede were often "capable of excesses contrary not only to the laws of England but to those of nature and humanity" (XVI, 346). By contrast to this crew, the worthy Cedric stands out as a representative of an antique fidelity and belief in freedom that is already vanishing in *Ivanhoe*.

Cedric's integrity is shared by all the Saxon characters: the honest Gurth and the loyal Lockesley and his band. Even Friar Tuck's moments of clerical hypocrisy are more than compensated by his sturdy valor—a valor never achieved by the vain and selfish Norman prelate, Prior Jorvaulx. But despite his preference for the Saxons, it is not with the extremes of either group that Scott's allegiance lies. Rather it is with chivalry in its ideal form as represented by the noble Wilfrid of Ivanhoe, who has mitigated the crudity of his Saxon forebears while retaining their stalwart virtues. Together with Richard Coeur-de-Lion, who embodies the dying world of knight errantry, Ivanhoe represents the primitivist virtues of honor and bravery in a society that is ceasing to care for the weak and oppressed.

Scott's attitude toward chivalry has come in for questioning in recent years. Far from being considered the great defender of the chivalric, he has been described as "stringently anti-chivalric," [29] though an admirer of its more moderate virtues of compassion and generosity. However, a closer examination of what Scott meant by chivalry shows that while he rejected its quixotism and its egotistical concern with fame, he did see in it the possibility for reconciling freedom and order. Scott defined chivalry in an essay he wrote for the *Encyclopedia Britannica* as the use of individual freedom to defend the social order. It thus mediates between the extreme individualism of hard primitivism and the social organization of a more developed civilization.

The complexity of Scott's attitude toward chivalry can be seen in the conversation between Ivanhoe and Rebecca as she describes for him the siege of Torquilstone. To his praises of war and glory, Rebecca counters by citing the cost of battle in human suffering. She seems, to the modern reader at least, to have the stronger case. But she is left silent by his final definition of chivalry. He tells her that it is

"the pure light of chivalry, which alone distinguishes the noble from the base, the gentle knight from the churl and the savage; which rates our life here far, far beneath the pitch of our honour, raises us victorious over pain, toil, and suffering, and teaches us to fear no evil but disgrace

[29] Francis R. Hart, *Scott's Novels: The Plotting of Historic Survival* (Charlottesville: University of Virginia Press, 1966), p. 152.

... Chivalry! Why, maiden, she is the nurse of pure and high affection, the stay of the oppressed, the redresser of grievances, the curb of the power of the tyrant. Nobility were but an empty name without her, and liberty finds the best protection in her lance and her sword." (XVII, 108–109)

The way in which chivalry bridges the gap between the leaders and the led, a major concern of most nineteenth-century medievalists, can also be seen in King Richard's and Ivanhoe's relations with their dependants. Richard, who has the whole of England in fief, comes off less well than Ivanhoe in this regard. While he has the welfare of his country at heart, his feats of chivalry are too freakish, "furnishing themes for bards and minstrels, but affording none of those solid benefits to his country on which history loves to pause" (XVII, 325). Ivanhoe, however, is the ideal master, for he combines his individualism with a sense of responsibility. The tournament, which on one level is simply a means by which Scott captures his readers' imaginations with pageantry and drama, is also symbolic of the way in which a chivalric hero like Ivanhoe can act to redress injustice. At Ashby de la Zouche, Ivanhoe fights to uphold Rowena's Saxon beauty; at Templestowe, more significantly, to defend Rebecca's innocence. Ivanhoe's strength protects not only the weakness of women but also the needs of his inferiors. At the end of the novel, Wamba and Gurth, "sharers of Wilfred's dangers and adversity [remain], as they had a right to expect, partakers of his more prosperous career" (XVII, 390–91). Chivalry in the field has turned to paternalism at home—a sublimation that lies at the heart of Scott's social philosophy.

Quentin Durward (1823) further explores the meaning of feudal society and, more than any other of Scott's books, implies the medieval-modern contrast. Scott is not so much interested here in presenting feudalism as a mode of social organization as in allegorizing it as a guide to human conduct. He returns to the theme that Goethe had enunciated in *Götz von Berlichingen* and that Burke had emphasized in his *Reflections:* that the death of chivalry meant the end of altruism and the beginning of self-interest as the approved motives of behavior.

In fact, some of his passages in *Quentin Durward* seem specifically directed against the utilitarians. The phrase "sum of happiness" in his opening sentence has a peculiarly Benthamite ring. He writes that

> the scene of this romance is laid in the fifteenth century, when the feudal system, which had been the sinews and nerves of the national defence, and the spirit of chivalry, by which, as by a vivifying soul, that system was animated, began to be innovated upon and abandoned by those grosser characters who centred their sum of happiness in procuring the personal objects on which they had fixed their own exclusive attachment. The same egotism had indeed displayed itself even in more primitive ages; but it was now for the first time openly avowed as a professed principle of action. The spirit of chivalry had in it this point of excellence, that however overstrained and fantastic many of its doctrines may appear to us, they were all founded on generosity and self-denial, of which if the earth were deprived, it would be difficult to conceive the existence of virtue among the human race. (XXXI, xxv)

The differences between a chivalric and a utilitarian society are exemplified in Scott's two main characters—Quentin Durward and Louis XI—the one symbolizing the era that is passing, the other, the period to come. Durward is pretty much of a cardboard chevalier, a mere lay figure in comparison with the complex delineation of Louis. But his loyalty, generosity, and idealism make him the hero of the book, albeit one of a Candide-like naïveté. Durward combines the courage and hardy virtues that he learned from his Scottish ancestors with the compassionate ethical code of his monastic education, and the result is both fidelity and endurance. Louis, by contrast, is presented as a completely antichivalric force, opposed to all medieval conventions and values. He prefers low amours to courtly love, barbers and hang-men to bishops and princes, mercenary soldiers to devoted knights. Several times Scott actually compares the king to Goethe's Mephistoph-eles, saying that both men are constantly employed in "under-valuing and vilifying all actions, the consequences of which do not lead certainly and directly to self-gratification" (XXXI, v–vi). Louis's

40

is the spirit that denies—denies the medieval principles of generous and disinterested action. He is "so guiltless of entertaining any purpose unconnected with his ambition, covetousness, and desire of selfish enjoyment, that he almost seems an incarnation of the devil himself, permitted to do his utmost to corrupt our ideas of honour in its very source" (XXXI, iv). Scott realizes that no system, particularly one which, like chivalry, takes no account of human frailty, can survive forever, and he is careful to give Louis credit for his devotion to the national welfare. But there is no question that Scott sees him as a malignant influence, destroying those "ties of religion, honour, and morality" (XXXI, xii), by which mankind is bound.

It is not only for Louis's opportunism that Durward's chivalry acts as a foil. As in *Ivanhoe*, Scott uses the book to examine a wide range of cultural patterns: the atheistic faithlessness of the gypsies, the brutality of William de la Marck, the undisciplined energy of Charles the Bold. His portrait of the rebellious citizens of Liege is especially interesting since it shows one aspect of Scott's reaction to the continuing fear of insurrection that troubled England for half a century after the French Revolution. In this novel Scott shows no sympathy for the insurgents. Although the better class of burghers shrinks from violence, those of lower education or more brutal natures quickly learn to imitate the behavior of de la Marck and his troops, proceeding from drunkenness to riot to the ultimate horror of assassination. The scene in which the bishop is struck down in his own episcopal hall by the headsman's axe is a deliberate anachronism on Scott's part and may have been intended to suggest the execution of Louis XVI. Scott's repeated reference to the bishop of Liege by his given name of "Louis of Bourbon" certainly suggests a parallel with the unfortunate monarch.

However, it is not violence alone that precipitates the bishop's death. The insurrection is also based on the mob's belief that King Louis will support their action. Quite as much as sheer lawlessness, then, the king's doctrines of utility and self-gratification are shown to destroy order. He paves the way for the mercenary armies that will ravage Europe in centuries to come and sets in motion a ruinous suspiciousness in international affairs. He is, in fact, his own worst foe since it is by disregarding his own obligations to his vassal Burgundy that he almost comes to ruin. In *Quentin Durward*, as in all his novels, Scott sees only chaos as coming from lawlessness or bad faith.

It should be noted, however, that Scott's hatred of a lawless mob does not extend to a legitimate peasantry or bourgeoisie. The same admiration for hardihood and independence that leads him to admire a potential freeman like Gurth at the beginning of the medieval period makes him sympathetic to the reasonable aspirations of the rising middle class at the end of the era. In *Quentin Durward* such bourgeois characters are peripheral to Scott's theme—although the unruly Liegeois are counterbalanced by the loyal syndic Pavilon—but in *The Fair Maid of Perth* (1828) and *Anne of Geierstein* (1829) a stalwart citizenry is essential to his story. Both novels praise such characters—townsfolk in one and mountaineers in the other—for insisting upon their traditional rights. *Castle Dangerous* (1832), too, with its portrayal of Wilkin Flammock, the Flemish steward, also shows Scott's persistent interest in middle-class characters.

In view of the serious attention that later writers such as Ruskin and Morris were to show in the craftsmanship of the Middle Ages, *The Fair Maid of Perth* is particularly interesting for its concentration on the medieval artisan. Harry Smith, whose surname indicates his occupation, takes great pride in his work. He wears armor only of his own making and boasts that he can take up a link in a coat of mail as well as his "mother could take up a stitch in the nets she wove" (XLII, 227). He is proud of being able to hurl a mighty hammer and can work off a horseshoe in a hundred strokes. Simon Glover, too, shows a craftsman's pride in his more delicate trade, frequently asserting the ancient honor of glovemakers. In a footnote to his novel, Scott quotes the inscription on the banner of the Perthshire glovers' guild: "The perfect honour of a craft, or beauty of a trade, is not in wealthe, but in moral worth whereby virtue gains renowne" (XLII, 127). In view of such later works as Lord John Manners's *A Plea for National Holy-Days*, it is interesting to observe that the smith's workmen are given St. Valentine's and other saints' days for holidays—a startling idea for Scott's readers in the years of the eighty-four-hour work week.

One of the most interesting aspects of *The Fair Maid of Perth* is the relation between Sir Patrick Charteris, the provost of Perth, and the good burghers such as Smith and Glover. Scott's characterization of Sir Patrick seems deliberately designed to suggest the nineteenth-century landholder to his reader. When a deputation of burghers approaches his castle just as Sir Patrick is planning to go hawking (the medieval equivalent of fox-hunting), he has "pretty much the same feelings that the modern representative of a burgh . . . [has at] the menaced visitation of his worthy electors at a time rather unseasonable for their reception" (XLII, 168). However, when the matter turns out to be serious, Charteris subordinates all selfish thoughts to his communal responsibility, for he is not only a typical aristocrat but a model one. He represents the burghers both in council and in action, places his military strength at their command, and protects Simon Glover and his daughter in an emergency. Foreshadowing Carlyle's Landlord Edmund in *Past and Present*, he is no mere game preserver but a man preserver.

If such novels as *Ivanhoe* and *Quentin Durward* emphasize the importance of order for Scott, both *The Fair Maid of Perth* and, more vividly, *Anne of Geierstein* show his profound concern with personal liberty and national independence. *Anne of Geierstein*, one of Scott's last published novels, shows that for all his belief in paternalism, Scott never forgot the value of liberty and nationalism. Although the book contains the usual aristocratic adventures of a Waverley Novel and an unusually large number of Gothic plot devices, the real story centers upon a group of Swiss freemen who are seeking to free themselves from the Burgundian yoke. Scott describes their simplicity in a manner reminiscent of Tacitus's *Germania;* they are as yet uncorrupted by luxurious food, drink, or behavior. In this way we see Scott, even in a novel published in the thirties, still making use of the "hard primitivism" and the related idealization of the Swiss that had been popular forty to fifty years earlier. The Swiss mountaineers, like the best of Scott's Highlandmen, show man organized into society but not yet corrupted by its vices.

43

The Swiss leader Arnold Biederman is one of Scott's most admirable characters. A nobleman who has renounced his title for the right of being a free citizen of the Swiss republic, Biederman combines the magnanimity of the aristocrat with the hardihood of the yeoman. Scott describes his figure and features as exhibiting "a primeval simplicity mixed with a certain rude dignity, arising out of his masculine and unaffected character." Both his clothing and his deportment are patriarchally simple and grand:

> But the figure of him who wore this homely attire, which seemed almost wholly composed of the fleeces of the mountain sheep and the spoils of animals of the chase, would have commanded respect wherever the wearer had presented himself, especially in those warlike days, when men were judged of according to the promising or unpromising qualities of their thews and sinews. To those who looked at Arnold Biederman in this point of view, he displayed the size and form, the broad shoulders and prominent muscles of a Hercules. But to such as looked rather at his countenance, the steady, sagacious features, open front, large blue eyes, and deliberate resolution which it expressed more resembled the character of the fabled King of Gods and Men. He was attended by several sons and relatives, young men, among whom he walked, receiving, as his undeniable due, respect and obedience, similar to that which a herd of deer are observed to render to the monarch stag. (XLIV, 59–60)

Biederman states that he has joined the people only to serve them better. He believes that when the commons are no longer awed by the vain pomp of title and ceremony, they will be able to regard the nobles, not as "wolves among the flock, but as sagacious mastiffs, who attend the sheep in time of peace, and are prompt in their defense when war threatens" (XLIV, 87). It is in this dual role of protector and defender that Biederman governs his people in peacetime and then leads his loyal band in its just demand for freedom.

Biederman's sense of connection between the leaders and the led is central to Scott's vision of the Middle Ages. It is symbolized by the ritual of the feudal feast—the bountiful meal at which all classes come

44

together to share in their leader's generosity. A feature of almost all Scott's medieval poems and novels, these elaborately described meals share certain characteristics: food is plenteous and offered to all, for bounteousness is one of Scott's cardinal virtues. Rank is carefully observed, however; the ministering nobles sit at the head of the table and give inferior place to the receiving populace. But there is no atomism; the interdependence of classes is woven into the texture of everyday life. As Scott writes in one of his novels of the very late Middle Ages, *The Monastery* (1820), in the fifteenth century "the idea of the master or mistress of the mansion feeding or living apart from their domestics was ... never entertained. The highest end of the board, the most commodious settle by the fire,—these were the only marks of distinction; and the servants mingled with deference indeed, but unreproved and with freedom in whatever conversation was going forward" (XVIII, 41).

The amount of food available in Scott's novels was probably very important in shaping nineteenth-century attitudes toward the Middle Ages. In none of them does anyone go hungry. No matter what the crisis, a fat haunch of venison, rich pasties, and stoups of wine are always lurking in the background. Describing the economy of a feudal castle in *The Abbot* (1820), Scott described the fare that its master provided for his retainers:

> Two bullocks and six sheep, weekly, were the allowance when the Baron was at home and the number was not greatly diminished during his absence. A boll of malt was weekly brewed into ale, which was used by the household at discretion. Bread was baked in proportion for the consumption of his domestics and retainers. (XX, 162)

All these images of the medieval world were so vivid for Scott's readers and so satisfying to their wishes that they took on a life of their own. Looking backward as they do to the medievalism of the eighteenth century, Scott's Middle Ages were nonetheless an important force in shaping nineteenth- and ultimately twentieth-century social values. To an increasingly staid and respectable society, they offered an outlet for vicarious adventure. To a society in which many were hungry—starving even—they presented a picture of universal abundance. To a society disturbed by its own commercialism and competitiveness, they suggested the possibilities of an interrelated social order and a chivalric protectiveness. Most important, they offered a new potential for leadership by showing a possible mode of action to those guiltily conscious of possessing knowledge, wealth, or title without having any corresponding duties to perform.

IV

Underlying Scott's interpretation of the Middle Ages was a highly consistent view of human nature. A conservative by temperament, Scott resisted throughout his life the notion that reason was invincible. The legendary and the local—the folk tales of a winter fireside—captured his boyish imagination and profoundly shaped his more mature view of man. Seeing men always as individuals rather than abstractions, Scott had no patience with utopian schemes for human betterment. Reason was invaluable, but it had to be built upon a more solid foundation of passion and custom. Like all traditionalists, he therefore distrusted it and preferred to have men guided by what had proved workable in the past rather than what might seem desirable for the future.

In view of this conception of human nature, it is not surprising that Scott admired Burke and praised his "prophetic powers." Leslie Stephen said that Scott transferred Burke's political ideas to literature,[30] and the medieval novels often do seem to illustrate the great conservative's aphorisms. Burke says that man in society must divest "himself of the first fundamental right of uncovenanted man . . . to judge for himself and to assert his own cause."[31] Scott shows us in all his poems and novels that man must make a covenant with society if he is not to be

[30] Leslie Stephen, *The English Utilitarians*, Series of Reprints of Scarce Works on Political Economy, no. 10, 3 vols. (London: London School of Economics and Political Science, 1950), II, 367.

[31] Burke, *Complete Works*, V, 122.

destroyed. Burke distrusts the "sophisters, oeconomists, and calculators," who, though a part of society, try to remake it according to their erring reason. Scott gives us the Machiavellian Louis XI, who by unloosing the loyalties that bind his nobles to him, fulfills Burke's prophecy that "when the old feudal and chivalrous spirit of *fealty* is ended," there will ensue, "that long roll of grim and bloody maxims which form the political code of all power." [32]

As his emphasis on "honor" shows, Scott does not believe that a narrow rationalism or self-interest can be the basis of society. He prefers to place his faith in the "affections" and loyalties. Burke writes that affection "must be the surest hold of our government" [33] and insists that the love of the state begins with the love of the limited circle in which we dwell. For such ideas, *Ivanhoe* is almost a demonstration or proof. The welfare of the state is shown to depend on the repetition on a larger and larger scale—recurring like ripples in a pool—of the relationship between Cedric and Gurth. The action is not resolved until Cedric yields to Coeur-de-Lion the same self-respecting loyalty that Gurth gives to him.

Like Burke, Scott also believed that the common man's love for the state, once established, had to be nourished and sustained by rituals and illusions, since government was otherwise too abstract a concept for him to grasp. Both for Scott and for Burke, as they later were for Disraeli and the Young Englanders, the best of these illusions were the customs and ceremonies of monarchy, and the Middle Ages the period at which they were most picturesque. In one of the familiar passages in the *Reflections on the Revolution in France*, Burke describes monarchy, ennobled by chivalry, as one of the great "superadded ideas, furnished from the wardrobe of a moral imagination, which the heart owns and the understanding ratifies, as necessary to cover the defects of our naked shivering nature, and raise it to dignity." [34] Scott, through his novels, delighted in painting the full panoply of the Middle Ages, especially these scenes in which all classes came together at a festival

[32] *Ibid.*, p. 153.
[33] *Ibid.*, III, 159.
[34] *Ibid.*, V, 151.

or ceremony presided over by monarch or noble. Among the tableaux that come to mind are the tournaments and games in *The Lady of the Lake, Ivanhoe, The Talisman*, and *The Fair Maid of Perth*, in which the glittering garments of the nobility enrich the buff coats of the yeomen and serve to remind the populace of the ceremonies of rule and the oneness of their society.

In idealizing the role of the lord as "hlafward," or loaf-keeper, Scott again initiates one of the significant ideas in nineteenth-century thought. In line with Burke, young England, and Disraeli, he thought it natural for an aristocracy of birth and property to rule society and considered the age of chivalry as a time when it ruled particularly well. In contrast to the parvenu manufacturers of his own age, who were too greedy to be trusted with power, he saw the hereditary nobleman—made cautious by the stabilizing power of property and generous by the traditions of rank—as a fit guide to society. Most of Scott's heroes—Cedric in *Ivanhoe*, Sir Halbert Glendinning in *The Abbot*, and leading figures in *The Betrothed, The Fair Maid of Perth*, and *Castle Dangerous*—believe that wealth is in part for the service of the poor. "What use," asks one of them, "the mountains of beef and oceans of beer which they say our domains produce if there is a hungry heart among our vassalage?" (XLVII, 286).

For all their charity, Scott's aristocrats are stern. Unjust demands must be put down, by force if necessary, and signs of rebellion swiftly repressed. Although sturdy individual citizens do appear in both the Scottish and medieval novels, Scott places little reliance on the lower orders. It is not without significance that Arnold Biederman, one of the best of Scott's aristocrats, compares his people to sheep, for it is the herd instinct that Scott fears. Repeating in his own voice ideas he had earlier translated in *Götz von Berlichingen*, he has one of the heroes of his later novels state that he is quick "to protect the commons versus oppression" when they are being wronged, but equally quick "to put them down when oppressing others" (XXXVI, 287). It is perhaps the implicit presence of this philosophy in his work that led Lockhart to state that Scott's "services, direct and indirect, toward repressing the revolutionary propensities of his age were vast—far beyond the comprehension of vulgar politicians." And a Tory historian wrote in *Blackwoods* that the "romances of Sir Walter Scott have gone far to neutralize the dangers of the Reform Bill."[35]

Scott's comments on the political situation of his own time show him applying the same criteria to his own period that he used for the Middle Ages. His main complaint about contemporary English society was its social atomism. He thought that the poor–rates, that overwhelming problem of the early nineteenth century, were caused only in part by the "devil-take-the-hindmost" economics of the manufacturers. Equally important as a cause was the breakdown of social feeling, which in an earlier state of society had made men willing to help people even remotely connected with them. He welcomed, therefore, such an occasion as the coronation of George IV, which, like the medieval feasts and festivals, brought all ranks together and gave a "happy holiday to the monotony of a life of labour."[36]

Since industrialism particularly tended to dissolve those bonds between master and man that he idealized in the Middle Ages, Scott was hostile to the growth of cities. He complained that a "Master calls together 100 workmen for this week and pays them off the next with far less interest in their future fate than in that of as many worn-out shuttles."[37] His surprisingly radical solution to the problems of unemployment was that manufacturers should be taxed "according to the number of hands which they employ on an average ... the produce [to be applied] in maintaining the manufacturing poor." If such a proposal should injure or limit business speculations, Scott cared not at all, since he believed that manufacturing was a lottery and not "a regular profession, in which all who engaged with honest industry and a sufficient capital might reasonably expect returns proportional to their advances and labour."[38] No wonder, then, that Scott, like Ruskin, celebrated a Middle Ages when factories did not exist and the

---

[35] Quoted in Crane Brinton, *The Political Ideas of the English Romantics* (London: Oxford University Press, 1926), p. 139.

[36] Lockhart, *Memoirs of Scott*, III, 550.

[37] Scott, *Letters*, VI, 103–104.

[38] Lockhart, *Memoirs of Scott*, III, 179.

guilds proclaimed that "the beauty of a trade is not in wealthe but in moral worth."

Scott's sympathy with workmen, however, was limited. The distaste he shows for the mob in his medieval works is only a literary expression of his very acute anxiety over the possibilities of uprisings in nineteenth-century England. Living in the shadow of the French Revolution, he could condemn dissatisfied Galashiels weavers as a *Jacquerie* or approve the Manchester magistrates' action at Peterloo. He thought the city rabble was "rendered effeminate and vicious by over-wages and over-living," [39] and in his angrier mood he must have envied such medieval characters as Götz for the summary way they treated a mob.

On the whole, though, Scott's attitude was temperate. His ideal was to have England retain as much as possible of the old feudal relations between the poor and their "natural leaders" that he praised in his novels and that prevailed at Abbotsford. There Tom Purdie, Scott's servant, "always appeared at his master's elbow on Sunday, when dinner was over, and drank long life to the laird and lady and all the good company in a quaigh of whiskey or a tumbler of wine." [40] During periods of unemployment Scott provided jobs for as many as thirty of the laborers in his neighborhood by setting them to work on his grounds, paying them piecework to assure their diligence. During the labor uprising of 1819, he planned for a corps of yeomen to be called "The Loyal Foresters," who would aid their lairds in defending their property.

Scott's own practice, then, shows how appealing the medieval myth of an ordered society might be. He never actually said that he was trying to reproduce at Abbotsford, or in England as a whole, the conditions of the Middle Ages. Later medievalists would do that. But it is clear that his attitudes toward industry and labor are outgrowths

[39] *Ibid.*, p. 180.
[40] *Ibid.*, p. 434. G. M. Young writes, "It was, I think, his deep and simple conviction that if the relations between the Duke of Buccleuch and Walter Scott and between Walter Scott and Tom Purdie had existed in France, there would have been no French Revolution because there would have been no need."

of the same mixed love and fear of the common man that were to characterize medievalist thought in general and that, at its best, resulted in an active concern for the popular welfare.

The Romantic movement has been called an attempt to bring color back in the world; medievalism, as it develops in Scott, is clearly part of the same attempt. Not only does it provide pageantry and drama, but, equally important, reduces society to a graspable human pattern of brotherly men and fatherly leaders. It is part of the same desire to feel at home in the universe that led Carlyle, who was deeply influenced by Scott, to write his two greatest books: *Sartor Resartus*, a search for a Father in Heaven, and *Past and Present*, a search for a father on earth.

It is not surprising that Scott's novels had such wide popularity and his medievalism such deep influence. His imaginative projection of history and society made the Middle Ages as real to his century as Athens and Rome had been to the minds of preceding centuries. Like the classical myth, his medieval myth appealed to some of the deepest desires of his age: its wish to make the individual life heroic and yet to unify and order society. It was related, too, as we have seen to the Romantic fear of time and to its converse, the desire for permanence and stasis. The phrase "Merry England," which was to become the medievalists' battle cry against the prevailing drabness of the day, was the prose equivalent for the "joy in widest commonalty spread" of the poets.

Romanticism, however, was not solely responsible for the unprecedented success of Scott's medievalism. His feudal community, with its paternalistic lords and contented commons, had real meaning for a nation looking for a way out from the profit of the few and the poverty of the many, and from the shoddiness and ugliness of life in general. Indeed, during the first half of the century, the problems of society were so intense that medievalism was primarily practical—a way to resolve the difficulties and dislocations of the Industrial Revolution. Only toward the end of the century, when the specific economic and social problems became less pressing while the general sense of alienation and depression increased, did medievalism more clearly return to its Romantic origins.

2

Historical Background: Cobbett

MEDIEVALISM WAS NOT only actuated by a desire for the ideal, it was also rooted in a nostalgia for the ordinary. Like the worship of nature, it was part of the yearning for a more pastoral England that was rapidly disappearing, along with the vestigial feudal social structure with which it was closely intertwined. Men who had been young at the beginning of the nineteenth century could remember a past that might almost be called medieval, far different from the bustling industrialism of their maturity. In contrast to the sixteenth or seventeenth centuries, the late eighteenth century was of course "modern" and thought of itself as such. But the nineteenth century was the true age of change: from agriculture to industry, from aristocracy to democracy, from belief to doubt. Before, all was so different as to belong to a different world. As Thackeray wrote in 1860:

> It was only yesterday; but what a gulf between now and then! *Then* was the old world. Stagecoaches, more or less swift, riding-horses, pack-horses, highwaymen, knights in armour, Norman invaders, Roman legions, Druids, Ancient Britons painted blue, and so forth— and these belong to the old period. I will concede a halt in the midst of it, and allow that gun-powder and printing tended to modernise the world. But your railway starts the new era, and we of a certain age belong to the new time and the old one. We are of the time of chivalry as well as ... of the age of steam.[1]

For some commentators the transition was merely a matter of remark

[1] William Makepeace Thackeray, *The Works of William Makepeace Thackeray* (London: Smith, 1911), XX, 72.

or even rejoicing. For others, however, the rapid overturn of ancient customs and institutions was a matter of deepest regret, in which an avowed desire to bring back the Middle Ages was intensified by an unstated longing for the simpler, more harmonious world of their youth.

How medieval was England on the eve of the nineteenth century? It is easy to overemphasize either the progressiveness or stagnancy of early industrial England, but survivals of medieval thought and customs are easy to find. As in the past, the nation was founded upon a Christian orthodoxy, in which the City of God was still publicly acknowledged to be at least as important as the cities of the world. The Church, though no longer part of the medieval church universal, was still established—so firmly established in the eighteenth century that it had grown careless of its position. Although no longer enforced by the dungeon and the stake, membership in it was still the basis of civil privilege, and dissidents from the Establishment had almost no legal power. New forms of Christianity were beginning to challenge Anglican supremacy both from within and without the Church, but it was only after great struggle in the nineteenth century that the heterodox gained a voice.

As a source of political power, land in the eighteenth century was almost as important as it had been in the twelfth. As in the Middle Ages almost until their end, the power of the king was nominal, that of the landholders real, though the rule of the landed gentry had superseded that of the great nobles of the Middle Ages. Upon that class almost all the power of the state had devolved: executive, legislative, judicial. As justices of the peace, they were responsible for the local militia; as commissioned officers, for the conduct of the army. Primarily, however, their source of strength was civil rather than military. In place of the martial retainers of the past, the landlords had substituted the "peaceful feudalism" of "an army of faithful voters,"[2] and with their aid fully controlled the Parliament.

Local government was particularly bound by tradition. Some parishes still maintained open vestries, a form of primitive democracy;

[2] Elie Halévy, *A History of the English People in the Nineteenth Century*, trans. E. I. Watkin, rev. ed. (London: E. Benn, 1949), I, 108.

almost all possessed the ancient manorial institutions of court-baron and court-leet. Most archaic of all customs—"perhaps," as Halévy puts it, "the final relic of a constitution of society anterior to the feudal system"[3]—were the annual meetings of the villagers to allot strips of land in the common fields.

Always, in fact, in considering the persistence of medievalism, we come back to the land. Like an aerial photograph which discloses traces of long-forgotten roads and fortifications, the surface of eighteenth-century England still gave evidence of its former feudal structure. Almost throughout that century the normal life of most English villages continued to be based on the open-field system. In 1700 half the land of England—most of it either in the northwestern districts around Cumberland and Westmoreland or in a central wedge running from Lyme Regis to the Tees estuary and from Southampton to Lowestoft —was still unenclosed and consisted mainly of earlier enclosures or the lord's domain land lying alongside the open fields. Only a little more land was enclosed between 1700 and 1760, and even the great wave of enclosures that began in 1760 took several generations to complete. As late as 1798 about 20,000 out of 23,000 arable acres in Middlesex were still cultivated by the open-field system, and in all of England some eight or nine million acres still remained either as open fields or commonage.[4]

Such antique modes of landholding encouraged the persistence of the medieval gradation of society into landlords, yeomen, and laborers and of the most primitive forms of husbandry. The changing seasons still saw the familiar three-course rotation of two crops and a fallow, and in spite of the efforts of progressive agriculturalists to introduce

[3] *Ibid.*, I, 236.

[4] See J. H. Clapham, *An Economic History of Modern Britain, 1820–1850*, 2nd ed., 3 vols. (Cambridge: The University Press, 1930), I, 9, 19–20; J. L. and Barbara Hammond, *The Village Labourer, 1760–1832*, 4th ed. (London: Longmans, Green, 1927), pp. 9, 18; William Smart, *Economic Annals of the Nineteenth Century, 1801–1820*, 2 vols. (London: Macmillan, 1901), I, 25. For more recent discussions of the effect of enclosures see Peter Laslett, *The World We Have Lost: England before the Industrial Age* (New York: Scribners, 1965); and M. Dorothy George, *England in Transition: Life and Work in the Eighteenth Century* (Baltimore: Penguin Books, 1965).

turnips and artificial grasses, the inevitable crops on fields which had to be cultivated by common consent were still wheat, barley, oats, and beans. Plowing was done with oxen that wore "simple heavy wooden yokes such as were used five hundred years ago."[5] Outside the eastern counties, where Jethro Tull had been influential, grain was likely to be sown broadcast, harvesting to be done by hand, and threshing with a flail.[6]

The homes of the yeomanry tended to be archaic, too, presenting an appearance that was Elizabethan, if not medieval. In his *The Rural Life of England*, written in 1844, William Howitt records that stone floors, pewter plates, naked tables, and straw beds could be found almost everywhere in England—found, as he describes it, in conjunction with the Old English Plenty that was part of the medievalist's creed. "The spots are not difficult to be found even now," he writes, "where the old oak table, with legs as thick and black as those of an elephant, is spread in the homely house-place, for the farmer and his family— wife, children, servants, male and female; and his heaped with the rude plenty of beans and bacon, beef and bacon . . . a table where bread and cheese, and beer and good milk porridge . . . or stirabout still resist the introduction of tea and coffee."[7]

Written in the Hungry Forties, a half-century after commentators had begun remarking that farmers no longer dined with their laborers, Howitt's description seems here to be idyllic rather than accurate as a portrait of the mid-nineteenth century, but it probably pictures the earlier period quite well. Certainly, in the late eighteenth century, when roads were not much better than they had been in the Middle Ages or, indeed, than "God had left them after the Flood,"[8] domestic life in many parts of rural England was perforce both simple and

[5] William Howitt, *The Rural Life of England*, 2nd ed. (London, 1840), p. 100.

[6] J. Alfred Eggar, *Remembrances of Life and Customs in Gilbert White's, Cobbett's, and Charles Kingsley's Country* (London: Simpkin, Marshall, Hamilton, Kent, 1924), mentions that hand harvesting continued until 1870 and threshing with a flail until 1880 in some parts of Surrey.

[7] Howitt, *Rural Life*, pp. 107–108.

[8] E. Lipson, *The Economic History of England*, 5th ed., 3 vols. (London: Black, 1931), II, 442–443.

self-sufficient. Each parish, almost every home, landlocked through winter frost and spring rains, had to provide almost all its own needs. Bread and beer, therefore, the staples of food and drink, were made at home, and though weaving was usually done by a town craftsman known simply as *"the* weaver," the hearthside spinning wheel only disappeared with the triumph of industrialism. So ancient indeed were the customs of the North that F. M. Eden mentions distaff spinning there into the 1790s.[9] Novelists as late as George Eliot and even Thomas Hardy record the persistence of these ways.

In the isolated rural areas, customs and superstitions, too, recalled an ancient world. On Christmas Eve, even in the nineteenth century, Devon carollers wassailed their apple trees, sprinkling the roots with cider and singing:

> Wassail the trees, that they may beare
> You many a plum, and many a peare;
> For more of the use of the fruit they will bring
> As you do give them wassailing.[10]

At Michaelmas, when farmers and servants flocked to the Statute Fair to make engagements for the coming year, other medieval traditions prevailed. Shepherds wore a hank of wool in their hats; milkmaids, a tuft of cow's hair; carters, a piece of whip cord. Plough Monday, one of the numerous holidays retained from the Middle Ages, must have looked like a morality play come to life. Servants and laborers, dressed as harlequins, their faces daubed white, red, and black, rushed through the village armed with wooden swords. One of their numbers was always dressed as a woman and carried a besom, while another drove a team of men-horses with noisy, though painless, blows.

Even in urban areas modernity was slow in coming. The economist J. H. Clapham cautions us against thinking that the average "town worker of the decade 1820–30 was . . . a person who performed for a

---

[9] Sir Frederick Morton Eden, *The State of the Poor*, 3 vols. (London, 1797), I, 559.
[10] Howitt, *Rural Life*, p. 470.

self-made employer in steaming air, with the aid of recently devised mechanisms, operations which would have made his grandfather gape."[11] More likely he worked for a small firm, using tools that had not been changed for centuries. When change did come—and it came unevenly to different parts of England—the basic social and family structures still remained static, retaining the patterns of medieval life long after the seeming arrival of industrialism.[12]

In many trades, relics of the guild system survived. The London companies—apothecaries, barbers, brewers, butchers, cooks, curriers, cutlers, innholders, masons, plumbers, stationers—were recognizable medieval institutions even in the early nineteenth century, and in many industries the apprentice system was still common. Apprenticeship rules in the hat industry were only repealed in the 1770s, and almost until 1800 a man still had to serve a five-year apprenticeship to expose his cloth for sale in the Leeds Cloth Hall. In some of the new industries, the ideals of apprenticeship had been successfully applied to the new conditions. One manufacturer, for example, made it a practice "to be in his warehouse before six in the morning, accompanied by his children and apprentices. At seven they all came to breakfast, which consisted of one large dish of water-pottage made of oatmeal. . . . At the side was . . . a basin of milk, and master and apprentices, each with a wooden spoon in his hand, without loss of time, dipped into the same dish and thence into the milk pan."[13]

Indeed, it would be a mistake to say that medieval social controls were ever completely abandoned. The Assize of Bread governed the weight and price of a loaf from 1266 to 1836, even though in actuality the bread was often adulterated. Centuries-old statutes against engrossing, forestalling, and regrating of corn were invoked as late as 1800 under special circumstances, and a statute of Edward III still regulated wages in the late eighteenth century. In all of these cases, the medieval carry-over persisted so long that it seemed almost to blend into the

[11] Clapham, *Economic History*, I, 74.

[12] Laslett, *World We Have Lost, passim.*

[13] Lipson, *Economic History*, II, 73. See also H. D. Traill (ed.), *Social England*, 6 vols. (New York, 1896), V, *passim.*

modern reform: into the laws regulating the purity of food, speculations on the market, and the security of labor. Over and over, as our medievalists well knew, "modern" reforms were but conscious or unconscious returns to older principles.

To the question of how much the continuing medievalism of English life affected the new feudalists, geography provides an interesting answer, for almost all of them came from a region that was particularly backward. In Sir Walter Scott's Lowlands, and indeed in all of Scotland, practically no land had been enclosed before his birth in 1771 and little enough by his death in 1832. The nineteenth-century Scottish peasant still paid his rents with feudal services as well as money, and Scott could rightly think of the duke of Buccleuch as a feudal laird in days when rents were usually paid in kind and use of the lord's mill likely to be compulsory.

In the area surrounding the Lake District, somewhat similar conditions existed, although the machinery of land tenure was somewhat different. For all his sturdy independence, the northern yeoman was in some respects a villein still. His land was burdened with dues and heriots; his time cut into by the "boon days" on which, if summoned, he might have to fetch and carry the lord's peat, plough or harrow his fields, reap his corn, make his hay, or carry his letters. Particularly in Cumberland, antique customs tended to prevail long after they had died out elsewhere. There hand spinning continued the longest; there unmarried laborers dined with their farmers almost into the reign of Victoria; there the parish priest took knife and fork and lived for a while with each of the farmers in his district.

Because these areas were so late in moving forward from the past, they gave early nineteenth-century observers the opportunity to see what one commentator has called the "sudden sunset" of the feudal era.[14] Scott's frequent references to the dying cottage industries, Coleridge's dislike of enclosures, and Southey's praise of medieval trade regulations are only a few of the ways in which writers tried to keep England from completely abandoning the customs and values

[14] Kenneth MacLean, *Agrarian Age: A Background for Wordsworth*, Yale Studies in English, Vol. CXV (New Haven: Yale University Press, 1950), p. 27.

with which they had grown up. Some of their ideas came simply from a sentimental fear of change—a rather reactionary desire to retain the thatched cottage and smock frock. Most of their medievalism, however, proceeded from a humanitarian concern for the welfare of the common man. If it stressed the necessary subordination of the lower orders, it also made sure that these lower orders had land to till, decent places to work, and the same solid prosperity their ancestors were thought to have enjoyed.

Most medievalists were learned men who balanced their nostalgic longings for the past with a wide knowledge of its literature and history. William Cobbett, however, had little of their sophistication or learning. A yeoman (to use a word he liked), a peasant (to use a word he hated), he represented with exaggerated intensity the reaction of the average rural Briton to the new nonfeudal world.

II

The countryside of Cobbett's youth offers no exception to the rule that medievalists tended to come from "medieval" areas, for his native Surrey was remarkably slow in embracing modern improvements. A Board of Agriculture report for 1794 chided the local farmers for "having so little business capacity that they preferred to sell their corn cheap to old customers than to accept better offers from persons with whom they were unaccustomed to deal." The report stated that 96,000 acres were still unenclosed and that in the unenclosed areas scarcely a turnip or a cloverblade was to be found.[15] The plows there were almost identical with those "used by their grandfathers"; drill-planting and horse-hoeing remained as unknown as they had been five hundred years before.[16]

The ancient town of Farnham, in which William Cobbett was born in 1763, was a particularly appropriate birthplace for him. Its two great landmarks were Farnham Castle and Waverley Abbey: the one

[15] William James and Jacob Malcolm, *General View of the Agriculture of the County of Surrey . . . Drawn up for the Board of Agriculture* (London, 1794), p. 1.
[16] *Ibid.*, p. 41.

suggesting the power of medieval England that Cobbett would praise; the other, the spoliations of Henry VIII that he would denounce. Even more important, however, as a symbol of medieval life was Farnham Common, on which in 1801 a hundred townsmen and cotters still enjoyed their ancient rights of pasturage and goosage[17]— a reminder of the old English right to the land that Cobbett was to claim once again for his countrymen.

Cobbett himself was a fitting inheritor of this tradition. He often said that his only claim of lineage was that he had been born "in old England." His grandfather had been a day laborer and had served one farmer for forty years. His grandmother, with whom Cobbett spent his boyhood Christmases, lived in a thatched cottage, made a turf fire, and used a rushlight for her evening illumination. Cobbett recalled that she gave him bread and milk for breakfast and apple pudding for dinner.[18]

It is perhaps worthwhile to quote at some length Cobbett's own description of the England he remembered, both for its intrinsic interest as a portrait of an era that had vanished and as a proof that he himself identified the world of the 1770s with the almost feudal past. He writes that

> in those "dark ages" that the impudent Scotch economists talk about, we had a great many holidays. There were all the fairs of our own place, and all the fairs of the places just round about. There were several days at Christmas, at Easter, at Whitsuntide; and we had a day or two at Hollantide, as we used to call it, which came in November, I believe, and at Candlemass. Besides these, there were cricket-matches, and single-stick matches; and all these were not thought too much. . . . I never knew a labouring man, in those "dark ages," go out to his work in the morning without a bottle of beer and a satchel of victual, containing cheese, if not bacon, hung upon his crook. . . .
>
> In the "dark ages," when I was a boy, country labourers' wives used

[17] Arthur Young, *An Inquiry into the Propriety of Applying Wastes to the Better Maintenance and Support of the Poor* (Bury, 1801), p. 5.

[18] William Cobbett, *The Autobiography of William Cobbett*, ed. William Reitzel, new ed. (London: Faber, 1947), p. 10.

to spin the wool, and knit the stockings and gloves that were wanted in the family. My grandmother knit stockings for me after she was blind. Farmers' wives and daughters, and servant maids, were spinning, reeling, carding, knitting, or at something or other of that sort, whenever the work of the farm-house did not demand them.

Accordingly, be it observed there wanted no schools, no Lancastrian or Bell work, no Tracts, no circulation of Bibles, to make the common people generally honest and obedient.[19]

Despite the apparent inconsistencies of his political views, Cobbett remained true to this timeless, rather stagnant background throughout his life. Both in his early Tory period and in his later, more prolonged and famous radicalism, Cobbett's real aim was to bring back the idyllic and prosperous world of the 1760s and return the nation to its ordered and agricultural past. Whether England in the 1760s was indeed as superior to post-Napoleonic England as Cobbett claimed has increasingly become a matter for debate among historians, some of whom believe it was a new awareness of poverty rather than an increase in the actual suffering of the poor that made the opening years of the nineteenth century seem so dreadful.[20] If so, much of the credit for this awareness must go to Cobbett and to the differences he saw, both real and fancied, between past and present. The contrasts he makes between the unenclosed fields of the Farnham countryside, with their sturdy yeoman populace, and the dispossessed tenants of the age that followed sound the keynote of medievalism, as does his comparison between the orderly and stable society of one era and the deracinated competitiveness of the next.

It is this loyalty to a past in which the common man had his necessities and comforts—and also his fixed station in life—that conditioned all of Cobbett's statements, both in his Tory and Radical phases. A more yielding man than Cobbett might have found the sixteen years he spent abroad from 1784 to 1800 in revolutionary America and France and the rapid changes of his new, industrialized century somewhat unsettling to his beliefs. Cobbett simply grew more pugnaciously British

[19] *Ibid.*, pp. 15–16.
[20] George, *England in Transition, passim.*

and old-fashioned as the world around him changed. If the rest of the world was marching headlong forward, he at least would simply shout the louder for the class system of old England: for "long-tried principles ... ancient families ... ancient establishments ... king ... laws ... magistracy .... church ... and country."[21] He wanted to make the "poor man proud of his inferiority" by giving him a "personal affection for his lord."[22] He declared in 1803 that England must revive her nationhood by bringing back the spirit of the Plantagenets. "The days of the Veres and Percies, and Cliffords, and Nevilles must return," he wrote, "and the glory of leading *vassals* into the *field* must once more be the responsibility of England's gentry."[23]

Such explicit medievalism was rare in Cobbett's earlier work, however, since Cobbett at first believed that the elimination of some relatively recent malpractices would be a sufficient solution to the nation's problems. Looking at the plight of the poor around him, Cobbett came to believe that the chief cause of England's misery was not the amount of wealth the country produced but the way in which that wealth was distributed. In 1804, long before Carlyle was to pose the "sphinx-riddle" of poverty in the midst of plenty, Cobbett was asking whether the "turnpike roads and canals, the amazing Manufactures of Manchester and Birmingham, the immense extent and riches of London" were enriching the nation as a whole or simply a small group of manufacturers and stockjobbers.[24] Under the rule of this new class, Cobbett claimed, corruption was openly practiced. It was the cost of this corruption, together with the financial waste of the Napoleonic Wars, that was impoverishing the common man by laying upon him a burden of intolerable taxation. Until that was eliminated, Cobbett was sure, the nation would continue to decline.

Graft and boodle were, of course, fairly easy to see. Newspapers

[21] John M. Cobbett and James P. Cobbett (eds.), *Selections from Cobbett's Political Works*, 6 vols. (London, n.d.), I, 469.

[22] Reitzel, *Autobiography of Cobbett*, p. 93.

[23] William Cobbett, *Selections*, introduction by A. M. D. Hughes (Oxford: Oxford University Press, 1923), p. 159.

[24] G. D. H. and Margaret Cole (eds.), *The Opinions of William Cobbett* (London: Cobbett Publishing Co., 1944), p. 62.

advertised the sale of pensions and sinecures; parliamentary seats were open to the highest bidder; Addington's son, aged twelve, held a £3,000 a year office; and a baroness earned a handsome sum as Sweeper of the Malls. Cobbett himself was offered a profitable slice of a public loan in order to purchase his opinion. As Cobbett looked closer, however, he began to realize that these episodes of corruption, for which he blamed the Pitt government, were but the surface manifestations of a vast shift in power. A *nouveau riche* class was using taxes and financial maneuvers to supplant the ancient aristocracy and then building Gothic ruins in their gardens to prove its rights to the soil. Although Cobbett's explicit medievalism did not develop in detail until later, all these early references show an unconscious identification of a chivalrous nobility with a desirable social order and a fear of a false aristocracy as usurping an unjust place.

Cobbett saw·in the triumph of the newly rich not only the death knell of aristocracy but the destruction of the yeoman class upon which England had depended for a thousand years. He claimed that banking and funding (paper money and taxation), the two chief devices by which the new upper classes achieved their power, worked particular hardship on the small tenant and landholder. Paper money drove prices up faster than wages could follow them, and borrowing imposed such high duties on vital consumer goods that Cobbett declared a man with an income of £20 a year might well spend £10 on candles, malt, bricks, and tea. Under this dual pressure, which was often aggravated by the escalating rentals of an inflationary period, Cobbett asserted, not without cause, that the small landowner and tenant were being forced to sell out and become laborers. He saw the disappearance of this group as a break in the historic continuity of England and as disruptive of the benevolent social order that he would later associate with the Middle Ages. He wrote in 1806:

> ... the *paper* system, has ... drawn the real property of the nation into fewer hands; it has made land and agriculture objects of speculation; it has, in every part of the kingdom, moulded many farms into one; it has almost entirely extinguished the race of small farmers; from

one end of England to the other, the houses which formerly contained little farms and their happy families, are now seen sinking into ruins, all the windows except one or two stopped up, letting in just enough light for the labourer, whose father was, perhaps the small farmer, to look back upon his half-naked and half-famished children, while, from his door, he surveys all around him the land teeming with the means of luxury to his overgrown and opulent master.[25]

However much Cobbett hated the new business class, manipulators of the beastly "Thing," as he called the national debt, he reserved some of his bitterest invective for the evangelicals and dissenters, by no means excluding the reformers among them from his wrath. He felt for them the sort of instinctive dislike that the Middlemarchers had for Mr. Bulstrode or Mr. Weller for the Rev. Mr. Stiggins. To Cobbett an evangelical manufacturer was a hypocritical miser who sweated honest laborers in steaming, lint-filled factories while uttering pious fears for the natives of Borrio-boola-Gha. (That the philanthropic aims of a Lord Shaftesbury came very close to his own he somehow managed to ignore.) The list of his complaints against the dissenters and their causes is at once ludicrous and shrewd. It includes "money and manufactures; the nasal twang of a methodistical nose; the extermination of bulldogs; the converting of negroes into saints; Sunday schools for making scholars of those whose business it is to delve; soup shops for feeding those who are too idle to work and too proud to beg; the abolition of tithes; thick handkerchiefs for ladies' bosoms. . . ."[26] He did not have much sympathy for high-and-dry Anglicanism, either, and to annoy both parties, he was willing to espouse any cause, even that of Catholic Emancipation. His later, pro-Catholic medievalism can thus be at least partly explained, like many of Cobbett's enthusiasms, as a dislike for something else.

III

Two forces, then, gradually drew Cobbett toward an interest in the Middle Ages. The first was his dislike for the newly rich and his desire

[25] Cobbett and Cobbett, *Selections*, II, 48.   [26] *Ibid.*, I, 295.

to return to a world in which rich and poor were symbiotically, rather than parasitically, related. The other was his acute dislike for contemporary religious tendencies. At first taking him back only as far as his idealized boyhood of the 1760s, these preferences—or prejudices, if you will—eventually attracted him to pre-Reformation England.

The immediate impetus for Cobbett's propagandistic medievalism may well have been given him by his reading of a *History of England* (1819–30) by John Lingard, a Catholic priest. But it is misleading to state, as G. D. H. Cole does in his definitive life of Cobbett, that "Cobbett was carried away" by the book, in which he "discovered for the first time that the medieval Church, and especially the monasteries, had performed important social functions, that the tithes had been destined for the care of the poor as well as the parson . . . and that the Reformation had ruthlessly swept away the communal world of the medieval Church without putting anything in its place."[27] Cobbett's work was not only implicitly promedieval in its hatred of capitalism and evangelicalism but actually explicitly so long before Lingard's book was published. All through his early writings—together, it must be admitted, with some scattered hostility—statement after statement appears praising the Middle Ages in comparison with the present. Knowing, for example, how valuable the waste, or commons, had been during the Middle Ages as a source of wealth and freedom for the poor, he asserted that "a family reared by the side of a common or forest" was far better off both for food and for environment than a "family bred in the pestiferous stench of a town."[28] And he told his readers that feudal vassalage was "not so degrading . . . as the vassalage of our manufactories."[29] Writing in 1811 Cobbett described the medieval Catholic clergy as wise, virtuous, and brave and praised the Church as the defender of the poor. He even began to hint at that period, as he would later vociferously insist, that medieval England was more prosperous and more populous than modern.

[27] G. D. H. Cole, *The Life of William Cobbett*, 3rd ed. rev. (London: Home and Vanthal, 1947), p. 289.
[28] Cobbett and Cobbett, *Selections*, IV, 262.
[29] *Ibid.*, II, 310.

Nevertheless, Lingard's book was useful in providing Cobbett with a factual basis for the very detailed and polemical medievalism he came to espouse. An annotated edition of Cobbett's *A History of the Protestant Reformation in England and Ireland* (1824–26), the work in which he most forcefully attacked post-Reformation England, lists scores of occasions on which Lingard is obviously the source of Cobbett's information and points out several passages in which the books show verbal parallels.[30] Cobbett himself did not hesitate to admit that he had read Lingard's book, at least in part, and referred to it on several occasions. Being Cobbett, however, he naturally followed up his admission with the remark that Lingard's work, although "able and good," would never "produce a thousandth part of the *effect*" that his would.[31]

Lingard's history does not account for either the tone or real theme of Cobbett's book. The sober cleric would have blushed to hear the Reformation referred to as "the thing . . . engendered in beastly lust, brought forth in hypocrisy and perfidy, and cherished and fed by plunder, devastation, and by rivers of innocent English and Irish blood"[32] or to hear Elizabeth's time called "the pauper and ripping-up reign . . . . of 'good Queen Bess'" (I, ix, 259). Nor could he have ever risen to the dazzling invective of calling Henry VIII a "royal PEACHUM" receiving parcels of plunder worth almost a million pounds from church and convent (I, vi, 178). More significantly, though, Lingard could not provide Cobbett with the all-important contrast between pre-Reformation wealth and modern poverty because he never made it. As Cobbett wrote in an early comment on the book,

> I lament that the Doctor, like other historians, has not informed us of the *prices* of *labour* and of *food* in the several reigns. This is a matter in which we are much more interested than in the intrigues of courts,

[30] Francis Aidan, Cardinal Gasquet (ed.), *A History of the Protestant Reformation in England and Ireland* (New York, n.d.), *passim*.

[31] William Cobbett, "To the British Catholic Association," in *Cobbett's Weekly Register*, LII (October 30, 1824), 288.

[32] William Cobbett, *A History of the Protestant Reformation in England and Ireland*, 2 vols. (London, 1829), I, letter vii, para. 192.

battles, and negotiations. If, for instance, a history of the *present day* were to give us the boastings about . . . our *"twice conquering France,"* . . . and about the *"Quarter's Revenue"* . . . if a history of the present were to treat posterity to this, and say nothing about the English and the Scotch *paupers* and the Irish *starvers;* were to say nothing about Englishmen being harnessed like horses to draw gravel . . . [or] of the *manure-eating* in Ireland . . . ; if posterity were to get this as a *history* of England in the reign of George the Fourth, what a lying history this would be! One page at the end of each reign telling us what men got for their work, and what they paid for their food would have been better calculated than all the rest of the history, to make us judge correctly of the goodness or badness of the Government.[33]

One of the sources of Cobbett's conclusions about the superior living standard of medieval England was Sir John Fortescue's *De Laudibus Legum Angliae,* a book to which he frequently refers. A disquisition on statecraft written for Henry VI and popular up to the nineteenth century, Fortescue's book sought to prove the superiority of the English over Continental forms of government by contrasting the prosperity of the comfortable English yeoman with the misery of the downtrodden French peasant. Other sources included Gilbert White's *Natural History and Antiquities of Selborne,* Sharon Turner's *History of England,* and Cobbett's own *History of Parliament from the Earliest Times to the Year 1803* (a work that now forms the opening volume of Hansard's *Parliamentary Debates.*) It is worth mentioning these books if only to show how varied the sources of medievalism were and how many different kinds of works contributed to the growing idealization of the past.

Although all of these scholarly productions were essential to *A History of the Protestant Reformation,* which is inconceivable without a prior corpus of knowledge, the trenchancy of Cobbett's writing there really depends on something else—the impact of immediate events on an angry mind. For one thing, Cobbett wrote the *Protestant Reformation* because he wished to defend the Irish Catholics, who he thought

[33] Cobbett, "To the British Catholic Association," pp. 272–274.

unjustly treated, and whose leader, Daniel O'Connell, was his ally. For another, he wrote it because his second exile to the United States from 1817 to 1819 had shown him that the modern world could still allow a society to remain prosperous and free if it avoided the pitfalls into which England had recently fallen. Mainly, Cobbett wrote his history as the propagandistic work that it is because his travels through England, the famous rural rides, had shown him more vividly than he had ever known it the degradation of his native land. In his home county of Surrey, for instance, he remembered a village fair at which the "white smock frocks, and red handkerchiefs, and nice clean clothes of the girls," used to serve as ornaments to the day. Stumbling upon it in a rural ride in 1822, he found there were "not a tenth part of the people, and these, in general ragged and dirty with some few girls drawn off in tawdry cottons, looking more like town prostitutes than country girls." And this, Cobbett concluded unhappily, "was a fair sample of the whole country."[34]

A History of the Protestant Reformation attempts to explain the beginnings of the degradation Cobbett saw around him. It is a wrathful denunciation of the way in which the people's birthright was sold and the Reformation divided a unified and wealthy country into two nations, "masters and slaves, a very few enjoying the extreme of luxury, and millions doomed to the extreme of misery" (I, v, 149)—or, as Cobbett also phrased it, how "this land of meat and beef was changed, all of a sudden into a land of dry bread and oatmeal porridge" (I, vi, 165).

Cobbett supports his thesis in many ways. One of them is to argue the superiority of medieval civilization by exaggerating the wealth of England in the Middle Ages. He calculates that the national wealth of England and Wales in 1804 was only about two-thirds of what it had been just before the Reformation, and it was far less equitably distributed. The typical medieval, landed gentleman, according to Cobbett, was worth perhaps four times as much as his successor in the nineteenth century, but his income was not disproportionate to that of the poor, all of whom had a decent competency.

[34] William Cobbett, "Letter to Lord John Russell," in *Weekly Political Register*, LII (October 16, 1824), 145.

One reason that all were comfortable in the Middle Ages was that wages and prices were in rational proportion, something no longer true in the age of manipulated currency. A medieval dung-cart filler, Cobbett asserts, "had more than the price of a fat goose and a half for a day's work, and ... [could] earn very nearly a pair of shoes every day ... a fat shorn sheep in four days; ... a fat hog, two years old, in twelve days; ... [and] a grass fed ox in twenty days." No wonder, then, that even poor men dined ordinarily on "beef, pork, mutton, and veal," and that the very plowmen had gloves to wear (I, xvi, 466). Go, tell this, says Cobbett bitterly, to the "poor souls ... who are eating horse-flesh and grains (draff) in Lancashire and Cheshire; who are harnessed like horses drawing gravel in Hampshire and Sussex; who have 3d a day allowed them by the Magistrates in Norfolk; who are, all over England, worse fed than the felons in the jails" (I, xvi, 460).

Between the crime rates of the Middle Ages and modern times Cobbett notes a great difference, for it is only since the Reformation that vagrancy and crime have become a major problem. Before then, men lacked the chief incentives to wrongdoing: hunger and despair. Confounding together all periods of the Middle Ages with equal impartiality, he notes that in Alfred's reign—Alfred, whom all Englishmen ought to revere—a bracelet could be hung by the roadside in utter safety and that in Fortescue's time judges could do their work in three hours a day. What a difference, Cobbett exclaims, between their times and ours. Now we build a treadmill on the very spot where Alfred lies buried and have so much work for our judges that a whole day of hearings scarcely suffices.

Not only were medieval Englishmen more prosperous and more honest than their modern descendents; they were also, Cobbett is sure, more numerous. As early as 1807 Cobbett had observed that areas which now were waste had once been under cultivation. As the years went on Cobbett became obsessed with the notion that these abandoned fields indicated a decrease in population since the Middle Ages. Casting about for further proofs of his idea, he was struck by the disparity he often observed between the medieval church and its modern parish. Time and again in his travels Cobbett paused to remark churches obviously built to hold five or even ten times the number of present inhabitants, or, indeed, to hold all the current parishioners, infants and invalids included, on the porch alone. Far from seeing that the loss of rural population had been more than compensated by the urban increases or from understanding that the medieval mind scorned a mean-sized church, Cobbett simply went on to claim that only "down-right idiots" could fail to be convinced that "England was not more populous before the 'Reformation' than it is now" (I, xvi, 453).

Actually, by the time Cobbett wrote *A History of the Protestant Reformation* enough was known about the historical growth of the English population to make his beliefs absurd. But Cobbett was not one to abandon an outrageous theory lightly, especially when that theory served to refute his archfoe Malthus. For, if he could show that Malthus was wrong in thinking that population grew geometrically, then he could also show that the source of England's current difficulties was not the improvident procreativity of the poor. And once he had shown that the poor were not to blame for their own misfortunes, then he could argue logically against the restraints and hardships wrought on them in Malthus's name. What is more, he could triumphantly fix the blame elsewhere—on the financial system, the "Thing," which he had so long denounced!

In other ways, too, Cobbett used the supposed superiority of the Middle Ages as a way of lashing out at present-day abuses. His own experiences of being once jailed and twice forced to flee England for expressing his beliefs made him particularly sensitive to what the twentieth century calls civil liberties. Everyone, he wrote, talks about the "liberties of England," but what are these liberties and where did we get them? They consist, he answers, in "the laws which regulate the descent and possession of property; the safety from arrest, unless by due and settled process; the absence of all punishment without trial before duly authorized and well known judges and magistrates; the trial by jury; the precautions taken by divers writs and summonses; the open trial; the impartiality in the proceedings" (I, xvi,

456). And they were given to us by our Catholic ancestors. It is we who have marred them with our unjust confiscations of Roman Catholic property, our summary arrests and trials, our suspensions of habeas corpus, our venal judges and packed juries, our treadmills, transportations, and hangings.

Besides, Cobbett asks, what is freedom, anyway? His definition— Tory and medievalistic, for all his radicalism—is that it is a form of security: the right to the "full and quiet enjoyment of your property," without which "you may call yourself what you will, but you are a slave." On this point, Cobbett says, our medieval ancestors took particular care:

> They suffered neither kings nor parliaments to touch their property without cause clearly shown. They did not read newspapers, they did not talk about debates; they had no taste for "mental enjoyment"; but they thought hunger and thirst great evil, and they never suffered any body to put them to board on cold potatoes and water. They looked upon bare bones and rags as indubitable marks of slavery, and they never failed to resist any attempt to affix these marks upon them. (I, xvi, 456)

Even in the matter of political rights, says Cobbett, once more using the Middle Ages to argue for parliamentary reform, our ancestors were better off than we. The chief reason for a parliament is to make sure that we are not taxed without representation and that all have a voice so that none are burdened unduly. To such justice modern England can make no claim, but the Middle Ages could. To be sure, even Cobbett cannot claim that all his Catholic ancestors had the vote, but then, he remarks, neither do a "fiftieth part of us." And they, he believed, had annual instead of septennial Parliaments. Furthermore, they had their church to guard them. "The whole of our history shows," he says, "that the Church was invariably on the side of the people, and that, in all the much and justly boasted of triumphs which our forefathers obtained over their kings and nobles, the Church took the lead," able to do so because it was powerful enough to be independent of all temporal powers (I, xvi, 456).

The Church was also responsible for the greater unity of medieval England, that Burkean sense of cohesion so important to all our new feudalists. In part, Cobbett thinks, this patriotism was the result of pride in English power, in the possession of Calais and Boulogne, and in the victories of Crécy and Agincourt—possessions and victories far surpassing those of the shrunken, cowardly England of George IV. But it came from other sources, too: from an attachment to the lovely and productive countryside, from a reciprocal faith between peasant and lord, from admiration and veneration for "ancient and magnificent proofs of skill and of opulence" (I, v, 155)—from churches and cathedrals, convents and monasteries, schools and colleges, castles and palaces.

What have we now in their place, Cobbett asks, to make men proud of the beauty and wealth of their country? Go into any parish or shire and see what has happened: "Look at the cloister, now become in the hands of a rack-renter, the receptacle for dung, fodder, and faggotwood; see the hall, where, for ages, the widow, the orphan, the aged, and the stranger, found a table ready spread; see a bit of its walls now helping to make a cattleshed, the rest having been hauled away to build a workhouse; recognize in the side of a barn, a part of a once-magnificent Chapel." If, in your musings, Cobbett continues, the voice of a screech owl should remind you of the oncoming of night and the need for shelter, then "look at the white-washed and dry-rotten shell on the hill called the 'gentleman's house'; and, apprized of the 'board-wages' and spring guns . . . jog away from the scene of . . . 'old English Hospitality'" to the nearest inn, where your reception will be "precisely proportioned to the presumed length of your purse" (I, v, 155).

It is these two forces, the monastery and the manor, or the Church and the land, that Cobbett sees as the source of medieval superiority. When their influence waned, modern degradation set in. The son and grandson of Farnham laborers, Cobbett was always convinced that agriculture was the true source of wealth and stability, and that all riches not directly derived from the earth were simply the product of some usurious sleight of hand. The reason, Cobbett thought, that medieval England was great was that neither aristocrats nor laborers ever loosened their Antaeus-grip upon the soil. But once the natural leaders of the land, the clergy and the landowners, ceased to reside in their localities and began to prefer the lively city and the fashionable watering place, England's greatness was finished.

Cobbett's bitterest example of the degeneration of the English clergy is taken from his native Farnham, which had served for nine hundred years as the seat of the bishop of Winchester's palace. He says that William of Wykham, the medieval bishop of Winchester, lived in what have been termed the "dark ages of monkish ignorance and superstition," but spent his income on providing churches, hospitals and education for the men of England. The present incumbent, however, uses his power far differently. He has already divided "twenty-four livings, five Prebends, one Chancellorship, one Archdeaconship, and one Mastership, worth perhaps, all together more than twenty thousand pounds a year" among ten of his relations and is now supplementing his income by allowing "SMALL BEER TO BE SOLD OUT OF HIS EPISCOPAL PALACE AT FARNHAM" (I, iv, 124). No wonder, then, thought Cobbett, that the poor were suffering, when the tithes which in the Middle Ages had been set aside for their support were used to enrich do-nothing churchmen. Under these circumstances, he believed that tithes should be abolished altogether.

Not only did the Reformation undermine England's traditional feudal paternalism but it created a society that was essentially unstable. According to Cobbett, revolution bred revolution. Henry VIII's Reformation, whereby religion was deposed for the sake of a king, showed Cromwell's men that a king could be deposed for the sake of religion. And once that had occurred and the king's divinity been unhedged, then the way was open for the three succeeding revolutions of 1688, 1776, and 1789—all of which Cobbett here denounced.

That Cobbett personally at this time favored the French and American revolutions is beside the point. What he wished to show was that each of these events had involved England in unnecessary military activity which had largely to be sustained by foreign mercenaries. To Cobbett, who had spent two years in prison for denouncing the flogging of English soldiers by German drillmasters, the presence of foreign troops on English soil was unforgivable. Far better to "pay 'pence to PETER' than pounds to Hessian Grenadiers," he declared. Given a choice, he preferred the "cloister to the barrack; the chaunting of matins to the reveille by the drum; the cowl to the brass-fronted hairy cap; the shaven crown to the mustachio; . . . the rosary, with the cross appendant, to the belt with its box of bullets" (I, iii, 90)—the medieval to the modern.

Fundamentally, Cobbett's objection to modern militarism was economic rather than emotional and was related to the complaints he had made against the Pitt government as early as 1802. He saw that the military expenditures involved in keeping an unpopular Protestant dynasty on the throne of England during revolutionary times had taxed England beyond its resources and created that national debt which had divided the nation into a few wealthy taxeaters and a multitude of starving taxpayers and which had turned the English nation, "once the greatest and most moral in the world," into a "nation of incorrigible thieves . . . the most impoverished, the most fallen, the most degraded that ever saw the light of the sun" (I, xvi, 478). Cobbett's praise of the Middle Ages is then a criticism of his increasingly materialistic society. Looking back over the three hundred years since the Reformation, Cobbett saw the wealthy gaining riches without responsibility and the poor becoming dispossessed and demoralized. Englishmen were losing their political rights and, more important, the heartiness, generosity, and sense of unity that had formerly sustained the nation. The government, unjust and unpopular, maintained itself in power by militarism, and the expenses of a standing army were leading the nation to ruin. The answer to the problems of the present lay in a return to the principles of the past.

IV

As history, Cobbett's study of the Reformation is often nonsense and his analysis of its effects as ridiculous in some ways as it is profound in others. An angry book, it is sometimes as stupid and silly as prejudice can make it; other times it is hammered out into a memorable expression of righteous wrath. It shows, however, the two main uses of the medieval ideal in the early nineteenth century: first, as a storehouse of arguments against specific contemporary abuses; second, as a standard against which to measure England's general inadequacy. Cobbett's major contributions to the medieval myth are his popularization of the belief in medieval prosperity, which would develop throughout the century, and his attempted rehabilitation of the medieval Catholic church.

Rural Rides (1830), too, has its share of foolishness and vituperation, but it is a far different and far better work. It evokes the English countryside with a simplicity, a vividness, and a personal directness that is always appealing. Writing with a countryman's eye, Cobbett will always pause to tell us of the crops: here the mangel-wurzel have been improperly seeded and hoed; here is a fine plantation of locusts; here a farmyard with straw so abundant that horses and cattle are bedded right up to their eyes. Occasionally, too, there is a burst of enthusiastic writing describing a fine canter or an all-day ride in the rain.

Again and again *Rural Rides*, the earliest sections of which antedate or parallel the writing of his book on the Reformation shows us the immediate occasion for one of Cobbett's generalities in the *History:* a church too large for its parish, a hillside once plowed in terraces, an estate dating to King Alfred's time now in the clutches of a detested banker, a new Gothic "ruin" on a parvenu's lawn, a jail in imitation of a church. The medieval-modern contrast is repeated, too, as in a passage beginning, "Talk of *vassals!* Talk of *villains* [*sic*]*!* Talk of *cerfs* [*sic*]*! . . .* did feudal times ever see any of them, so debased, so absolutely slaves, as the poor creatures who, in the '*enlightened*' North, are *compelled* to work fourteen hours in a day, in a heat of *eighty-four degrees;* and who are liable to punishment *for looking out at a window of the factory!*" [35]

The medievalism of the *Rural Rides*, however, is not a mere repetition of that in *A History of the Protestant Reformation*. There, Cobbett

[35] William Cobbett, *Rural Rides*, ed. G. D. H. and Margaret Cole, 3 vols. (London: P. Davies, 1930), I, 167–168.

had been concerned with making a generalized outline of the reasons for the superiority of the past and the inferiority of the present. Here his instances are much more particularized, given in minute documentary detail rather than broad strokes and caricature. The social problems of the present are much more specifically stated and solutions from the past are applied to them.

For one thing Cobbett now tends to make a wider indictment. It is not merely the plundering Reformation gentry or the wealthy manipulators of the funds that have impoverished the masses, but Cobbett's own class, the farmers, too. They have tried to ape the customs of the rich and have been able to do so only at the expense of the poor. At farmhouses, Cobbett complains, where "plain manners and plentiful living" once prevailed, all is now as "bare-faced upstart as any stock jobber in the kingdom can boast of." The parlor has replaced the hall and mahogany furniture, the oaken table; carpets cover the well-sanded floor; a bell pull calls the footman or parlormaid to attention. The children are made to be gentlefolk; the laborers degraded to slaves. Echoing a familiar question, Cobbett asks why farmers no longer feed and house their work people as they formerly did. His answer is simple: it is cheaper to give them wages; for the farmer can pay them so little that even though he has a house they can inhabit and a kitchen they can eat in, he will still save money. It is not that the land produces less, Cobbett continues, that makes for poverty, but that there is a new distribution of wealth. The farmer now sits alone at his mahogany table with "*wine-decanters* and *wine-glasses*, and '*a dinner set*'" while his workers go hungry in hovels. "Judge then," he says, "of the *change* that has taken place in the condition of these labourers! And, be astonished, if you can, at the *pauperism* and the *crimes* that now disgrace this once happy and moral England" (I, 276–77).

Cobbett's solutions to the problems of the nation—particularly to this problem of poverty in the midst of plenty—take many forms. Parliamentary reform is a necessity; cutting the national debt by economy and lowered interest rates is another; eliminating tithes is a third. All of these involve some appeal to the past, or the supposed past—to the England of more equitable county representation, of annual parliaments, of solid agricultural wealth, of a resident clergy. His medievalism shows most clearly, however, in his plans for regenerating the land itself.

To begin with he wishes to see a return to small landholding. Although he is too good a farmer to deny the value of enclosures in making for efficient cultivation, Cobbett is also too much a philanthropist not to see that pauperism increases when one farm can occupy what was once forty farms. Like Robert Southey and Arthur Young, he advocates what is known as the cottage system, a modified form of feudal landholding, whereby farmers let small tracts of land to their tenants at a minimal rate—say one pound a year for a quarter acre. Cobbett remarks in 1826 that this custom is a growing and a good one:

> ...it is a little step towards *a coming back* to the ancient small *life* and *lease* holds and *common-fields* ... the "*dark age*" people were not so very foolish, when they had so many *common-fields*, and when almost every man that had a family also had a bit of land, either large or small. It is a very curious thing, that the enclosing of commons, that the shutting out of labourers *from all share* in the land; that the prohibiting of them to look at a wild animal, almost at a lark or a frog; it is curious that the hard-hearted system should have gone on, until, at last, it has produced effects so injurious and so dangerous to the *grinders* themselves, that they have of their own accord, and *for their own safety*, begun to make a step towards the ancient system. (II, 422)

Once this step is made, other things can be done by both the tenant and owner. For one thing the tenant can defeat the manufacturers and the taxgatherers by returning to the system of making as many things at home as possible. He can make beer for a penny that would cost him sixpence because of the excise rates, shoes for five shillings instead of ten shillings, soap for threepence instead of sevenpence. He can bake his own bread, plait his own straw for hats, knit his own wool into stockings. Machines, Cobbett admits, are valuable if they help men do things more easily at home. But "if the machine be *elsewhere:*

if it be worked *by other hands;* if *other persons* have the *profit* of it, and if, in consequence of the existence of the machine, we have hands at home, who have *nothing to do,* and whom we *must keep,* then the machine is an injury to us, however advantageous it may be to those who use it, and whatever traffic it may occasion with foreign States" (II, 376). In the past Englishmen were rich because wives and daughters stayed home, spun and wove, while the men worked in the fields. Now they are forced to be idle, to consume without producing, and to starve without hope.

Just as Cobbett vehemently opposes the removing of industry from the home, so, naturally, he disapproves of removing trade from the village. In the "dark ages" the fairs and markets, which his ancestors had wisely instituted and carefully supervised, brought consumer and producer into close contact with one another. No middlemen were there to raise prices without adding value or to lower quality by deceit. In the fairs and markets there were no tricks or "traffickings." Instead there were wise and just laws to prevent the manipulators of money— the forestallers and regraters—from profiting at the expense of the poor. Such laws, Cobbett thinks, should be enforced again.

As we might expect, Cobbett's ideal world is not only agrarian but paternalistic. He wishes to bring back not only the medieval economy but the medieval social system. Although Cobbett the Radical demanded equal political rights for all, Cobbett the Tory still believed in degree and gradation and thought that the rich were responsible, because of their greater wealth and opportunities, for the economic and moral well-being of the poor. Especially during the tumultuous agricultural uprisings of 1830, when England seemed on the brink of revolution, Cobbett kept insisting on the need for love between "lords and gentlemen" and the "common people," for "happy cottages" and "cheerful farm-houses" (III, 870). Not by mere frightened charity, placating gifts of money and bedding—"scare-blankets" the people called them—would farmers once more be able to "go to sleep without starting at every moment at the thought of fires." They would have to renew their relations with the people (II, 678). This could be done in part *"by keeping the young men, young women, the boys and the girls,*

78

in the farm-houses, as was formerly the case all over England; by giving a young man from *fourteen to seventeen pounds a year wages, with board and lodging in the house,* with table-cloth and knife, fork and plate, laid for him, twice in the day, with bread and cheese for supper, and with beer to drink with his meals" (III, 867–68). Brought up under such conditions young people would be "moral and well-behaved," for they would have been educated under the spirit that animated the apprentice system, which made it the master's bounden "duty to make [his servants] rise early, keep good hours, be industrious and careful, be cleanly in their persons and habits, be civil in their language" (II, 670). Only when society is reformed in this way, says Cobbett, will the Reformation-created gulf between master and slave be closed and the sufferings and indignities of the current age be removed.

V

With the publication of the last of the *Rural Rides* in 1832, Cobbett's medievalism and, indeed, his life span were almost complete, although he would further develop some ideas in *Cobbett's Legacy to Labourers* (1835) and *Cobbett's Legacy to Parsons* (1835). Taken as a whole his contributions to the new feudalism formed a fairly coherent pattern, for which the shaping force was always his yeoman background. Following up some hints in his earlier writings, Cobbett idealized the Middle Ages in *A History of the Protestant Reformation* as an agrarian Utopia under the dual guidance of a benevolent church and a benevolent gentry and went on to trace the decline of England from this high point ever since the Reformation. The succeeding *Rural Rides* showed how England could bring back the age of gold by means of land reform, home industries, and a general anticommercial program. That the world he envisaged was very much like the world of 1760, seen through the improving lens of distance, is unimportant, for the world of 1760 was very medieval, indeed.

Far less excusable is Cobbett's artifice in declaring that the Middle Ages were all good. Unlike most other nineteenth-century medievalists whose inaccuracies were usually the result of the inadequacy of current historiography, Cobbett deliberately made mistakes. A comparison of his work with Lingard's shows how he distorted the facts at his command, for even Lingard knew that taxes and tallages were almost as severe in the Middle Ages as they were in his own times, that "deathless landlords" were not always the most charitable landlords, that John Ball's followers in the fourteenth century could be as violent as Captain Swing's followers in the nineteenth. That Cobbett did not know as much about the faults of the Middle Ages as G. G. Coulton, for example, was to know seventy-five years later is to be expected.[36] But he might, at least, have stayed close enough to his sources to avoid the charge of deliberate misrepresentation.

Cobbett's remedies for the present are subject to the same sort of criticism as his analysis of the past. It was perhaps excusable in the early nineteenth century to think that England's future might still be with the cottage and the spinning wheel rather than the factory and the power loom; at least, it was an error he shared with some of the wisest men of his time. But to say, as Cobbett did, that he never voluntarily went into any manufacturing place and had no intention of doing so, was to show a stubborn obscurantism.

And yet it is hardly surprising to find Cobbett hostile to industrialism. From its earliest period the Romantic movement had loved the country and hated the towns. Blake's lines about the "dark Satanic mills" show the early identification of manufacturing with the diabolical, just as his vision of the New Jerusalem shows an early association between "green and pleasant fields" and the celestial. In terms of the medieval movement this Manichaean dualism continued throughout the century to equate the Middle Ages with pastoral bliss and the modern period with industrial damnation. The pervasiveness of this idea can be seen in the fact that one of its earliest exponents was William

[36] The controversy between G. G. Coulton and Cardinal Gasquet, much of which is reproduced in Coulton's *Ten Medieval Studies* (Boston: Beacon Press, 1959), is interesting, since Gasquet was an editor and an admirer of Cobbett's. Much of the evidence Coulton musters in opposition to Gasquet's views of the Middle Ages can be used as a corrective to the extreme partisanship of *A History of the Protestant Reformation.*

Cobbett, who had probably never read any Romantic poem and may never even have heard of the Romantic poets.

All in all, though, Cobbett's strengths far outweigh his weaknesses. He was not a reasonable man; he was an angry man—angry for the right cause at the right time. When he said he never went into places of manufacture, it was simply a dramatic device to show how unendurable he thought them, just as his diatribes against the potato were an advertising slogan to focus public attention on the miserable diet of the poor. Besides, the faults he found were prescient, since the poverty and alienation he found increasing in his own lifetime were precisely the faults that persisted.

His solutions were in some ways prescient, too. From the Middle Ages Cobbett derived the great lesson of responsible leadership that he never tired of repeating against the Scotch "feelosophers" who believed in laissez faire. Quoting Sir William Blackstone, he wrote that for the poor to "'demand a supply sufficient to all the necessities of life from the more opulent part of the community is dictated by the principles of society,'" and he expanded this idea to show how it was associated with feudal tenures. He claimed that since all property was held in trust from the state, all property owners had the same responsibility the state had "to give protection to all the citizens, or persons living under it . . . against hunger, nakedness, and all those things which expose life and limb to danger."[37]

Cobbett himself thought that the way to give this protection was to revive the paternalistic aristocracy of the past, to make the holders of land responsible for the welfare of all who tilled it for them. History showed that this was not to be. But in proclaiming to the world in publications whose circulation reached into the tens of thousands the injustices of a civilization that housed its farm hands in mud-floored cottages, that fined its mill workers a shilling for opening a window, that hanged a starving woman for stealing potatoes from a cart, Cobbett anticipated the ideas of Carlyle and Young England and helped to make way for the paternalistic state of the future. He was, as Cole says, unable to bring back the past. But "the last great tribune

[37] William Cobbett, *Legacy to Labourers* (London, 1835), p. 124.

of the agrarians was . . . also the first great tribune of the industrial proletariat." [38]

[38] Cole, *Life of Cobbett*, p. 434. Cobbett was hardly alone in wishing a return to agrarianism. One of Mrs. Barbauld's poems, for example, envisions an England returned to pastoralism which will attract American tourists.

3

Broadening the Vision: The Lake Poets and Some Contemporaries

COBBETT'S WRITINGS about the Middle Ages show clearly how historical facts could be twisted to support modern premises. But it would be a mistake to think that other historical writing in the Romantic period was notably objective. The ideal of re-creating the past as it really was—did not gain popularity until quite late in the nineteenth century. And though an English historian could write as early as 1795 that historical conclusions needed to be based on a nation's "antient and authentic historical monuments,"[1] English historical writing almost up to modern times is largely a record of political opinions. The Middle Ages in particular lent themselves to historical polemics, since both Whigs and Tories could use the British past to support their own interpretations of the British constitution. Thus, while there is no question that factual information about the Middle Ages was constantly increasing, it is often difficult in the early nineteenth century to separate the development of historical fact from the entanglements of political opinion. The new history not only contributed to medievalism; it was part of it.

The affinities between Toryism and medievalism are not hard to understand. The emergence of the Tories as a recognizable political

[1] Thomas Preston Peardon, *The Transition in English Historical Writing, 1760–1830* (New York: Columbia University Press, 1933), pp. 291–292. For a full discussion of the preservation and publication of government records see Peardon's final chapter. For a study of the contributions of private learned societies see Harrison Ross Steeves, *Learned Societies and English Literary Scholarship* (New York: Columbia University Press, 1913).

faction had taken place during the seventeenth century when the country gentlemen sided with the Stuart cause; and in the eighteenth and nineteenth centuries this early loyalty had developed into a general allegiance to the Crown, the Church, and the land itself. Thus, if the seventeenth century saw the Tories defending the Royalist position, the eighteenth saw them reading *The Patriot King*, and the nineteenth defending throne and empire. Similarly, the Tories' initial hostility to Puritanism expressed itself more generally as antagonism to granting any privileges to Dissent, on the one hand, or to Catholicism on the other, right up to their final defeat on this issue in 1830. But the most significant quality of the Tory gentleman was his abiding attachment to the land. Although Toryism did in the nineteenth century attract both merchants and members of the working class, the backbone of the party continued to be the country gentleman. Attached to the land, jealous of his time-honored role as squire and magistrate, opposed to the dangers of centralization, the typical Tory was, with a few significant exceptions, hostile to unnecessary alterations. By temperament and by training he was very likely to agree with Lord Falkland's statement: "When it is not necessary to change, it is not necessary to change."

Given these various loyalties, the attraction of the Middle Ages for Tory historians is not difficult to understand since they saw their own class privileges rooted in the medieval past. They saw the Middle Ages, too, as a period when traditional loyalties had developed, if not to the Crown, then to a feudal hierarchy which imposed an order upon society. Although they hated Romanism, they managed to find comfort in the predominance of an *English* church somehow existing amidst popish corruption throughout the medieval period. Moreover, they manipulated the past to support their ideas. By underemphasizing the amount of freedom that Englishmen had enjoyed under Saxon, Norman, and Plantagenet rule during the Middle Ages, they defended the Stuarts against the charge of absolutism and—much more important—argued against the extension of liberties that had followed the Stuart overthrow. For if they could prove that the Stuarts' power had had no constitutional limits, then the Whigs had not had the right to depose the Stuarts for exceeding them. And if the Whigs had been wrong, then the Revolution of 1688 had been merely an act of politics, not principle, and all subsequent consequences, including the Reform Bill of 1832, were historically unjustified.

Many of these Tory attitudes are illustrated by Sharon Turner's *The History of the Anglo-Saxons from the Earliest Period to the Norman Conquest* (1799–1805), in many respects a pioneer work. Although marred by dreamy discussions of the race of Japhet and hampered by the limits of the knowledge then available, the book marked a tremendous advance in methodology and content over previous histories. Scott and Wordsworth valued and used it; Coleridge called Turner the "most honest" of English historians; and Southey believed that "so much new information was probably never laid before the public in any one historical publication."[2] Turner himself claimed that his work was two-thirds new, based on hitherto unexamined manuscript sources.[3]

Turner's section on King Alfred affords a good example of his attitude. Always a king of blessed memory, Alfred approached canonization in the early nineteenth century. He was the subject of poems by the poets Henry Pye and Joseph Cottle and formed the basis for innumerable reflections on the greatness of the English spirit. Turner joins this tradition by making Alfred's reign into a model for monarchs. Although he narrates with full documentation the events of Alfred's life and times (the story of the burnt oatcakes, for example, is cited from four different sources), Turner is mainly concerned with his role as a king. He sees Alfred as an ideal ruler who used his power to impose order on the turbulence of his society. He analyzes and praises his code of laws, his administration, and his earnest pursuit of justice. Most of all, he praises his efforts to improve the moral state of his people by educating both clergy and laity.

This emphasis on Alfred's creation of a strong central government

[2] William Wordsworth, *Poetical Works* (London, 1904), p. 721. Samuel Taylor Coleridge, *The Complete Works of Samuel Taylor Coleridge*, ed. W. G. T. Shedd, 7 vols. (New York, 1884), VI, 57. Robert Southey, *Selections from the Letters*, ed. John Wood Warter, 4 vols. (London, 1856), I, 338.

[3] Sharon Turner, *History of the Anglo-Saxons from the Earliest Period to the Norman Conquest*, 5th ed., 3 vols. (London, 1828), I, v–vi.

betrays Turner's Tory bias. He is not so much interested in liberty as in law, not so much concerned with the antiquity of English freedom as with the glory of her hereditary monarchy. By no means an absolutist, he nonetheless has a very limited conception of how limited a monarchy should be.

Throughout the history Turner's Toryism appears quite consistently. He specifically opposes the idealization of the Anglo-Saxon freeman indulged by such Whigs as Thomson and Mrs. Macaulay. With a typically conservative insistence on the limitations of human nature, he writes that

> we must not let our minds expatiate on an ideal character which eloquence and hope have invested with charms almost magical. No utopian state, no paradox of an almost pure republic as reason can conceive, but as human nature can neither establish nor support is about to shine round us when we describe the Anglo-Saxon freeman. A freeman amongst our ancestors was not that dignified independent being, "lord of the lion heart and eagle eye," which our poets fancy under this appellation; he was, rather, an Anglo-Saxon not in the servile state. (III, 86)

As Turner reminds his readers on many occasions, however, most Anglo-Saxons were in the servile state—bereft of liberty, rights, and comforts.

In the preface to the third edition of his study which appeared in 1820, Turner states that he has received many inquiries from his readers about the Anglo-Saxon witenagemot, or national council.[4] This curiosity about the witenagemot was related, of course, to the increasingly urgent matter of parliamentary reform and showed how closely the past was being scrutinized for solutions to contemporary problems. Turner's answer is interesting, for it shows how cleverly,

---

[4] Another frequent question involved the population of Saxon England. This, too, was related to a current problem since the acceptance of the Malthusian theory —with all its economic implications—depended on proof that the English population had indeed increased. See the chapter on Cobbett for a further discussion of this question.

though perhaps unwittingly, he could manipulate history to support his views. He states that after many years' investigation he has concluded that the Anglo-Saxon witenagemot very closely resembled the nineteenth-century Parliament. He thinks that such an assembly was one of the happiest inventions political wisdom ever devised for representing the best interests of the people and ensuring the progress of their society. In a burst of pious enthusiasm, he declares that such parliaments are "the nearest human imitation of a superintending Providence which our necessities or our sagacity have yet produced" (III, 184).

In so idealizing a mere Saxon assembly, Turner would seem at first to outdo the most outrageously Whiggish historian of the previous century. But a closer look at his argument shows its fundamental Toryism. What he is really interested in proving is the similarity in membership between the witenagemot and "our present parliament, in [that] the orders who attended as representatives, were chosen by classes analogous to those who now possess the elective franchise" (III, 180). Only the serfs were not directly represented, and, like Coleridge and other nineteenth-century medievalists, Turner thinks that the clergy and crown served quite adequately as their spokesmen. The implication of all this is clear: as the franchise was in the Middle Ages, so should it remain in the nineteenth century—in spite of Cartwright, Burdett, Cobbett, and Hunt.

Two points in *The History of the Anglo-Saxons* are particularly worth noting since they represent attitudes that were prevalent at the very beginning of the nineteenth century but that were soon changed by contemporary conditions. For one thing, Turner believed that Alfred's police system—which essentially made each member of a community responsible for the behavior of his neighbors—was intolerably restrictive. But as we shall see, this rigid supervision of society was precisely what some later medievalists wished to revive in the frightening days of riots and rick-burning that followed. For another, he was also more certain of English prosperity. *The History of the Anglo-Saxons* is a work of the late 1790s and early 1800s, a period when agricultural distress, though often severe, was probably not so acute nor the "horrors of the Industrial Revolution" so well known as they were to be a generation later. Turner could, therefore, still be sure that the standard of living enjoyed by nineteenth-century Englishmen was superior to that of their medieval ancestors. Looking about him, he could claim that ordinary farmers fared better than Anglo-Saxon thegns and knights and that the "cottages of day-labourers have many more conveniences and their life fewer privations than most of the Anglo-Saxon classes of society enjoyed" (III, 80).[5]

By contrast to Tory historians such as Turner, the Whig historians consistently emphasized the freedom achieved during the Middle Ages. Members of a rising mercantile class, whose sympathies were with industry, representative government, and religious dissent, the Whigs idealized the Middle Ages in order to prove the antiquity of British liberties. They saw the bold spirit of the Saxon freeman as the inspiring force of English history: in Alfred's time it had created the witenagemot; in John's, it had demanded the liberties of Magna Charta. According to them, the "Glorious Revolution" of 1688, far from being historically unjustified, was simply the last logical step in the limitation of monarchy and the assertion of popular freedom.

The greatest of the Whig historians was Henry Hallam. His *View of the State of Europe during the Middle Ages* (1818) reflects the growing knowledge about the Middle Ages themselves, but it also anticipates the spirit of 1832. He cannot help, of course, seeing what Scott and Turner saw in the Middle Ages: that feudalism was a school of honor and that lord and vassal were bound by ties of loyalty and affection. But he is much more interested in showing that the feudal relationship, far from being altruistic, was actually based on a series of businesslike contracts that protected the liberties of society. Contractualism pervades Hallam's entire interpretation of medieval history. He reminds his readers that whatever obligations the possession of a fief "laid upon the vassal of service to his lord, corresponding duties were imposed by it on the lord toward his vassal."[6] The rights of each station in

---

[5] Turner's later work, *The Sacred History of the World* (1832) does show an awareness of the hardships of the factory laborer.

[6] Henry Hallam, *View of the State of Europe during the Middle Ages*, new ed., 3 vols. (London, 1872), I, 167.

society were fixed by law so that even the lowly villein, who had virtually no freedom within the manor itself, could nonetheless plead against his lord in open court.

In view of his inherent constitutionalism, it is no wonder that Hallam criticizes those historians who for party reasons term Magna Charta "the result of an uninteresting squabble between the king and his barons" (III, 158). He saw it confirming the civil rights of all freemen and declared it "beyond comparison the most important event in our history" (II, 326). To Magna Charta, to the impartiality of English justice, and to the power of Parliament to control the royal purse, Hallam attributes the continuity of his nation's freedom, even in periods when other nations had sunk into tyranny.

Like his fellow Whig historian, Thomas Babington Macaulay, Hallam is committed to a belief in progress. He states that he will "refute the deliberate errors of other historians" who do not see the "long and uninterruptedly increasing prosperity of England as the most beautiful phaenomenon in the history of mankind" (II, 269). He cannot help but sneer at the smoky, chimneyless medieval dwellings and at the paucity of medieval comforts. But the pressure of contemporary conditions is against him and forces him to modify his view. Because he is writing in the years of depression following upon 1815, the Whig Hallam is forced to admit what the Tory Turner, writing earlier, had not yet realized: that the "labouring classes . . . were better provided with the means of subsistence in the reign of Edward III or Henry VI than they are at present" (III, 372). Then, he notes, a man worked a week for four bushels of wheat; now it takes him ten or twelve days. Then, a laborer earning eighteenpence a week could buy his family twenty-four pounds of meat; now, a laborer earning twelve shillings a week can afford only half that amount. In spite of all his Whiggish faith in progress and prosperity, such statistics as these force Hallam to admit that manufactured goods and modern conveniences have not really improved the workman's lot and that he is much worse off than his medieval ancestors in purchasing power and the ability to support a family.

It is interesting to note the sources of Hallam's information on this

comparative medieval prosperity, for they point up the close connection between scholarship and social philosophy that marked the whole
nineteenth century. The primary source for Hallam's figures on
medieval wages and prices is Sir John Cullum's *The History and
Antiquities of Hawstead and Hardwick*, which first appeared in 1784
and was published in a second edition in 1813.[7] Cullum, an Anglican
clergyman, begins his book with a conventional discussion of local
genealogies and ecclesiastical histories, but eventually moves on to
consider the ever-pressing question of the poor rates. Cullum is the
earliest medievalist to consider the effects of the end of the domestic
system. He explains the contemporary rise in poor rates by the passing
of the cottage industries, which has made it impossible for women and
children to earn more than a few pence a day spinning yarn. In passages
anticipatory of Cobbett, he recalls the more prosperous past when
"harvest days must have exhibited one of the most cheerful spectacles
in the world."[8] Even though times were disorderly then, men were
at least paid enough for their labor to buy substantial food. Pork and
bacon, which Cullum says are today the delicacies of Suffolk laborers,
were part of the daily diet of the fourteenth-century yeoman, and the
"laziest lubber [could] . . . earn more than the most industrious workman can at present."[9]

For some reason, Cullum's rather specialized antiquarian researches
were widely read, probably for the light they cast on the contemporary
issue of poverty. His figures are cited in both Thomas Ruggles's
History of the Poor (1793–94) and Sir Frederic Morton Eden's *The
State of the Poor* (1797),[10] as well as in Hallam's history. Eden's work,
which was very much studied in the early nineteenth century, is one
of the first books to treat poverty scientifically: to record the incomes

[7] Hallam cites Sir John Cullum, *The History and Antiquities of Hawstead and
Hardwick*, 2nd ed. (London, 1813), pp. 258–259, for his figures on wages and
wheat prices.
[8] Cullum, *History and Antiquities*, p. 223.
[9] *Ibid.*, p. 258.
[10] Thomas Ruggles, *The History of the Poor*, 2 vols. (London, 1793–1794), I,
16–18. Sir Frederic Morton Eden, *The State of the Poor*, 3 vols. (London, 1797),
I, 17–18.

of the poor, examine their budgets, and tabulate their condition (diet, dress, housing, fuel, occupations) as methodically as possible. Comparing his data from the 1790s with what he could discover about the Middle Ages, Eden concludes that the poor had certain definite advantages in medieval times. He writes:

> However deplorable, therefore, the effects produced by the want of personal freedom may have been, every individual in the kingdom had an appropriate fund to look to for sustenance; and . . . however degraded the condition of the great mass of people . . . might be, they were still, unless in extraordinary cases of national misery, assured of the bare necessities of life. The villein . . . if unable to work, was maintained by his lord; as the pauper is now supported by his parish.[11]

Of course, no one of these books completely changed men's attitudes toward the Middle Ages, and not all of them together might have done so if the sharp lessons of adversity had not taught Englishmen to hold their tongues a little about the superiority of the present. Little by little, however, the increased knowledge of the past, combined with the increasing woes of the present, helped wear away centuries of hostility toward the medieval past. A nation that had seen the poor rates increase by 50 percent in the three years following the war, could not afford to be contemptuous of a period in which the poor, though far from free, were at least secure. Historical knowledge, therefore, ceased to be the province of the antiquarian; it became a sourcebook for sermons—and those of no unfrightening nature—on the values of medieval life.

II

In spite of the Gothic atmosphere of such poems as "Christabel" and "The Rime of the Ancient Mariner," Samuel Taylor Coleridge is not so obviously a medievalist as Scott or Cobbett; and yet his contributions here, as in so many other fields, are, to use John Stuart Mill's word, "seminal." Both his criticism of his own day and his

[11] Eden, *State of the Poor*, I, 59.

occasional comments on the Middle Ages are richly suggestive and show the new medievalism, if not fully matured, at least in active growth.

Curiously enough, the conservative Coleridge resembles the Whig Hallam in some of his judgments about the Middle Ages. At a lecture given in January 1818, the year of the publication of Hallam's *View of the Middle Ages*, Coleridge anticipates some of that historian's ideas about medieval freedom. Like Hallam, he sees feudalism as a "chain of independent interdependents,"[12] in which the power, and consequently the liberty, of each rank of society are limited by law. Going beyond Hallam, he sees the feudal system not merely as a historical justification for English liberty, but as a solution to the universal human problem of reconciling liberty and law. A note taker at his lectures records a naïve effusion of praise for the medieval past:

> I see the grandeur, the freedom, the mildness, the domestic unity, the universal character of the middle ages condensed into Alfred's glorious institution of the trial by jury. I gaze upon it as the immortal symbol of that age;—an age called indeed dark; but how could that age be considered dark, which solved the difficult problem of universal liberty, freed man from the shackles of tyranny, and subjected his actions to the decision of twelve of his fellow-countrymen. (IV, 237)

Coleridge claims that the "Goths," as he calls medieval people in general, were more fortunate in their liberty than the Greeks, since their institutions did not involve the contradictions of liberty and slavery. Disregarding the prevalence of serfdom in the Middle Ages, he says that the medieval state was happy and lasting. As he describes it:

> The Goths said. . . . You shall be our Emperor; but we must be Princes on our own estates, and over them you shall have no power! The Vassals said to their Prince, We will serve you in your wars and defend your castle; but we must have liberty in our own circle, our cottage, our cattle, our portion of land. The Cities said, We acknowledge you for our Emperor; but we must have our walls and our strongholds,

[12] Coleridge, *Complete Works*, IV, 288.

and be governed by our own laws. Thus all combined, yet all were separate; all served, yet all were free. Such a government could not exist in a dark age. Our ancestors may not indeed have been deep in the metaphysics of the schools; they may not have shone in the fine arts; but much knowledge of human nature, much practical wisdom must have existed amongst them, when this admirable constitution was formed. (IV, 237)

Even in this passage, the political differences between Hallam and Coleridge are apparent. Quite as much as he wants to preserve the freedom and identity of each class, Coleridge also wants to merge all classes into the unity of the state. Like most medievalists, he shares the typically conservative belief in the need for a community. He thinks that without local attachment, men are merely locusts who devour, rather than husbandmen who conserve, the riches of the earth. He is quite naturally, therefore, interested in the Middle Ages as the source of permanence and tradition—of all those rites and customs, "faith, freedom, heraldry, and ancestral fame" (VI, 65)—that reinforce men's sense of nationhood.

In his *Lay Sermon Addressed to the Higher and Middle Classes* (1817), Coleridge blames England's current distresses and unrest on the loss of this very sense of nationhood. He ascribes the economic hardships of the postwar period, not to any superficial changes in government funding or spending but to a fundamental change in the structure of English society. Like Cobbett, he sees the increasing pauperization of the poor—their inability to find work at adequate wages, or indeed to find any work at all—as the result of the breakdown of the ancient forms of landholding that had existed in England since the Middle Ages. Under the ancient communal system practically no class of society had been without right to some bit of arable land and access to the waste for pasturage. With the advent of the modern system of "enclosures," however, at the end of the eighteenth century, "communal farming" was being replaced by more commercial ventures. It was the "extension of the commercial spirit into our agricultural system" that Coleridge calls "the groundwork of our calamity" (VI, 215) and the cause of England's disintegration as a nation.

Coleridge's discovery that in the counties where farms of one or two thousand acres were numerous, the poor rates were also highest was, of course, no discovery at all. Cobbett had expressed it most vigorously, but the depopulation of the English countryside had been apparent even half a century before when Oliver Goldsmith wrote "The Deserted Village." [13] The close relationship between a peasantry sinking into pauperism "step for step with the rise of the farmer's profits and indulgences" had been the subject of innumerable treatises, including the Board of Agriculture Report for 1816—to cite only the document of which Coleridge made most use.

What is important, though not unique, in Coleridge is his realization that the changed relationships between landowners and farm laborers, which were destroying the old feudal interreliance of the classes, were actually part of a broader moral change that was undermining the whole fabric of the nation. Like Burke and like Scott, he saw the end of feudalism as the end of chivalry and generosity and the substitution of mere profit-and-loss calculation. In a passage that Scott would have liked, Coleridge tells of a conversation he had with a Highlander by the shores of Loch Katrine. According to this speaker, one of the local lairds had raised a company for the war because of "the love that was borne to his name" and had gained preferment as a result. Only a "small part of those that he took away" came back again, and of those who did return, "some [were] blind, and more in danger of blindness." What were their thanks, the Highlander asked? "Why that their fathers were all turned out of their farms before the year was over, and sent to wander like so many gipsies, unless they would consent to shed their gray hairs, at ten pence a day, over the new canals." Once, if a price had been set on the laird's head, the Highlander continued, "he needed but have whistled, and a hundred brave lads would have made a wall of flame round him with the flash of their broad-swords! Now if the French should come among us . . . let

[13] Rural depopulation owing to the spread of enclosures had been a frequent theme in English literature ever since the sixteenth century. As Sir Thomas More wrote in his *Utopia*, "sheep . . . become so great devourers and so wild, that they eat up and swallow down the very men themselves. They consume and devour whole fields, houses, and cities."

94

him whistle to his sheep and see if they will fight for him!" The same loss of patriotism is voiced by another Scotsman whom Coleridge quotes as saying simply that "it kills a man's love for his country, the hardships of life coming by change and with injustice" (VI, 211–12).

Although Coleridge does not specifically refer to the Middle Ages for his solution to the problems brought about by the rise of the commercial spirit, his answer is essentially medieval. Unlike Cobbett, however, who wishes to return to the old system of landholding, he realizes that history is irreversible. Thus, his solution is more spiritual than pragmatic. He wants the "higher and middle classes" to remember their responsibility to make the profits of their estates "a subordinate consideration to the living and moral growth that is to remain on the land—I mean a healthful, callous-handed but high-and-warm-hearted tenantry, twice the number of the present landless, parish-paid laborers, and ready to march off at the first call of their country" (VI, 217).

By the time Coleridge wrote his essays *On the Constitution of the Church and State* (1830)—a work suggested by, but not restricted to, the question of Catholic Emancipation—his disillusion with the current condition of England had become more complete. He is still concerned there with England's loss of nationhood and the alienation of her people, but his criticism is broader. He sees all the intolerable manifestations of modern life—"game laws, corn laws, cotton factories, Spitalfields, the tillers of the land paid by poor rates, and the remainder of the population mechanized into engines for the manufactory of more rich men"—as the indirect product of that loss of faith and substitution of "mechanic philosophy" that has been going on since the sixteenth century. He sees government in the nineteenth century reduced to a mere "anarchy of minds" and the idea of a state dissipated in a cloud of tract societies and conventicles, Lancastrian schools, mechanic institutes, and lecture bazaars. The result of this confusion of values is degradation and vice: "Gin consumed by paupers to the value of about eighteen millions yearly: Government by clubs of journeymen; by saint and sinner societies, committees, institutions; by reviews, magazines, and above all, the newspapers; lastly, crimes quadrupled for the whole country, and in some counties decupled."

It involves, in short, the giddy madness of an uncontrollable "magic wealth machine" which converts "the strength of the nation . . . into an intolerable weight of pauperism" (VI, 64–66).

Coleridge's one hope in this darkness is again born essentially of the Middle Ages. No merely mechanical appeal to political science or popular suffrage will do for him, although he favors the Factory Acts. He believes instead in the far more basic reform of the human heart, in a great work of education to be accomplished by what he calls the National Church. This National Church, or to use Coleridge's more accurate name "Nationalty," in many ways resembles the church universal of the Middle Ages, and must in part have been suggested by his readings in St. Thomas and the other scholastics. Like the medieval Catholic church, it is an estate of the realm, with wealth and power to support it, dedicated to preserving the nation's spiritual life. Unlike the Catholic church, however, its function is not purely theological, nor even necessarily Christian. Its "clerisy" comprehends all learned men, and its function is to promote "culture" in its broadest sense:

> . . . to preserve the stores and to guard the treasures of past civiliza-
> tion, and thus to bind the present with the past; to perfect and add to
> the same, and thus to connect the present with the future; but especially
> to diffuse through the whole community and to every native entitled
> to its laws and rights that quantity and quality of knowledge which
> was indispensable for both the understanding of those rights, and for
> the performance of the duties correspondent. . . . (VI, 52)

Coleridge believes that the medieval Catholic church had the organization to bring the light of learning into every parish and during the Middle Ages was often the chief voice of freedom; but, like most of his contemporary medievalists, who somehow managed to reconcile admiration for the Middle Ages with hatred for its religion, he thinks it failed through avarice and superstition. Henry VIII, too, he believes, missed the opportunity to create a Nationalty out of the medieval institutions he destroyed. According to Coleridge, he should have distributed the wealth of the Church, not into private hands, but to the nation:

> 1st, to the maintenance of the Universities and the great liberal schools: 2dly to the maintenance of a pastor and schoolmaster in every parish: 3rdly, to the raising and keeping in repair of the churches, schools, and other buildings of that kind; and lastly, to the maintenance of the proper, that is, the infirm poor, whether from age or sickness: one of the original purposes of the national reserve being the alleviation of those evils, which in the best forms of worldly States must arise . . . from the institution of private properties. (VI, 67)

Coleridge believes that much of England's current tragedy has arisen from this failure to set aside a saving remnant of wealth for the Nationalty, but he does not think the situation is irremediable. The Church of England still has the power her medieval predecessor had to instruct and protect the nation. It must still, as in the Middle Ages, be responsible for the great task of tending to the poor and sick and for the more complex responsibility of turning men into citizens. As Coleridge puts it, the pastor, together with the schoolteacher, much give each man the knowledge necessary to a "free subject of a civilized realm." In even the remotest parish, the clergyman must set a moral example, must be a "*nucleus* round which the capabilities of the place may crystallize and brighten" (VI, 70–71). Because he moves among his people as a family man and neighbor and is equally at home in the mansion and the cottage, he can be a leader in the all-important task of submerging class loyalties into a sense of nationhood. Reminding men that they are members of one nation, he can thus educate them to serve that nation with their best selves.

Coleridge, then, looks to the past for two things: social order and spiritual direction. Like so many nineteenth-century thinkers, he is concerned by both the material and moral impoverishment of the world around him. Seminal as always, he turns to the Middle Ages for a solution. This discussion has possibly overstressed the medieval portion of his thought; Coleridge himself, it must be admitted, often

97

seemed to prefer the age of the Caroline divines to that of Dante and Aquinas.[14] But it is worthwhile, perhaps, to draw the lines a little heavily and make explicit what was only implicit, for that was precisely what the medievalists who followed him were to do.

III

In one of the central passages of the Preface to *Lyrical Ballads*, William Wordsworth states that he has chosen humble or rural life for his poetry "because in that condition of life our elementary feelings coexist in a state of greater simplicity" and "because in that condition the passions of men are incorporated with the beautiful and permanent forms of nature."[15] As this quotation makes plain, Wordsworth is basing his poetic theory on the relationship of the simple or primitive to both the natural and the permanent. He is thus continuing the eighteenth-century tradition of linking primitivism, so often equivalent to medievalism, with the major Romantic themes of time and nature. However, in spite of the equation in the Preface between the primitive, the natural, and the eternal, Wordsworth's poetry is seldom specifically medieval. Perhaps because of the tragic possibilities of a changing order, he is more interested in the period of flux between the pastoral and stable mid-eighteenth century and the increasingly uprooted and industrialized era that followed it. "The Ruined Cottage," "The Last of the Flock," "Michael," and even "Goody Blake and Harry Gill" are all tragedies of a dying culture.[16]

How oriented Wordsworth was to using the Middle Ages for

[14] Like most of his contemporaries Coleridge is too anti-Catholic to accept the religious life of the Middle Ages without sharp criticism. Thus in the early years he can write in *The Friend:* "Monsters and madmen canonized and Galileo blind in a dungeon! It is not so in our times, Heaven be praised."

[15] William Wordsworth, *The Poetical Works of Wordsworth*, ed. Thomas Hutchinson, rev. Ernest de Selincourt (London: Oxford University Press, 1950), p. 735.

[16] It is interesting to note that Goody Blake tries in this poem to exercise her traditional rights of turbary, or wood-gathering. Coleridge writes that Wordsworth's "'Michael' furnishes important documents of the kindly ministrations of local attachment and hereditary descent."

purposes of social commentary can be seen in his prose, especially that written during the economic depression and political agitation of the late teens. In these writings he discusses the final disappearance of the Middle Ages quite directly. Like Cobbett and Coleridge, he sees the responsible small landholder, descendant of the medieval freeman, being replaced by a new agricultural and industrial proletariat, whose ignorance and insecurity make it the prey of demagogues and rabble-rousers. Despite his earlier liberal politics, the mature Wordsworth fears democracy. He believes that the people are "already powerful beyond the increase of their information and their improvement in morals." [17] In fact, he is far from convinced that even the new middle class has sufficient wisdom and altruism in proportion to its power, and as a result turns back toward medieval society for a solution. Once again what can be termed a new feudalism is suggested as the answer to England's woes. Writing to Lord Lonsdale in 1818, Wordsworth states that he "cannot but be of the opinion that the feudal power yet surviving in England is eminently serviceable in counteracting the popular tendency to reform." [18]

Wordsworth also finds a source of stability in the surviving ecclesiastical power of the Church of England. Like the sixteenth-century Anglicans who had revived the literature of the Anglo-Saxon church to justify their separation from Rome, Wordsworth wrote the *Ecclesiastical Sonnets* (1822) to combat the agitation for Catholic Emancipation. His chief aim in this verse history of Christianity in England is to show the continued existence of an authentic English church, during the Middle Ages and to find lessons for his own time. The conversion of Edwin suggests the antiquity of England's union of church and state; the bravery of the knights and crusaders shows how this union prompted the moral vigor of the country; and such incidents as the interdict and the persecution of Wycliffe show the dangers involved in bowing to the tyranny of Rome.

[17] William and Dorothy Wordsworth, *The Letters of William and Dorothy Wordsworth: The Middle Years* (1806–1820), arr. and ed. Ernest de Selincourt, 2 vols. (Oxford: The Clarendon Press, 1937), II, 830.
[18] *Ibid.*

After tracing the history of the church from medieval times to his own, Wordsworth tries to picture the ideal church of the nineteenth century. Characteristically, the church is rural and, in some ways, what we have come to call medieval. Wordsworth implies that he would like the nineteenth-century church to be like that of the Middle Ages. It should serve as the center for the traditional life of the village and also unite that simple life with the mainstream of national culture. The ancient buildings—cathedrals, abbeys, churches—remind him of England's holy heritage, while the parsonage suggests the old English virtues: "A genial hearth, a hospitable board." [19]

The question of Catholic Emancipation turned Wordsworth's attention to the medieval church; the passage of the Reform Bill turned it to medieval society. He believed that one of the greatest choices facing his world was that "between the feudal and monarchical governments and the representative and republican systems," [20] and he was convinced that the electoral reforms of 1832 were but the first step in a complete levelling of society. If the ten-pound ratepayer could vote, he asked, why not the ten-shilling? the tenpence? anyone? He saw the constitution of England, that object of "sublimest contemplation," about to be destroyed under such onslaughts, which would give the vote to those who had grown up without "being trained in habits of attachment either to the Constitution in Church and State, or what remained of the feudal frame of society." He feared that such changes would "inevitably bring on a political and social revolution." [21] No wonder, then, that in the poems written in 1833 and published in *Yarrow Revisited* (1835) Wordsworth is constantly looking back to an earlier and more stable England.

Like Coleridge's *Constitution of Church and State*, these poems involve a realization of the spiritual superiority of the past and a grudging admission of the value of the medieval Catholic

[19] Wordsworth, *Poetical Works*, p. 349.
[20] William Wordsworth, *The Prose Works*, ed. Alexander B. Grosart, 3 vols. (London, 1876), I, 262.
[21] William Wordsworth, *The Letters of William and Dorothy Wordsworth: The Later Years* (1820–1850), arr. and ed. Ernest de Selincourt, 3 vols. (Oxford: The Clarendon Press, 1939), II, 587.

church in establishing that superiority. "O Fancy," Wordsworth
writes:

> what an age was *that* for song!
> That age, when not by *laws* inanimate,
> As men believed, the waters were impelled,
> The air controlled, the stars their courses held;
> But element and orb on *acts* did wait
> Of *Powers* endued with visible form, instinct
> With will, and to their work by passion linked.[22]

In such an age the "bold credulities" of faith raised churches filled
with the beauty of God and made them the center of life for "peasant
and mail-clad chief" alike. The churches and their lands served as
islands of peace and wealth where industrious monks turned moors
into meadows, clothed the naked, fed the hungry, and mitigated the
harshness of feudal rule with their own gentle justice. Although
the strolling minstrel with his harp might sometimes be chided, the
monasteries were still glad places where travelers could rest and feast-day
throngs rejoice.

In some of his poems Wordsworth seems to be using medieval
material for a specifically modern application. His appeal to the memory
of King Alfred and the long tradition of English liberty seems directed
against the newly passed Reform Bill; while his praise of medieval alms-
giving is apparently directed against the arguments being made for the
scientifically harsh new Poor Law. On the intellectual level, however,
the most important poems in the series are those contrasting the unhappiness of modern England with the joyousness of her medieval past.
The Romantic poets had almost to a man bewailed the loss of spontaneity and joy that came with personal maturity. Wordsworth here,
like almost all the other medievalists, seems to be making a parallel
statement about national youth and maturity, finding, like so many
of his contemporaries, that modern England was dominated by "discontent, and poverty, and crime." Ruefully, Wordsworth writes,
"They called Thee MERRY ENGLAND, in old time" (363).

---

[22] Wordsworth, *Poetical Works*, p. 368.

The measure of Wordsworth's fears for the present and his reliance on the spirit of the past can best be seen in the sonnet "Lowther," a characteristic medievalist utterance:

> LOWTHER! in thy majestic Pile are seen
> Cathedral pomp and grace, in apt accord
> With the baronial castle's sterner mien;
> Union significant of God adored,
> And Charters won and guarded by the sword
> Of ancient honour; whence that goodly state
> Of polity which wise men venerate
> And will maintain, if God his help afford.
> Hourly the democratic torrent swells;
> For airy promises and hopes suborned
> The strength of backward-looking thoughts is scorned.
> Fall if ye must, ye Towers and Pinnacles,
> With what ye symbolize; authentic story
> Will say, Ye disappeared with England's Glory!

(374)

IV

Medievalism, particularly as it appeared in Wordsworth, often seems like a frightened response to the terrors of the French Revolution and all the subsequent fears of revolt that agitated England during the turbulent teens and twenties. But such an analysis is far too simple. There is no question that a return to feudal power was often explicitly offered as a barrier against change, and yet it is equally clear that medievalism was not simply a mask for reaction. If anything, it was allied with utopianism, though with a utopianism that created the ideal out of the past rather than the future. What distinguished medievalism from other forms of utopianism was not that it was less visionary —since medievalism, for all its dependence on history, was primarily a myth—but the temper of mind of its adherents. This temperament, which we have identified as Burkean, combined an idealistic desire to create a secure and harmonious state with a realistic belief that reason alone could not achieve that goal. Robert Southey provides an interesting example of this kind of thinking. He used the Middle Ages as subject matter during both his radical and his reactionary periods and in his continuing medievalism illustrates a consistent attitude toward human nature that connects and helps to reconcile his seeming contradictions.[23]

The earliest of his works, the fragmentary *Harold* of 1791, is in some ways the most explicit in its medieval-modern contrast and is clearly the product of Southey's enthusiasm for the French Revolution. Dealing with the Robin Hood story, the poem shows Coeur-de-Lion as an essentially democratic monarch who favors the outlaws in their rebellion against church and state and contrasts this ideal Richard with the repressive and reactionary leaders of his own day. *Wat Tyler* (written in 1794 and published to embarrass Southey in 1817) is also essentially revolutionary, based largely on material taken from the second part of *The Rights of Man*. In the poem, John Ball serves as the spokesman for Southey's egalitarian radicalism:

> Ye are all equal: nature made ye so.
> Equality is your birthright. . .
> .   .   .   .
> Boldly demand your long-forgotten rights,
> Your sacred, your inalienable freedom.
> Be bold—be resolute—be merciful.
> .   .   .   .
> And there will be a time when this great truth
> Shall be confess'd—be felt by all mankind.
> The electric truth shall run from man to man,
> And the blood-cemented pyramid of greatness
> Shall fall before the flash. . . . [24]

---

[23] Southey's medieval scholarship should not be underestimated. His early readings exposed him to such figures as Bishop Percy, and the historical notes to his poems and translations show that he kept abreast of the latest scholarship. His *Book of the Church* led him to examine English monastic material, and he wrote a number of reviews of books on the Middle Ages for the *Quarterly Review*. His library contained an extensive number of primary and secondary works relating to the medieval period.

[24] Robert Southey, *The Complete Poetical Works of Robert Southey* (New York, [1850]), pp. 105, 109.

On the surface *Joan of Arc* (begun in 1793 and prepared for publication in 1795) appears to continue his essentially Godwinian view of history. As a study of a people's revolt against oppressive invaders it seems the perfect vehicle for Southey's early thought. It is medieval and therefore primitive and heroic. It is democratic and therefore concerned with the common man. It is revolutionary and therefore associated with the blissful dawn of 1789. Most important, by being all of these, it affords Southey the opportunity to make an indirect attack on the England of the 1790s, which possessed none of these virtues, since it was neither heroic, democratic, nor free.

The poem is thus a deliberately antinational epic. Both in the fifteenth century and in his own, Southey thinks that the kings of England dragged their subjects into an unjust war with France. He does not care if any of his readers object to his portraying the defeat of England, for no one should wish an unjust cause to succeed. His attitude toward the Hundred Years' War is as unconventional as his attitude toward the current one with France is unpatriotic. He turns the popular conception of British heroism, based on Shakespeare's history plays, quite upside down: his Englishmen carouse on the night before Agincourt, his Joan is a saintly heroine, his Henry V is a provoker of discord.

In this early study of the Middle Ages, Southey is extravagantly antimonarchical. The future author of *A Vision of Judgment* calls kings "the murderers of mankind" and devotes the ninth book of his poem to a grisly description of the torments reserved for monarchs who force their subjects into war.[25] His Dauphin Charles is a cowardly sensualist who cares more for his mistress than his country, and the sycophantic courtiers of France parody the "placemen" and pensioners of eighteenth-century England. The poet sees in

[25] Robert Southey, *Joan of Arc: An Epic Poem* (Bristol, 1796), p. 351. Southey eliminated the ninth book entirely in the revised edition. Coleridge, in a letter written in 1814, reacted to *Joan of Arc*, to which he had contributed some portions, in this way: he was "astonished ... at the transmogrification of the fanatic Virago, into a novel-praising proselyte of the Age of Reason, a Tom Paine in Petticoats."

both ages a do-nothing aristocracy weakening and impoverishing the nation:

> [They] for themselves and their dependents seize
> All places and all profits, and they wrest
> To their own ends the statutes of the land.[26]

Nevertheless, by late 1794, even before *Joan of Arc* was published, Southey was already becoming afraid of revolution. He wrote that there were "bad men and mistaken men in England who do not know that revolution should take place in the mind."[27] This increasing timorousness has long been seen in the revisions Southey made for the 1798 edition of *Joan*, but they are actually present in the first edition, too, and show his ambivalent feelings toward the masses. This ambivalence shows quite plainly in Southey's description of a dying soldier:

> blood and mingled gall
> Flow'd from the wound; and writhing with keen pangs,
> Headlong he fell; he for the wintry hour
> Knew many a merry ballad and quaint tale,
> A man in his small circle well beloved,
> None better knew with prudent hand to guide
> The vine's young tendrils, or at vintage time
> To press the full-swoln clusters; he, heart-glad,
> Taught his young boys the little all he knew,
> Enough for happiness. The English host
> Laid waste his fertile fields: he to the war,
> By want compell'd, adventur'd,—in his gore
> Now weltering.[28]

The reference to the "merry ballad and quaint tale" and the evocation of olden times in this passage show that, for all his radical impatience

---

[26] Southey, *Joan of Arc*, p. 380.

[27] Geoffrey Carnall, *Robert Southey and His Age: The Development of a Conservative Mind* (Oxford: The Clarendon Press, 1960), p. 33.

[28] Southey, *Joan of Arc*, p. 384.

with monarchy, Southey is already idealizing feudalism. The king sitting aloof in his castle is evil, but the lord keeping a hospitable hearth in his castle is good. As Southey's famous request to include servants in the pantisocracy suggests, he was not really an egalitarian. He cared deeply for the common man; but, even in his radical period, he seldom forgot the difference between the common man and the uncommon, between the peasant or yeoman and his lord. As another of his verse epitaphs shows, he saw loyalty to a superior as an unquestionable virtue:

> the dying man
> In his Lord's castle dwelt, for many a year
> A well-beloved servant: he could sing
> Carols for Shrove-tide, or for Candlemas,
> Songs for the Wassel, and when the Boar's head
> Crown'd with gay garlands, and with Rosemary
> Smoak'd on the Christmas board, he went to war
> Following the Lord he loved, and saw him fall
> . . . and expired,
> Slain on his master's body.[29]

Only a few years later Southey would actually make the relationship between servant and master into an analogy of that between man and God. In the fragmentary *Robin Hood*, which he wrote with his wife in 1805, he compares a vassal's duty to an "earthly liege-lord" with the greater one that all men must discharge to God.[30]

Order and degree, obedience and loyalty—these are the conservative virtues that Southey began celebrating even in his seemingly radical period. They are not based on dislike or ill will for the common man, but on a disillusion with the power of reason to cope with human difficulty. Such ideas often occur as a reaction to a revolutionary society; they are most likely to occur when the masses seem to threaten the individual. Such a philosophy, for all its weakness and

---

[29] *Ibid.*, p. 394.
[30] Robert and Caroline Southey, *Robin Hood: A Fragment* (Edinburgh, 1847), p. 31.

misuses, is often a defense of individualism, a reaction on the part of a gifted or sensitive person lest he be swallowed up by the masses. Recognizing the irrational in man, such thinkers try to protect man against himself. It is by such a paradoxical attempt to defend the individual by placing strong curbs on his individualism that Southey's medievalism develops.

Although neither of his other two poems about the Middle Ages, *Madoc* (1805) and *Roderick, Last of the Goths* (1814), has much bearing on medievalism in this sense, all his prose written after 1810, the year in which he wrote Scott that they agreed on almost all issues of contemporary politics, shows these tendencies. He sympathizes deeply with the agricultural laborer reduced to hunger and despair by the new economic system and pities the factory workers condemned to the damp cellars and cold garrets of the poor. The children especially grieve him—taken by the wagonloads from the workhouse to work all night in oppressive, lint-choked factories. But, in spite of his pity, he still fears the new proletariat and, like many other Englishmen of his generation, reads "revolution" in the light of the blazing ricks. Quite consistently in his prose Southey looks to the Middle Ages for examples and ideas to help forestall revolt.[31] He thinks that it was the survival of feudal feelings, long after the decay of actual institutions, that accounted for the sweetness and calm of English rural life before the nineteenth century. He writes that

> long after the lord had ceased to require the service of his vassals in war, and to estimate his power by the number of men whom he could bring into the field either for or against his sovereign, the bond between them continued unbroken. They who were born upon his lands looked to him as their natural protector; the castle or the manor-house was open to them on festival days, and from thence they were supplied in sickness with homely medicines, and that good diet, which, as old Tusser says, "with wisdom best comforteth man."[32]

[31] For instance, see Robert Southey, "The Poor," in *Quarterly Review*, XV (April, 1816), 187–235. Reprinted in Southey, *Essays, Moral and Political*, 2 vols. (London, 1832).
[32] Southey, *Essays*, II, 112–113.

Like most of the early medievalists, Southey thinks that the recent failure of the landed classes to fulfill these responsibilities any longer is one of the main causes of England's degradation. Their desire to attend "more regularly at Vanity Fair," as he puts it, has led them to sell or enclose their estates in order that they may live luxuriously upon the proceeds. Unfortunately, their profits often meant ruin for the peasants, who, losing their land, lost all self-respect, too, and became candidates for the workhouse, the gaol, or the *Jacquerie*.

It is not surprising, then, that as early as 1817 Southey was at work on a book, eventually entitled *Sir Thomas More; or Colloquies on the Progress and Prospects of Society* (1829), whose major theme was the contrast between past and present. The book, over which Southey lingered for a dozen years before publication, was the repository for most of his animadversions on his own times: the national debt, poor rates, manufactures, Protestant nunneries,[33] plague, Catholic Emancipation. The chief problem considered, however, is the conflict between feudalism and democracy, which both he and Wordsworth agreed in thinking the greatest challenge of the day. In the *Colloquies*, Sir Thomas More is the voice of the past and the voice of reason as well. He is a particularly suitable mouthpiece for Southey, since he, too, lived in a period of social disintegration and was also the advocate of a form of feudalism. His adversary is the nineteenth-century man, Montesinos, who is wise enough to live in the Lake Country, but is otherwise much in need of instruction.

Montesinos begins by offering More his straw-man's argument for progress. He thinks that "a state of society is conceivable almost as superior to that of England in these days, as that itself is superior to the condition of the tattooed Britons, or of the Northern pirates."[34] He goes on to express his faith in continued material prosperity and his belief in the ultimate perfection of society through freedom and education.

[33] A revived interest in monasticism, among both Protestants and Catholics, is one by-product of the medieval revival.

[34] Robert Southey, *Sir Thomas More: or Colloquies on the Progress and Prospects of Society*, 2 vols. (London, 1829), I, 29–30. For convenience I have deleted internal quotation marks.

More's answer to this speech voices the recurrent doubt of the nineteenth century in its own well-being. It might almost be set down as a point-by-point refutation of Mill's "Speech on Perfectibility," or in a lesser key, the whole Podsnap-chorus of English self-praise. He deliberately exaggerates. Not only is the future darker than the present; the present is darker than the past. The majority of Englishmen are neither in "a happier [nor] more hopeful condition at this time than their forefathers were when Caesar set foot upon this island" (I, 45). Their physical condition is worse; their intellectual condition not much better.

> . . . they remain liable to the same indigenous diseases as their forefathers and are exposed moreover to all which have been imported. . . . They are worse fed than when they were hunters, fishers, and herdsmen; their clothing and habitation are little better, and in comparison with those of the higher classes, immeasurably worse. Except in the immediate vicinity of the collieries, they suffer more from cold than when the woods and turbaries were open. They are less religious than in the days of the Romanish faith; and if we consider them in relation to their immediate superiors, we shall find reason to confess that the independence which has been gained since the total decay of the feudal system, has been dearly purchased by the loss of kindly feelings and ennobling attachments. (I, 59–60)

More asserts that in spite of his slavery the medieval serf was really far better off than today's free laborer, claiming that if he lacked the joys of liberty, he lacked its insecurity, too. The serf had no threat of unemployment and no fear that the master he had served throughout his life would let him or his family go hungry. Southey would have agreed with Cobbett and Carlyle that such emancipation was too often "mere liberty to starve to death."

Southey further declares through his spokesman More that the passion for money which leads the modern master to overtask his laborers was unknown in medieval times and that, as a result, the medieval master had "no motive for cruelty, scarcely any for oppression" (I, 72) toward workers who were bound to him by custom and loyalty. He reiterates in the *Colloquies* the view familiar to readers of More's *Utopia* that it was only after the Wars of the Roses, when the trading spirit superseded "the rude but kindlier principle of the feudal system" (I, 79), that calculation replaced feeling and that owners freed their serfs to avoid having to care for them. The result of this, he points out, is the disorganized society of modern times, with its impoverished urban population and degraded agricultural poor.

Like Coleridge, Southey sees a loss of values, rather than a mere change of system, at the root of society's decay. He believes that for all his barbarism, medieval man knew that "the improvement of his moral and spiritual condition ought to be the first concern of every intellectual creature" (I, 155). He relied on religion rather than "liberal opinions" to guide him—liberal opinions being Southey's phrase for the "incentives to vice, impiety, and rebellion" put forth by an irresponsible press (I, 35).

As a result of his religious loss, modern man can now only build cotton mills where once he created cathedrals. Southey sees the ugliness of nineteenth-century architecture as a symptom of materialism. He compares the new houses of the manufacturing towns, "naked and in a row," unfavorably with the stone cottages of the yeoman, with their "weather-stains, lichens and moss," rosebushes, hollyhocks, and beehives (I, 173)—forgetting that both dwellings probably had undesirable drainage systems. Southey also anticipates Ruskin and Carlyle—for whom, as for Cardinal Newman, he was an important thinker—in his criticism of the quality of British manufactured goods. Where the medieval artisan took pride in his work, modern factory owners seem to vie only in the cheapness and flimsiness of their products. "Everyone endeavours to purchase at the lowest price, and sell at the highest. . . . Bad as the feudal times were, they were less injurious than these commercial ones to the kindly and generous feelings of human nature" (II, 246–47). He calls the manufacturing system "a wen, a fungus excrescence" that must be cut off at any price.[35]

---

[35] *Ibid.*, p. 171. Note the word "wen" borrowed from Cobbett's famous epithet for London.

Even in the matter of health Southey finds the Middle Ages—or at least the period before the Reformation—superior to his own. At least then man had enough respect for human life to isolate the sick in pest houses. Now they are all crowded together in filthy, wretched cities, free like Carlyle's Irish widow, to spread infection throughout the land. Worse than the dangers of infection, however, are the dangers of revolt. Far from sympathizing with the methods of Wat Tyler, the mature Southey is terrified of the mob. The word *Jacquerie* occurs again and again in his writings, as it does in the contemporary letters of Wordsworth and Scott, each time bearing the direst connotations. At any moment, Southey fears, the cellars of St. Giles, Spitalfields, and Pimlico may open and pour forth a retributive mob of near-savage revolutionaries. He cannot even estimate the destruction of the "hordes whom your great cities . . . would vomit forth" (I, 114).

At bottom, it is this fear of revolution that distinguishes the medievalism of Southey's maturity from that of his youth and that leads him to idealize control rather than freedom. The duties of government, he writes, are "patriarchal, that is to say, parental: superintendence is one of these duties and is capable of being exercised to any extent by delegation and subdelegation" (I, 105). Medieval society functioned effectively because both the civil and religious structures allowed for such a hierarchy of supervision. Even serfdom was excusable. For if the serfs "were regarded in some respects as cattle, they were at least taken care of; they were trained, fed, sheltered, and protected, and there was an eye upon them when they strayed." Better servitude, Southey continues, than the present condition of the working classes, "unowned, unbroken to any useful purpose, subsisting by chance or by prey, living in filth, mischief, and wretchedness, a nuisance to the community while they live and dying miserably at last" (I, 93–94).

Like all the major medievalists, Southey does not advocate an impossible return to the practices of the past, but he does wish to revive its principles of supervision and social harmony. To begin with, he relies on the state for positive action. He thinks that wealth should be transferred by taxation from excessively rich individuals, who cannot make use of it, to the state, which can apply it to public works and charities. Such a policy, he claims, would be far more effective than the poor rates in eliminating the scandal of men's dying of hunger in the streets and would create vast new sources of wealth for the people as a whole.

Although such ideas obviously anticipate the income taxes and public works programs of the twentieth century, the notion of wealth as a concern of the state rather than the individual derives from the Middle Ages. Similarly medieval and modern in conception is Southey's interest in co-operative societies, which looks forward to the Rochdale movement and backward to the manor and guild. Southey, who had visited Robert Owen's mills at New Lanark, devotes almost a chapter in the *Colloquies* to the possible workings of a co-operative. He describes in detail how joint purchasing and preparing of food, for example, would save time and money—both of which the workers might dedicate to self-improvement.

Southey's solution to the agrarian problem as a whole is like Cobbett's. It involves a return to the medieval system of small holdings, since his basic quarrel is with the inequities created by enclosure. He believes that if the landlords would only rent or sell small strips of land to their peasants, they would create a sturdy and secure yeomanry in place of a starving and dangerous rabble. This agriculturalist tradition, which reappears in William Morris later in the century, recurs in English thought down to the 1930s.

All of Southey's recommendations show how consistent he was in both his "radical" and "reactionary" phases. Behind both periods lies a concern for the people, their welfare and their security. In the early days of *Wat Tyler* and *Joan of Arc*, Southey thought that under their own leaders the people might achieve Utopia. But even then he was dreaming for them of a simpler life, such as that of the Middle Ages, in which their lives would be guided by a few leaders. As he grew older—and as the popular reactions to the French and Industrial revolutions became intensified—Southey's love for the people grew increasingly tinged with fear. His very sense of responsibility for the masses led him to believe that they themselves were irresponsible. Again, therefore, he looked to the Middle Ages, hoping there to find a

guided society sufficiently secure and affluent to be free from the threat
of riot or revolution.

V

Southey's *Colloquies* are probably best remembered because of
Thomas Babington Macaulay's attack in the *Edinburgh Review* of
1830. Macaulay takes exception to almost every one of Southey's
views, but the fundamental difference between the two men is in their
concept of government. For Macaulay the patriarchal and paternal
state is simply a meddling busybody interfering with the natural
progress of society. Left alone, he thinks, the world will not plunge
into Southey's prophesied ruin; it will rather blossom into incredible
prosperity. Far from looking backward, he predicts for the year 1930,
"a population of fifty millions, better fed, clad, and lodged than the
English of our own time"—a population that will travel by railway,
sail by steam, and have in its houses "machines constructed on principles yet undiscovered."[36]

Macaulay is too busy refuting Southey's pessimistic views about the
future in his review to spend much time berating him for his idealization of the past. There is no doubt, however, that his faith in laissez
faire and mechanical progress made him hostile to the Middle Ages.
Nearly twenty years after the Southey essay, in the opening volume
of his *History*, he delivered a diatribe against medievalism:

> It is now the fashion to place the golden age of England in times when
> noblemen were destitute of comforts, the want of which would be
> intolerable to a modern footman, when farmers and shopkeepers
> dieted on loaves the very sight of which would raise a riot in a modern
> workhouse, when men died faster in the purest country air than they
> now die on the coast of Guiana. We too shall be outstripped and in
> our turn be envied. . . . [It may become the mode] to talk of the reign
> of Queen Victoria as the time when England was truly merry England,
> when all classes were bound together by brotherly sympathy, when

[36] Thomas Babington Macaulay, *Critical and Historical Essays Contributed to
the Edinburgh Review*, 3 vols. (London, 1848), I, 267.

the rich did not grind the faces of the poor and when the poor did not envy the splendour of the rich.[37]

Utilitarians as well as Whigs found the assumptions of medievalism at war with their beliefs. As might well be expected, the young John Stuart Mill, who called Southey's *Colloquies* "the gloomiest book ever written by a cheerful man,"[38] also disliked the Middle Ages. His speech on the "Utility of Knowledge," delivered in 1823, condemns the new feudalism as a mask for tyranny. He states that "the appeal from the ages of civilization to the age of barbarism is made . . . by those alone who now, as then, would wish to see the great mass of mankind subject to the despotic sway of nobles, priests, and kings."[39] Instead of conserving the past, he proposes to overthrow the last vestiges of feudalism by disestablishing the Church and radically altering the constitution.

It was not the Whigs and utilitarians alone, however, who resisted the return to the past. Even those who should have been medievalists often were not. William Lisle Bowles—poet, antiquary, philanthropist, and Tory—is an excellent example of a man who had every qualification for becoming a medievalist but did not. He was an acquaintance of Coleridge's, wrote a poem about Harold the Saxon, produced a scholarly study of a medieval abbey, believed in the parochial clergy, and feared the rebellious poor. And yet, he insisted that the Middle Ages were inferior to modern times: that there were fewer people and fewer churches, less learning and less benevolence, and a much lower standard of living. Reversing the statistics cited in Cullum and Hallam, Bowles claimed that it took the medieval laborer nine weeks to earn the price of a bushel of wheat where now it takes only one.[40]

But in spite of all this hostility, the tide of medievalism was rising. The very fact that Mill in 1823 and Macaulay in 1848 found the need

[37] Thomas Babington Macaulay, *The History of England from the Accession of James II*, Everyman's Library, 4 vols. (London, n.d.), I, 328.

[38] John Stuart Mill, *The Spirit of the Age*, introduction by F. A. Hayek (Chicago: University of Chicago Press, 1942), p. 3.

[39] John Stuart Mill, *Autobiography* (London: Oxford University Press, 1952), p. 274.

[40] William Lisle Bowles, *Parochial History of Bremhill in the County of Wilts* (London, 1828), p. 18.

to write against it shows how strongly the idealization of the past held the English mind for at least a quarter of a century. And even Mill and Macaulay had to admit that the feudal system was the best that could have been achieved by England in that stage of her development.

The effect of the Middle Ages and medievalism on the cultivated mind can perhaps best be seen in the evolution of Thomas Love Peacock, John Stuart Mill's fellow official at India House. A classicist and something of a utilitarian, he would seem at first glance to be well armored against contemporary medievalism. But his novels show a very interesting evolution indicative of the pervasiveness of medievalism and the way in which it eventually transcended party lines. Starting from a skeptical analysis of the doctrine of progress, they lead at last to a surprisingly convincing medievalism.

In his earliest novel, *Headlong Hall*, Peacock is obviously mocking both the past and the present. Foster, the perfectibilitarian, delivers several fatuous speeches on the power of railways and roads, tunnels and canals, machines, manufactures, and everything modern to attest the "progress of mankind in all the arts of life and . . . their gradual advancement toward a state of unlimited perfection."[41] Escot, the deteriorationist, counters with equally opinionated views on the superiority of man's natural state. "Give me the wild man of the woods," he cries, "the original, unthinking, unlogical savage"; for there is good in him. In contemporary man, "sophisticated, cold-blooded, mechanical," there is none (I, 36). Although the deteriorationist seems at times to have a slight edge in the argument, the reason is probably that satire always favors the pessimist. On the abstract issue of progress, Peacock clearly shares the view of his genial spokesman, Mr. Jenkison, that "there is not in the human race a tendency either to moral perfectibility or deterioration" (I, 11). In the practical matter of current-day society, however, Peacock's attitudes are quite different: society had developed new faults, and they could and should be corrected.

Headlong Hall, which was written in 1816, develops the controversy

[41] Thomas Love Peacock, *The Works of Thomas Love Peacock*, ed. H. F. Brett-Smith and C. E. Jones, Halliford edition, 10 vols. (London: Constable, 1924), I, 9–10.

over the idea of progress in its eighteenth-century terms of primitivism versus civilization. *Melincourt*, written a year later, still uses this framework and borrows outrageously from the primitivists by introducing Sir Oran Haut-Ton, a very human ape and perfect Noble Savage, into the corrupt world of Regency England, using his simplicity to set off the vices of society. But Peacock also anticipates nineteenth-century approaches to the issue of progress by showing the superiority of the allegedly dark Middle Ages to modern times. In one place he writes that "the days of feudality [are] commonly called the dark ages, and the nineteenth century [is] commonly called the enlightenment age: why, I could never discover" (II, 17). In another he has his heroine declare that she thinks it desirable to find "as true a Knight-errant in a brown coat in the nineteenth century, as in a suit of golden armour in the days of Charlemagne" (II, 24). And he identifies chivalry with "truth and liberty—disinterested and benevolence—self-oblivion—heroic devotion to love and honour—protection of the feeble, and subversion of tyranny"—all of which, as another of his characters points out, is really the rankest Jacobinism (II, 85).

But if Peacock picks up in these early novels the newly favorable attitude toward the Middle Ages that was becoming more and more current, he is also equally aware of the silliness of some of its other aspects. Like Jane Austen's *Northanger Abbey* (1817), his *Nightmare Abbey* (1818) mocks Gothic architecture and Gothic novels. Peacock not only saw the absurdity of the Gothic craze, but was still suspicious both in *Melincourt* and *Nightmare Abbey* of the ties between medievalism and what might be called obscurantism in religion and politics. Although he favors the Middle Ages, he nonetheless distrusts the medievalists. His penetrating portrait in *Nightmare Abbey* of Coleridge as Mr. Flosky is a brilliant extrapolation and exaggeration of the ideas implicit in the *Lay Sermon Addressed to the Higher and Middle Classes*. He describes Flosky as one who

> had been in his youth an enthusiast for liberty, and had hailed the
> dawn of the French Revolution as the promise of a day that was to
> banish war and slavery, and every form of vice and misery, from the

face of the earth. Because all this was not done, he deduced that nothing was done; . . . that the overthrow of the feudal fortresses of tyranny and superstition was the greatest calamity that had ever befallen mankind; and that their only hope now was to rake the rubbish together, and rebuild it without any of these loopholes by which the light had originally crept in. (III, 10)

Yet, even in this work, Peacock is too aware of the value of praising the past in order to castigate the present to be wholly antimedieval. Mr. Toobad, the Manichaean millenarian, serves as a mouthpiece for Peacock's own criticisms of his "enlightened age." "What do we see," asks Mr. Toobad pointedly, "which our ancestors saw not, and which at the same time is worth seeing?"

We see a hundred men hanged, where they saw one. We see five hundred transported, where they saw one. We see five thousand in the workhouse, where they saw one. We see scores of Bible Societies, where they saw none. We see paper, where they saw gold. We see men in stays, where they saw men in armour. We see painted faces, where they saw healthy ones. We see children perishing in manufactories, where they saw them flourishing in the fields. We see prisons, where they saw castles. . . . In short they saw true men, where we see false knaves. (III, 106)

In fact, so much in accord was Peacock with Mr. Toobad's way of thought that he had begun work, before publishing *Nightmare Abbey*, on a novel called *Calidore*, a sort of *Connecticut Yankee* in reverse, in which the naïve comments of a visitor from Arthur's court to modern England serve as a bitter commentary on the times.

The use of the Middle Ages as "the vehicle of much oblique satire on all oppressions that are done under the sun" (I, cxvi) is the avowed purpose of Peacock's completed medieval fantasy, *Maid Marian* (1822). The work owes its existence to the late eighteenth-century republication of medieval material. It is particularly indebted to Ritson's *Robin Hood* and to a collection called *Robin Hood's Garland*, which had been reprinted approximately thirty times in the preceding thirty years. Apart from some sharp words on Southey and some mild burlesque of Scott, however, the satirical material in *Maid Marian* is scanty. Much more satire is to be found in the *Misfortunes of Elphin*, published in 1829, the year of Southey's *Colloquies*.

Peacock bases this novel on the romance of Taliesin from the *Mabinogion*, adding an introduction and conclusion of his own devising. Within this framework, he packs all kinds of satire, oblique and direct. The speech of Seithenyn the Drunkard, for example, on the advantages of not repairing the dike which keeps Elphin's lands from the sea, is a masterly parody of the Tory position and is said to be based on George Canning's speech on the British constitution. Seithenyn complains that the embankment has been criticized by "perverse people, blind to venerable antiquity: that very unamiable sort of people, who are in the habit of indulging their reason. But I say, the parts that are rotten give elasticity to the parts that are sound. ... If it were all sound, it would break by its own obstinate stiffness: the soundness is checked by the rottenness, and the stiffness is balanced by the elasticity. There is nothing so dangerous as innovation" (IV, 16).

Although this passage gives comfort to the antitraditionalists, the rest of the novel does not. Peacock's comparison between medieval and modern times is bitter indeed. Poor Middle Ages, he says ironically, when the science of political economy was still "sleeping in the womb of time!" The people then never had to learn the "advantage of getting into debt and paying interest," for they lacked the inestimable benefits of paper money whereby a "safe and economical currency . . . is produced by a man writing his name on a bit of paper, for which other men give him their property, and which he is always ready to exchange for another bit of paper, of an equally safe and economic manufacture." What money they had, Peacock goes on, they managed to keep; and what power they had, they achieved, even "as we do," by the use of force. The powerful took from the weak, and called "something or other sacred and glorious, when they wanted the people to fight for them" (IV, 50–51).

If human nature, however, was the same then as now, there were nonetheless many blessings to be had for living in the Middle Ages. Preindustrial England, Peacock declares, "had no steam-engines, with fires as eternal as those of the nether world, wherein the squalid many, from infancy to age, might be turned into component portions of machinery for the benefit of the purple-faced few. They could neither poison the air with gas, nor the waters with its dregs: in short, they made their money of metal, and breathed pure air, and drank pure water, like unscientific barbarians" (IV, 51). And he goes so far as to add that medieval astronomy, science, and medicine were no more foolish than his own and their courts infinitely more expeditious than Chancery. Besides, the Middle Ages had neither poorhouses nor game laws:

> The people lived in darkness and vassalage. They were lost in the grossness of beef and ale. They had no pamphleteering societies to demonstrate that reading and writing were better than meat and drink; and that they were utterly destitute of the blessings of those "schools for all," the house of correction and the treadmill, wherein the autochthonal justice of our agrestic kakistocracy now castigates the heinous sins which were then committed with impunity, of treading on old footpaths, picking up dead wood, and moving on the face of the earth within sound of the whirr of a partridge. (IV, 59–60)

Distressed by the gloominess of modern life, Peacock eventually plumps for the Merry England of the past, remarking that the phrase Merry England "must be a mirifical puzzle to any one who looks for the first time on its present most lugubrious inhabitants" (IV, 110).

The chief ideas in these passages are the preferability for the common man of the medieval to the industrial living conditions and the superiority of responsible feudal rule to that of a partridge-preserving "kakistocracy." Both ideas are very closely related to the major principles of medievalism in general, the strongest ties being to Cobbett. But while Peacock clearly aligns himself here with the critics of progress, his ideas are expressed only parenthetically and are not part of the structure of the novel. By 1834, however, he is so imbued with the new feudalism that he selects a medievalist to be the central figure of a novel. Mr. Chainmail in *Crotchet Castle* has a few crotchets of his own, such as an absurd interest in lineage; however, but he is as much of a hero as Peacock ever allows himself to create. Unlike the majority of "game-bagging, poacher-shooting, trespasser-pounding, footpath stopping, common-enclosing" country gentlemen, who are "an ornament to the world and a blessing to the poor" (IV, 56), Chainmail lives in a "large hall, adorned with rusty pikes, shields, helmets, swords, and tattered banners, and furnished with yew-tree chairs, and two, long, old, worm-eaten tables, where he dines with all his household, after the fashion of his favorite age" (IV, 60). He is clearly meant to win out in his dialogues with Mr. MacQuedy (pronounced "Q.E.D."), the philosophic radical. To MacQuedy's assertion that the Middle Ages was a "period of brutality, ignorance, fanaticism, and tyranny," Chainmail gives a convincing and Peacockian answer. "No, sir," he responds:

> Weigh the evidence of specific facts; you'll find more good than evil. Who was England's greatest hero; the mirror of chivalry, the pattern of honour, the fountain of generosity, the model to all succeeding ages of military glory? Richard the First. There is a king of the twelfth century. What was the first step of liberty? Magna Charta. That was the best thing ever done by lords. . . . And as to the people, I content myself with these great points: that every man was a good archer, every man could and would fight effectively with sword and pike, or even with oaken cudgel: no man would live quietly without beef or ale; if he had them not, he fought until he either got them, or was put out of condition to want them. They were not and could not be, subjected to that powerful pressure of all the other classes of society, combined with gunpowder, steam, and *fiscality*, which has brought them to the dismal degradation in which we see them now. (IV, 118–20)

Although MacQuedy's assertion that the friars were lecherous is never directly controverted, Chainmail seems to have the better end of the argument when he asks if the spirit that built medieval churches "and connected with them everywhere an asylum for misfortune and a provision for poverty" was not better than the commercial spirit, which turned all the business of modern life into a scheme of profit and processes of fraud and extortion!" (IV, 123).

The concluding scene of *Crotchet Castle* takes place at a Christmas feast at Chainmail Hall after the fashion of the twelfth century. In fine Peacockian manner most of the characters are gathered there, and they are not disappointed in the scene. Light streams through the stained-glass windows, a great fire blazes, and pennons and banners flutter in the draughty air. The gentry sit at the high table; the domestics and retainers, at the low. At a signal, the harper strikes up an ancient tune, and the boar's head, plum pudding, turkeys, sausage, geese, capons, tongues, hams, mince pies, and baron of beef are borne to the table in a grand procession.

In the midst of this display of old English plenty, modern poverty intrudes. There is a succession of voices and cries from outside and a chorus of voices shouting "Captain Swing" at the door. The modern *Jacquerie* has arrived. Chainmail is sympathetic with the assailants, for he knows that in every age the cause of revolt is "poverty in despair." But he is also firm in defense of his lands. "My spears and swords!" he cries, "these assailants are all aliens to my land and house. My men will fight for me." Guests and retainers snatch the rusty pikes and spears from the walls and, sallying forth from the "fortress of beef and ale," soon put the rabble to rout. "The Twelfth century," Chainmail remarks when they return, "has served them well . . . [for] its manners and habits, its community of kind feelings between master and man are the true remedy for these ebullitions" (IV, 199–204).

In its seriocomic way the scene epitomizes many of the elements of nineteenth-century medievalism. The trappings are all there—the feudal feast, the beef and ale, the kind and affectionate relations between master and man—and the underlying idea is there, too: that the medieval social structure, rapidly passing away in England, must be recaptured in modern terms if England is not to plunge into a revolution born of poverty and despair.

4

Faith and Order: Carlyle

LIKE SCOTT, like Wordsworth, and most of all like Cobbett, whose social origins resembled his own, Thomas Carlyle was born into an environment in many ways belonging to the past. If Cobbett's Farnham was still steeped in medieval sights and customs, Carlyle's Ecclefechan was almost equally old-fashioned. Near the town were the remains of a Roman station, whose inscriptions the young Carlyle was sometimes called on to translate; farther off, on the road to Dumfries, stood the ruined tower of some supposed ancestors of his, the feudal Carlyles of Torthorwald; and everywhere in that border area were to be seen mementos of that last burst of Scotland's medieval pride, the "Forty-five," which had so fired the imagination of Walter Scott. Even the great city of Edinburgh, the "Athens of the North," where Carlyle, like Scott, went to school, still housed the medieval citadel of the Old Town, whose high-backed buildings made a fortress of the ridge between Holyrood and Edinburgh castles.

Scottish social customs, too, in many ways resembled those of Cobbett's Surrey. Scotland was the last great area in the United Kingdom to be enclosed on a large scale, and as late as 1794, the year before Carlyle's birth, peasants were still protesting against the medieval relics of boon work and thirlage. Thatched roof for thatched roof, simple diet for simple diet, Carlyle's childhood was the northern counterpart of Cobbett's Old English upbringing.

And yet, the very fact that Carlyle was of the North rather than the South and that his birthdate was 1795 rather than 1763, made a tremendous difference in his early impressions of life and his eventual solutions to its problems. Between Cobbett's birth and his, Arkwright's spinning frame, Crompton's spinning mule, Cartwright's power loom, Whitney's cotton gin, Cort's reverberatory furnace, Watt's steam engine, and Maudslay's slide rest were invented, revolutionizing the textile industry and making possible the raw materials, tools, and transportation for a new civilization. This civilization, especially because of his seventeen-year absence from it, Cobbett never fully comprehended; he was probably nearly forty before he saw Manchester or Birmingham. Carlyle, however, was born in the manufacturing North and had the images of the industrial revolution imprinted on his memory at least from his teens. Cobbett's medievalism was wholly agrarian, a memory of the past; Carlyle's would be industrial, an anticipation of the future.

Carlyle was more like the Lake poets than Cobbett, however, in the ultimate reasons for his medievalism. Cobbett was quintessentially a materialist, believing only in what he could plainly see. For him the flitch of bacon hanging from the rafters and the round of cheese on the shelf—the small farm and the untaxed cottage—meant the difference between happiness and unhappiness. Carlyle, on the other hand, was a product of both English Romanticism and German Idealism. Born into a pietistic Scotch family and reared for the ministry by religious parents, he spent most of his life searching among the new nineteenth-century philosophies for his lost faith. His writings are all an attempt to find and express the unseen order of the universe.

The story of Carlyle's original loss of faith during his student years is well known. The lectures he heard at the University of Edinburgh exposed him to what he would later call a "sick, impotent Skepticism,"[1] for the vitality of eighteenth-century rationalism had burned itself out in Scotland without providing any substitute. Carlyle's professor reading his notes to a classroom empty except for Carlyle was the perfect symbol of a society in decay, just as his perseverance in attending class was a sign of his own desperation. Even in its prime, though, the rationalist tradition could not have satisfied Carlyle, for it was much too passive. God, to repeat the old metaphor, was a mere watchmaker,

[1] Thomas Carlyle, *Works of Thomas Carlyle*, Edinburgh Edition, 30 vols. (New York: Scribners, 1903–1904), I, 90.

who had set the universe ticking and then gone out of business. Man was a Lockean receiving apparatus, whose profoundest thought could be reduced to a series of vibrations. Politically, the state, stripped of any Burkean mystique, was a purely geographical entity, whose outlines might be redrawn to the convenience of its conquerors and whose function was to provide minimum police protection—"to keep the pigs from squealing," as Carlyle inelegantly phrased it.[2] Economically, too, society functioned as a machine. According to Adam Smith, production entailed consumption; consumption entailed production. Overproduction lowered prices; lowered prices raised consumption. Wages moved up and down by an iron law. History was neither the record of God's providences nor man's diversity, but simply proof that man and his world, though eventually somehow progressing, were always basically the same.

For the young Carlyle, such materialism was devastating. He could no longer believe that God Almighty came down and made wheelbarrows in a shop; nor could he find in psychology, politics, economics, or history any evidence of purpose, and without purposive movement mankind could not be helped. All led to inaction—even his own lack of faith. The unhappy doubter soon learned that his doubts were irremediable. He could not, he declared, "believe one jot better, though he were brayed in a mortar."[3]

If Scottish rationalism developed Carlyle's doubts, German Idealism helped solve them. Carlyle read extensively in the works of the Germanic Romanticists during the 1820s, and the ideas he found there not only gave him a positive philosophic basis for his thought but also biased him in favor of the Middle Ages. According to the German Romantic viewpoint, God was not a "great unintelligible perhaps" but a certainty; not a *was* but an *is;* not a watchmaker but the mainspring of the universe, ever-moving and moving everything. Man was very much God's creature, neither a "Patent-Digester" nor a "Logic Mill," but a dynamic being, able to use his mind to pierce the mass of phenom-

[2] Thomas Carlyle, *Letters of Thomas Carlyle, 1826–1836,* ed. Charles Eliot Norton, 2 vols. (London and New York, 1889), II, 216.

[3] Emery Neff, *Carlyle* (New York: W. W. Norton, 1932), p. 32.

ena that crowded his consciousness and perceive behind it the pattern of God's universe.

Because God continually manifested himself in appearances, whose meaning man could exert himself to grasp, the Romantic reading of politics, economics, and history was active where the neoclassical was passive. Particularly in Johann Gottlieb Fichte, the first Idealist he studied, Carlyle found the idea that certain men—geniuses, or "heroes," as he later called them—were better able than others to see the moral significance of life and apply this vision to the everyday concerns of society. These men were totally unselfish, since they put duty always before happiness. They were therefore entitled to that power over other men which selfish men wish. Through them the state achieved an active role. Especially in *Die Staatslehre*, Fichte showed these extraordinary men controlling the political life of the nation. In his *Der Geschlossene Handelsstaat* he described how they would arrange its economic activities. As he wrote in *Die Staatslehre*, "To force men into a state of law, to place them by force under the yoke of the law, is not only the right but also the sacred duty of all men who have the necessary knowledge. In case of necessity, a single man has the right and the duty to compel all humanity." [4]

Under a philosophical system such as Fichte's, history became a record of periods of faith (when men appreciated greatness) and periods of doubt (when they did not). The Middle Ages had been rejected by the eighteenth-century German rationalists, as by most of their English counterparts, as superstitious and crude. But the new romanticism now idealized the medieval past as a period of heroic action and belief. Interested as he was in all aspects of German thought, Carlyle was perforce drawn into its medievalism as well. His readings in Herder, Goethe, Novalis, and Schlegel—all of whom had already had some English influence through Coleridge—directly affected his unpublished *History of German Literature* (1830–33) and indirectly colored almost all his mature work.

The first great medievalist in Germany was Johann Gottfried von

---

[4] Quoted in Louis Cazamian, *Carlyle*, Les grands écrivains étrangers (Paris: Bloud, 1913), p. 45. My translation.

Herder, whose earliest collection of German folk poetry appeared in the late 1770s. To the intellectual map maker Herder is invaluable as a sort of crossroads where the fairly simple antiquarianism of researchers such as Bishop Percy enters into German thought and changes over into the scholarship of Franz Bopp and Jacob Grimm, on the one hand, and the theorizing of Novalis and Friedrich von Schlegel, on the other. Carlyle, who read at least four of Herder's works during the winter of 1823, was especially able to appreciate him because his own Burgher background, similar to Herder's German pietist upbringing, predisposed him to seek similar values in the past and to see the past imaginatively rather than rationally. The past thus became for both men a standard by which to judge the present. Herder used his picture of medieval greatness to castigate his contemporaries for their subjection to France; Carlyle used his to establish a whole series of criticisms of modern life. Herder idealized the Middle Ages as a time when the community as a whole was capable of selecting its natural leaders to defend the "germanic principle of trial by peers, meet punishment, . . . community of property and . . . liberty." [5] Carlyle viewed the Middle Ages as a time when men knew, as they no longer do, how to choose and reverence a hero. Similarly, Herder's interpretation of the later Middle Ages as a period in which leadership by primogeniture rather than worth caused this ancient society to degenerate parallels the picture of late medieval chaos that Carlyle gives in the Abbot Hugo portion of *Past and Present*—itself an allegory of the decay of leadership in early Victorian England.

The effect of Goethe, who had been Herder's pupil, on Carlyle's medievalism is somewhat harder to trace, in spite of his obvious influence on Carlyle. Certainly, the antirationalism of *Faust*—the rejection of the eighteenth-century cavalier Mephistopheles as the spirit that denies, and the contrasting idea of medieval faith and aspiration—must have indirectly shaped Carlyle's image of the Middle Ages. Goethe's conception of the leader as the practical man doing the task at hand ("hier oder nirgends ist Amerika") was at least as important

---

[5] John Godfrey [*sic*] Herder, *Outlines of a Philosophy of the History of Man*, trans. T. Churchill, 2 vols. (London, 1803), II, 562.

as Fichte's ideas in developing Carlyle's belief in hero worship, both medieval and modern. For more specific debts, however, *Götz von Berlichingen* is once again important. Carlyle read it in 1822 and it no doubt showed him the same feudal values it had shown to Scott: the unity of the people and the leaders in the Middle Ages and the function of such leaders as defenders of the people's freedom and well-being. Ancestor of many another nineteenth-century hero, the sturdy Götz is surely one of the forebears of Carlyle's medieval landlord Edmund, if not of the heroic Abbot Samson himself.

Carlyle's explorations of German literature also familiarized him with the work of the whole so-called Berlin-Jena group—Wackenroder, Tieck, Novalis, Fichte, Gries, and the Schlegels—all of whom idealized the art and culture of the Middle Ages and attempted to reproduce it by collections and studies of German medieval literature and by tales and poems loosely imitative of the "gothic." Carlyle wrote about almost all these figures in his two volumes entitled *German Romance,* which he finished in 1826, but Novalis and Friedrich von Schlegel were probably most important in developing his medieval sympathies.

Novalis's most significant defense of the Middle Ages, *Die Christenheit oder Europa,* which Carlyle probably first read in 1829, begins with the following passage:

> Those were fine, magnificent times when Europe was a Christian country, when one Christendom inhabited this civilized continent and one common interest linked the most distant provinces of this vast spiritual empire.—Dispensing with great secular possessions, *one* sovereign governed and united great political forces.—Immediately under him was an enormous guild, open to all, which carried out his commands and eagerly strove to consolidate his beneficent power. Every member of this society was everywhere honoured; and if the common people sought from him comfort or help, protection or advice, ... he in turn gained protection, respect and audience from his superiors. ... Mankind could serenely go about its daily business on earth, for these holy men safeguarded the future, forgave every sin and obliterated and transfigured life's discolorations. They were the experienced pilots on the vast uncharted seas, in whose care

mankind could disparage all storms and count on safely reaching the
shores of its true home. . . . Peace emanated from them.[6]

Even without the rest of the essay to sustain and develop its theme,
this opening paragraph makes clear Novalis's position as a medievalist.
For him the essence of medieval society was its Christian unity.
Each nation was bound together within its borders by an active
clergy, and all nations were bound together despite their borders by
the cohesive power of the papacy. Far from viewing society as a
composite of individually responsible citizens, Novalis saw it hier-
archically or corporately. The mass of men abandoned their decisions
to an enlightened priesthood, which in turn was guided and sustained
by a smaller number of priestly leaders.

A society so ordered, Novalis thought, was crowned by universal
peace. Its antithesis was the spirit of revolt—Lutheranism, Jacobinism,
rationalism—which unfortunately had led Europe into crisis after
crisis for the past three hundred years. Appalled by the horrors of the
French Revolution and the Napoleonic Wars, Novalis hoped for a
rebirth of essential Christianity, not necessarily in its "accidental" old
papal forms, but as a visible church uniting all Europe "without
consideration of national frontiers, a church eager to become the
mediator between the old and the new world, receiving into its bosom
all souls thirsting for a spiritual life."[7]

Apart from his cosmopolitanism and Catholicism, which Carlyle
could not accept, most of Novalis's ideas were bound to appeal to
the order-seeking Carlyle, who was looking in the past, as everywhere,
for faith and leadership. He was thus able to use not only Novalis's
fundamental political beliefs but also his application of them to the
Middle Ages. The idea of veneration, for example, with its implication
of hero worship, is repeatedly echoed in Carlyle. And even Novalis's
praise of relics as a mode of showing admiration for sainthood, or
goodness, appears in dramatic form in the chapter "St. Edmund,"

---

[6] Quoted and translated in *The Political Thought of the German Romantics,
1793–1815*, ed. with an intro. by H. S. Reiss (New York: Macmillan, 1955),
pp. 126–127.

[7] *Ibid.*, p. 141.

in *Past and Present*. Most important, Carlyle shares Novalis's con-
demnation of modern rationalism, with its idle spectator of a god, in
contrast to the living deity of the Middle Ages. He uses Novalis's
image of the mill as a metaphor for the mechanical universe on several
occasions. The strikingly phrased contention in *Die Christenheit oder
Europa* that "out of the infinite creative music of the universe, it
[modern rationalism] made a uniform rattling of a gigantic mill, which,
driven by the current of chance in which it floated is supposed to be a
mill-in-itself, without builder or miller and thus truly a genuine
perpetuum mobile, a mill grinding itself,"[8] appears more than once in
Sartor Resartus, where it gains added emphasis as a pun on the Utilitarian Mill. In the chapter called "The Everlasting No," Carlyle writes,
"to me the Universe was all void of Life, of Purpose, of Volition, even
of Hostility: it was one huge, dead, immeasurable Steam-engine,
rolling on, in its dead indifference, to grind me limb from limb. O,
the vast, gloomy, solitary Golgotha, and Mill of Death."[9]

Novalis's dream of the new, deathless Christendom to rise from
the ashes of rationalism is, of course, the phoenix-vision of all Romantics. It was distinguished in Novalis and in many of his contemporaries by being based on the imagined structure of the Middle Ages.
Carlyle found similar medieval associations in the work of another
Roman Catholic by conversion, Friedrich von Schlegel, whose works
he studied. Ascribing the richness of medieval life to the fructifying
contact of German heroism with Christian idealism, an idea previously
expressed by Herder, Schlegel saw the Middle Ages as one of history's
great eras. He believed that any reasonable man was bound to be
convinced that "great characters (abounding almost more than in any
other period of history), important interests, mighty motives, and
lofty feelings and ideas," all characterized western Europe from the
eleventh to fourteenth centuries. He further believed that religion
was the basis of that superiority. Then, he continued, religion underlay

---

[8] *Ibid.*, p. 133.
[9] Carlyle, *Works*, I, 133. Note his use of the steam engine to characterize the
modern world. Carlyle typically uses mechanical imagery to describe contemporary
society and images borrowed from nature to characterize the Middle Ages.

statecraft; now the state is atheistic. Then "principle was predominant"; now "opinion." No comparison, he concluded, can be more "profitable and instructive" than that between medieval greatness and our own decay.[10]

Carlyle also borrows from the Germans, though he might have found it in some of the earlier English medievalists, the familiar notion of "hard primitivism." He discerns in the "dark Forests" of Tacitus's period "those *German manners*, features of a rude greatness" by which "the old corrupt world was to be swept away as an abomination, and a new world under fairer omens for mankind to evolve itself."[11] Free, however, from the eighteenth-century bias which confused primitivism with barbarism, Carlyle declares that from the fourth or fifth centuries on there were no "dark ages," since Europe was athirst with "that noble zeal for knowledge . . . which is the best fruit and proof of culture."[12] His view of chivalry, the flower of that culture, would have satisfied any of his German mentors, both in its praise of the past and its implied criticism of the present. Under chivalry, he wrote,

> for the first time the grand principles of order, or subjection to rule were universally inculcated, and the maintenance of them made a habit and a social duty. Thus Strength thus harnessed itself in the yoke of reason. . . . It [chivalry] was a translation into Practice of whatever was noblest in the sentiments of mankind. . . .
>
> Here at last were old German Valour and Christian Humility harmoniously blended; and the new European man stood forth, all points a man . . . [bound by] that solemn vow to fight for the widow and orphan, to defend Holy Church and Truth. Everywhere to stand in the breach where might was threatening Right, what was it but a recognition of the infinite celestial nature of Virtue. . . . The moral philosophy of the twelfth century might put that of the eighteenth century to shame; for the one knew and practically asserted what the

[10] Friedrich von Schlegel, *The Philosophy of History*, trans. James Burton Robertson, 3 vols. (London, 1835), II, 152–154.

[11] Thomas Carlyle, *Carlyle's Unfinished History of German Literature*, ed. Hill Shine (Lexington, Ky.: University of Kentucky Press, 1951), p. 15.

[12] *Ibid.*, p. 76.

other had well-nigh forgotten, that beyond the sphere of sense there is an Invisible Kingdom in man.[13]

As a lesson in German romanticism and medievalism this passage might stand by itself. It hardly needs pointing out that almost all the ideas Carlyle had acquired in a decade of reading are here touched upon. The spiritual nature of the universe, man's need to recognize it, and his need to subordinate himself to those best able to understand it are all implicit here, as is the belief that the Middle Ages was the period when all these ideals were best realized.

The German idealists could provide Carlyle with a metaphysical solution to his search for order. But they were unaware of the special difficulties posed by an industrial civilization. All the figures whom he studied were born in the eighteenth century, long before Germany made her belated entrance into modernity at the end of the nineteenth century; and it has been accurately said that for them the "love of the middle ages was a kind of homesickness."[14] For the application of medievalism to the problems of contemporary society Carlyle was indebted to the writings of the Saint-Simonians, whose conception of history enabled him to cope with his changing environment. According to Saint-Simonian thought, civilization was both cyclic and progressive. It was cyclic because it alternated between organic (or good) eras when society was held together by universal faith in its ideas, and critical (or bad) eras when it was rent by disbelief. But society was also progressive because it was gradually moving toward a harmonious Golden Age in which the state would provide all men with guidance and security. For Carlyle this view of history was important, for it presented him with a society at once conservative and dynamic—founded on religion and yet directed toward social progress, allowing for change but rejecting revolution. Any real understanding of Carlyle's medievalism must therefore take this influence into account.

Some of this cyclic progressivism Carlyle had already seen in the German philosophers, notably Fichte and Goethe, but nowhere were

[13] *Ibid.*, pp. 69–70.
[14] Gottfried Salomon, *Das Mittelalter als Ideal in der Romantik* (Munich: Drei Masken, 1922), p. 48.

these ideas applied to history with as much detail as in the writings of Claude Henri de Saint-Simon. Briefly, Saint-Simon saw history divided into three organic epochs: the classical, the medieval, and the industrial. Of the classical period nothing need be said. But his opinion of the Middle Ages, which he described as far superior to all that existed before that era, is extremely important for Carlyle. Like Novalis and like the French theocrats, Joseph de Maistre and Louis de Bonald, Saint-Simon saw the medieval world as a single political body, rendered peaceful and unified by the superintendent hierarchy of the Roman Catholic church. Far from being a time of barbarity, ignorance, or superstition, the medieval era was far superior to post-Napoleonic Europe in its ability to maintain peace.

Saint-Simon believed that within its borders, too, the medieval state was in many ways the superior of the modern. Whereas modern France might lose her nobles, ministers of state, marshals, cardinals, archbishops, prefects, judges, and 10,000 richest landowners without the slightest harm to the nation, since these men were governors in name alone, medieval France could have survived no such loss. Her leaders led. Society was primarily military and religious, and landholding and power depended on giving either military or spiritual protection to the lower classes—on being, to adopt Carlyle's symbolic characters, either a Landlord Edmund or an Abbot Samson. Under such ministrations, Saint-Simon realized, the lower classes might not have been free, but at least they enjoyed a security lacking to their nineteenth-century descendants.

For all his praise of the past, Saint-Simon did not wish to revive it. His progressive view of history and his whole melioristic temperament precluded such a desire. As he wrote in a famous passage that Carlyle would one day quote: "L'âge d'or du genre humaine n'est pas derrière nous, il est au devant, il est dans la perfection de l'ordre social; nos pères ne l'ont pas vu, nos enfants y arriveront un jour; c'est à nous de leur frayer la route."[15] All his researches into the past are devoted to just this task of pointing the road to the future. The Middle Ages were

[15] Henri de Saint-Simon, *Oeuvres choisies de Comte Henri de Saint-Simon*, 3 vols. (Brussels, 1859), I, 247.

important because they showed him that this society must be founded on faith. They were also important because they showed him that it must be organized. Although power need no longer be concentrated in the hands of the military or theocratic castes, the same underlying principle must apply: the possessors of society's wealth and wisdom must rule. Who these men were in the nineteenth century seemed quite clear to Saint-Simon, and they were not the traditional noblemen and priests. The possessors of wisdom were the scientists; the possessors of wealth were the industrialists. Into their hands he delivered the state: "pour organiser la société de la manière la plus favorable aux progrès des sciences et à la prosperité de l'industrie, il faut confier le pouvoir spirituel aux savants, et l'administration du pouvoir temporel aux industriels" (III, 33).

From their neofeudal organization of society, Saint-Simon and his followers expected great benefits for the masses. The waste of laissez faire, so pointedly analyzed by Jean Charles Sismondi, would disappear. In its place, as in Fichte's *Geschlossene Handelsstaat*, an industrial elite would direct each man toward the work most suited to his talents and apportion this work for the greatest good of society. In the same way the Crusades had helped in the Middle Ages to unify the European community, Saint-Simon hoped a campaign by the industrialized nations to aid their backward neighbors would guarantee peace in the future. In all lands, in short, society would accomplish its great aim: "L'amélioration la plus rapide possible du sort de la classe la plus pauvre" (III, 328). Clothed in medieval analogies, then, Saint-Simon's doctrines lead straight into the future—to socialism, on one hand, and paternalistic capitalism, on the other. For Carlyle they provided a conception of social order that was to pervade his entire work.

II

English influences, as well as French and German ones, also helped shape Carlyle's medievalism. He read Gothic novels and admired the works of Scott. He wrote in one of his essays that Scott's portraits of the Middle Ages were popular because they offered the nineteenth century, an age "destitute of belief, yet terrified of Scepticism," the contrast of "rough strong times wherein these maladies of ours had not arisen." They made the modern reader wish that he, too, "had lived in those times, had never known these logic cobwebs, and felt [himself] a man among men alive" (XXVI, 77–78). Scott's novels also provided him with a persuasive description of a paternalistic age, which like his reading of what he termed Burke's "noble conservatism" presumably reinforced his sense of medieval chivalry (XXVIII, 42). Southey's political philosophy also met with Carlyle's approval; he found much in Southey's "Toryism which was greatly according to [his] heart; things rare and worthy, at once pious and true." [16]

Coleridge also, for all Carlyle's criticisms of his ideas may have been an influence. Such a passage as this seems very similar to the ideas, though not the tone, of Coleridge's *Constitution of Church and State:*

> For, alas, on us too the rude truth has come home. . . . Are these millions guided? We have a Church, the venerable embodiment of an idea which may well call itself divine . . . it is a Church well furnished with equipments and appurtenances; educated in universities; rich in money; set on high places that it may be conspicuous to all, honoured of all . . . . This Church answers: "Yes, the people are taught." This aristocracy, astonishment in every feature, answers: "Yes, surely the people are guided. Do we not pass what Acts of Parliament are needful; as many as thirty-nine for the shooting of the partridge alone. Are there not treadmills, gibbets, even hospitals, poor–rates, New Poor Laws?" So verily answers the Church; so answers Aristocracy, astonishment in every feature.
>
> Fact meanwhile, takes his lucifer-box [and] sets fire to the wheat-stacks. (XXVIII, 155)

Surprisingly enough, it is Cobbett, whom Carlyle praised for his humaneness and great love for the poor, who seems the most immediate English influence on *Past and Present. A History of the Protestant*

[16] James Anthony Froude (ed.), *Reminiscences by Thomas Carlyle* (New York, 1881), p. 515.

Reformation and *Rural Rides* seem to have been at the back of his mind when he came to write *Past and Present*, for they make the same contrast between the world of the monastery and that of the poorhouse, between medieval security and modern poverty that Carlyle makes in his far greater book. On one occasion, at least, it seems possible to detect a faint verbal echo between Carlyle and Cobbett:

Cobbett	Carlyle
They [English agricultural workers] have "liberty" to choose between death by starvation (quick or slow) and death by the halter.	Gurth is now "emancipated" long since; has what we call "Liberty." Liberty when it becomes the "Liberty to die by starvation" is not so divine! [17]

One great advantage that Carlyle had over Cobbett as a historian was his respect for historical fact, and in this he took advantage of the increasing availability of documentary material. Throughout the eighteenth century and well into the nineteenth, the condition of the government records had been a national disgrace. It was found in 1836, for example, that during his thirty-one years in office the secretary of the Record Commission had removed the seals from many important documents for his private collection and that the commission itself was alleged to have spent £200,000 in the period without achieving a thing. Some improvement occurred during the 1830s when the Record Commission publications were issued by the historian Francis Palgrave.[18] But there were still literally rats in the Record Office until a new commission, headed by Carlyle's former pupil Charles Buller, arranged for the proper cataloguing and storing of documents.

Private organizations, too, during the 1830s began trying more vigorously to discover and publish the remains of England's past. Between 1834 and 1846 twelve new antiquarian societies were formed, including the Surtees, Abbotsford, English Historical, Camden, Aelfric, and Caxton. Among the most successful of these was the

[17] William Cobbett, *Rural Rides*, ed. G. D. H. and Margaret Cole, 3 vols. (London: P. Davies, 1930), II, 116. Carlyle, *Works*, X, 212.

[18] Palgrave is interesting in that some of his ideas in the essay "Fine Arts in Florence" (1840) anticipate Ruskin's in *The Stones of Venice*.

Camden, founded to "perpetuate and render accessible, whatever is valuable, but at present little known amongst the materials for the Civil, Ecclesiastical, or Literary History of the United Kingdom."[19] The *Chronica Jocelini de Brakelonda*, Carlyle's sourcebook for the medieval section of *Past and Present*, was the Camden's thirteenth publication when it appeared in 1840.

Carlyle's uses of this work and of several other sources as well are meticulously examined in Grace Calder's study of *The Writing of Past and Present*, and there can be no quarrel with her verdict that "though he adds to Jocelin's narrative warnings for the behoof of his contemporaries, he does not alter the content of the historical picture as given by Jocelin," retaining throughout the book "an extraordinary fidelity to his source."[20] The warnings, however, are interesting since they came not so much from his reading as from his personal experience of the "condition of England." Carlyle's knowledge of these conditions was not, as for some other medievalists, merely secondhand, for he was born to know poverty. His boyhood in Ecclefechan and his student years in Edinburgh inured him to rough lodging and cheap food, but many of his friends and relatives, unable to provide themselves even with such a low standard of living, were forced to change their occupations or emigrate to the New World. Carlyle himself was obliged by straitened circumstances to spend seven years at Craigenputtock. Not until 1839, indeed, did he declare himself free from the terrors of utter destitution.

In spite of his experiences as a farmer, Carlyle seldom expended his pity on the agriculturalist. Poverty on the land was perhaps too familiar to be terrible. It was the city and the factory that compelled his imagination from the first. London, he agreed with Cobbett, was a "monstrous Wen," thick with smoke, clogged with vehicles, where even the middle class were ill-lodged in "houses, thin as shells, with the floors all twisted" and ill-fed on watery milk, muddy water, and rotten eggs and potatoes.[21]

[19] Quoted in Grace J. Calder, *The Writing of Past and Present: A Study of Carlyle's Manuscripts*, Yale Studies in English, no. 112 (New Haven: Yale University Press, 1949), p. 27.

[20] *Ibid.*, p. 48.

[21] Carlyle, *Letters, 1826–1836*, II, 7.

Manchester was a vast, reeking den of conflict, hunger, and despair; Birmingham, the basis for a dramatic portrait of an industrial hell:

> A dense cloud of pestilential smoke hangs over it for ever, . . . and at night the whole region burns like a volcano spilling fire from a thousand tubes of brick. But oh the wretched one hundred and fifty thousand mortals that grind out their destiny there! In the coal mines they were literally naked, many of them, all but trousers, black as ravens: plashing about among the dripping caverns or scrambling amid heaps of broken mineral. . . . In the iron mills it was a little better. . . . Here they were wheeling charred coals, breaking their ironstone, and tumbling and boring cannon with a hideous shrieking noise such as the earth could hardly parallel; and through the whole, half-naked demons pouring with sweat and besmeared with soot were hurrying to and fro in their red nightcaps and sheet iron breeches, . . . hammering or squeezing the flowing metal as if it had been wax.[22]

The social conditions preceding 1842, the year in which Carlyle wrote *Past and Present*, were particularly bad, almost the worst in England's history. A series of bad harvests beginning in 1837 had sent the price of wheat up a third over what it had been in the early thirties and helped make paupers of almost a tenth of the population, a tragedy to which a series of bank failures in 1838 and the closing of the cotton factories in 1839 had also contributed. Poor Law relief which had been £1,000,000 in 1836 was £5,200,000 in 1842. In some areas men subsisted on boiled nettles, and in one village, horrible to record, "the starving people dug up the putrid carcase [*sic*] of a cow rather than die of hunger."[23]

Carlyle's reaction, like Southey's and Scott's in 1819 and 1830, was one of mixed sympathy and fear. "The distress of the people of Britain," he wrote, "excels all that they have ever known."[24] So cold and sickly a winter he had not seen, with even the honest poor compelled

[22] Thomas Carlyle, *Early Letters of Thomas Carlyle, 1814–1826*, ed. Charles Eliot Norton (London, 1886), p. 312.

[23] See Thomas Carlyle, *Past and Present*, ed. A. M. D. Hughes (Oxford: Oxford University Press, 1921), pp. vii–xiii.

[24] Thomas Carlyle, *New Letters of Thomas Carlyle*, ed. Alexander Carlyle, 2 vols. (London and New York: J. Lane, 1904), I, 257.

to acts of theft. But as the sleety winter progressed into a dismal summer, he began to fear that the general discontent might soon break into revolt. In August he wrote to his wife that monarchy was rapidly becoming obsolete and that England was on the brink of anarchies and other nameless horrors.[25] Working at the same time on his projected biography of Oliver Cromwell, he wrote to Emerson in the same month that it was hard to be in two centuries at once and, with a heart "sick and sore" in behalf of his "own poor generation," to make the seventeenth century seem relevant to the nineteenth.[26] Cromwell's society failed somehow to offer the appropriate contrasts and parallels to his own. His writing slowed as he looked for the right symbol with which to express his nightmare visions.

The inspiration came in September 1842 when Carlyle visited in rapid succession the workhouse of St. Ives and the ruins of St. Edmund's Abbey. The differences between the two places epitomized for him the decline of England since the Middle Ages. In the workhouse healthy inmates sat enchanted in their "Bastille," victims of a do-nothing government and a laissez faire economy; in the abbey they had once received wise government in their prosperity and ample charity in their need. Carlyle seized on this contrast both as artist and social critic and expanded it into a comparison between a vital and ordered past and a chaotic and impotent present. From it was born *Past and Present*, the "most remarkable fruit in English literature of the medieval revival."[27]

III

Carlyle begins his book with a description of the condition of England which is meant to shock the reader so that he remembers it throughout the subsequent discussions of past, present, and future.

---

[25] Thomas Carlyle, *Letters to His Wife*, ed. Trudy Bliss (Cambridge, Mass.: Harvard University Press, 1953), p. 154.

[26] Thomas Carlyle, *The Correspondence of Thomas Carlyle and Ralph Waldo Emerson, 1834–1872*, ed. Charles Eliot Norton, 2 vols. (Boston and New York, 1894), II, 10–11.

[27] Oliver Elton, *A Survey of English Literature, 1780–1880*, 2 vols. (New York: Macmillan, 1920), III, 240.

In three stages he builds up a memorable image of horror. First, a paradox: "England is full of wealth and multifarious produce, supply for human want in every kind; yet England is dying of inanition." Then, an ironic report by the Picturesque Tourist on the workhouses ("pleasantly so named because work cannot be done in them"), which reproduces Carlyle's experience in September at the workhouse of St. Ives. And finally, a Dantesque scene from the inmost circle of Hell, the trial at the Stockport Assizes where a mother and father were found "guilty of poisoning three of their children to defraud a burial society of some £3 8s due on the death of each child." In prosperous Britain, he writes,

> A human Mother and Father had said to themselves, What shall we do to escape starvation? We are deep sunk here in our dark cellar; and help is far.—Yes, in the Ugolino Hunger-tower stern things happen; best-loved little Gaddo fallen dead on his Father's knees! The Stockport Mother and Father think and hint: Our poor little starveling Tom, who cries all day for victuals, who will see only evil and not good in this world: if he were out of misery at once; he well dead, and the rest of us perhaps kept alive? It is thought, and hinted; at last it is done. And now Tom being killed, and all spent and eaten, Is it poor little starveling Jack that must go, or poor little starveling Will?—What a committee of ways and means. (X, 4)

With this dreadful text for his lay sermon, Carlyle can go on to explain that England's basic weakness is that her leaders, like the nobility Saint-Simon had criticized in France, have ceased to lead. The aristocracy is interested only in preservation of game and corn laws; the millocracy, only in making money. Neither remembers its duty to assure its tenants and workers of the simple social justice of "'a fair day's–wages for a fair day's–work'" (X, 18). The result of their callousness is that the English horse is a good deal better off than the English man, for he at least is assured food and a stable, while millions of Englishmen go naked, hungry, unroofed, and what is worse, unbound by social ties. No wonder, Carlyle insists, that revolution is upon us.

In these opening chapters of *Past and Present*, Carlyle is more concerned with pointing his finger at England and saying "thou ailest here and here" than with finding any remedy for these ailments. One thing he does make clear, however, is that the reform must be spiritual. If the proximate cause of all this suffering is that man has forgotten social justice, the final cause is that he has forgotten God, that he is possessed of the inane idea that nature is dead, an ancient eight-day clock, "still ticking, but dead as brass" (X, 29). Going back to his Goethe and his Fichte, Carlyle places his hope in leaders whose spiritual wisdom teaches them the practical thing to do. His final wish, therefore, in this section is for "Hero Kings, and a whole world not unheroic" (X, 36).

To show what heroes can do Carlyle goes back in the second book of *Past and Present* to the "world not unheroic" of the Middle Ages. As he had done in so early a work as the *History of German Literature*, he compares the spiritual chaos of the present with the heart-whole faith of the past. But he now fills out the general theme with details, significant in themselves and useful for their contrast with modern times. Drawing heavily on Jocelin's chronicle, he transforms his record of St. Edmund's Abbey into what might be called a morality play for moderns, except that "morality play" is too abstract a term for the fullness of life and scene that he presents, and "Everyman," too weak a name for his heroic protagonists.

The first hero on whom the time-curtain rises is the good Landlord Edmund, who ruled a large tract of land in the eastern counties. A real man, Carlyle insists, he lived the ordinary life of his time: wore leather shoes and a sturdy body-coat, procured his breakfast, and somehow managed to reconcile the contradictions of life. But his reality is asserted only to make more effective the contrast between him and his nineteenth-century successors. Carlyle remarks with his customary irony that many things are not known about him: "With what degree of wholesome rigour his rents were collected we hear not. Still less by what methods he preserved his game . . . and if the partridge-seasons were 'excellent,' or were indifferent. Neither do we ascertain what kind of Corn-Bill he passed, or wisely-adjusted Sliding–scale." What is known is that far from busying himself merely with tailors and wine merchants, he stood bravely in defense of his own. When certain "Heathen Physical-Force Ultra-Chartists, 'Danes' as they were then called, [came] into his territory with their 'five points,' or rather with their five-and-twenty thousands points . . . of pikes," he resisted the incoming anarchy to the utmost. "Cannot I die," said he, and did so, barbarously tortured, but in his martyrdom eventually triumphant over them (X, 53–54).

No wonder then that in an age of hero worship Edmund needed no yeomanry-cavalry to keep his tenants in order:

> For his tenants, it would appear, did not in the least complain of him; his labourers did not think of burning his wheat stacks, breaking into his game-preserves; very far the reverse of all that. Clear evidence, satisfactory even to my friend Dryasdust, exists that, on the contrary, they honoured, loved, admired this ancient Landlord to a quite astonishing degree,—and indeed at last to an immeasurable and inexpressible degree; for finding no limits or utterable words for their sense of his worth, they took to beatifying and adoring him! "Infinite admiration," we are taught, "means worship." (X, 52)

Landlord Edmund is for Carlyle a typically heroic character of the early Middle Ages. After telling his story, which culminates with the founding of St. Edmund's Abbey, Carlyle skips several hundred years to describe the slipshod state of the abbey in the twelfth century, a state suggestive of England in the nineteenth. The ideal, Carlyle asserts in one of the bursts of hard-headed pragmatism that are as typical as his mysticism, "had always to grow in the Real, and to seek out its bed and board there, often in a very sorry way" (X, 57). Three centuries after its founding, St. Edmund's Abbey's way was of the sorrowfulest. The abbot was one Hugo—old, as Jocelin informs us, somewhat blind, and the victim of his flatterers' zeal and his own idleness. "Wrapt in his warm flannels and delusions," he had let the monastery's account books fall into a dreadful state (X, 58). As with the complacent Whig leaders of the 1830s, his expenditures each year exceeded his income, until at his death there was no money left in his exchequer and a national debt, so to speak, of £1,400.

Abbot Hugo dead, who was to replace him? Who was to lead the abbey—or England—out of chaos? This is an important question for Jocelin, who devotes many pages of his chronicle to narrating the conversations and transactions involved in electing his successor. It is important to Carlyle, too, who retells his story with great care. As an artist he could not help but be delighted by the life breathing from Jocelin's gossipy pages—the *dixit quidam de quodam* ("said one monk of another") that enliven his record. But as a sermon-writer he was even more impressed by the meaning behind these discussions. For elections are but another form of hero worship, and hero worship is the only significant social act. "Given the men a People choose," Carlyle asserts, "the People itself, in its exact worth and worthlessness is given" (X, 75).

Besides, Carlyle's generation was particularly interested in the mechanics of election. The Reform Bill had been the chief political accomplishment of the 1830s, and the question of extending this reform agitated the English political scene until late in the sixties. Carlyle, therefore, makes a point of showing that the devices of "midwifery," as he terms the mode of election, are relatively unimportant, not to be compared in importance to the spirit in which the choice is carried out.

Judged by this test, the medieval monastery is far superior to modern society, for it can choose a true hero for its leader. The new Abbot Samson possesses all the Carlylean virtues: faith, energy, discipline, and compassion. His first words on ascending to the difficult task of restoring order to the abbey are "miserere mei Deus," since he knows that if spiritual strength is granted him, adequate deeds will follow. However, he also knows that it is the duty of every leader to watch the account books. Faced with Abbot Hugo's accumulated debts, "boundless seemingly as the National Debt of England" (X, 87), Samson immediately institutes radical economic reforms—just as Carlyle hoped Prime Minister Robert Peel would do. There are only two ways, Carlyle points out, to reduce debt: "increase in industry in raising income, increase in thrift in laying out" (X, 91). Samson applies both with an intelligence and vigor that might well serve as a model to the current English government.

As his nineteenth-century descendants should also be, Samson is interested in justice as well as economics. The reaping tax had once driven women to rush out after the tax collectors like "Female Chartists," shrieking and waving their distaffs. Under Samson that tax ceases to be a burden on the poor, as does the Lakenheath eel toll and other exactions. Everywhere, in short, that "Disorder may stand or lie," Carlyle says, Abbot Samson "is the man that has declared war on it" (X, 92). If his monks are remiss in carrying out their duties toward his people, he chastises or even replaces them. If the courts are venal, he brings justice to them. If Parliament has fallen into decay—"some Reform Bill, then as now, being greatly needed"—he fights for reform, although in opposition to King John himself (X, 105).

At times, indeed, the very efficiency of Samson's justice shows a ruthlessness frightening to modern readers who have grown more skeptical than Carlyle about the value of substituting abstract authority for human values. Witness the affair of old Dean Herbert, who

> in a too thrifty manner had erected a windmill for himself upon his glebe-lands at Haberdon. On the morrow, after mass, our Lord Abbot orders the Cellararius to send off his carpenters to demolish the said structure . . . Old Dean Herbert, hearing what was toward, comes tottering along hither to plead for himself and his mill. The Abbot answers: "I am obliged to thee as if thou hadst cut off both my feet! By God's face, *per os Dei*, I will not eat bread till that fabric be cut to pieces. Thou art an old man, and shouldst have known that neither the King nor his Justiciary dare change aught within the Liberties without consent of Abbot and Convent: and thou hast presumed on such a thing. . . . Away, away, before thou gettest home again thou shalt see what thy mill has grown to!" The very reverend the old Dean totters home again in all haste; tears the mill in pieces by his own *carpentarii*, to save at least the timber; and Abbot Samson's workmen, coming up, find the ground already clear of it. (X, 113)

For Carlyle, however, all that is dictatorial in Samson's actions is redeemed by his ability to see, speak, and do the truth. In all his actions, a deep piety and reverence is apparent—most obviously so in his capacity for hero worship, for reverencing the divine in human shape. Using the strange light he could handle so well, Carlyle paints as the climax to Samson's abbacy his unveiling of the body of Landlord Edmund, of whose tradition he is the inheritor. We see him in the hushed midnight church unveil the loculus, look upon the linen-clad body, not daring to behold the sacred flesh, and reverently touch the eyes, the nose, the hand, the feet. "What a scene," Carlyle concludes, "shining luminous, effulgent, as the lamps of St. Edmund do, through the dark Night . . . the Convent all asleep, and the Earth all asleep,— and since then, Seven Centuries of Time, mostly gone to sleep" (X, 123).

It is with these seven centuries, or rather the difference between them—between, that is, the twelfth and nineteenth centuries—that Carlyle is mainly concerned. However brilliantly his narrative of St. Edmund's Abbey goes and however alive his characters based on Boswell-Jocelin become, sheer history is not his aim. His underlying theme is always past and present, the contrast between a medieval society that deifies St. Edmund and a modern one that lets Robert Burns gauge ale barrels in Dumfries. This medieval-modern comparison appears in dozens of brief or oblique references: some rather trivial, as is his description of riotous young knights as "young scamps, in the dandy state," eternally present in society "whether cased in iron or in whalebone" (X, 111); some, as we have seen, serious comments on corn laws, game preserving, or parliamentary reform. Even his little saint's life narrative of St. Edmund's appearance to a recreant knight engaged in a duel becomes the basis for a bitter apostrophe to his contemporaries of the "Age of Flunkeyism" for their blindness to spiritual truth.

Faith is the key to Carlyle's medievalism. Like many of the English and Continental medievalists he had read, he sees the Middle Ages as a period of belief—belief as distinguished from mere religious observance. Abbot Samson's faith is evidenced not in his creed or his rituals, but in the thousand daily acts that show his belief in a meaningful universe. "Practical-devotional," Carlyle calls it, and with his usual use of the medieval-modern contrast goes on to differentiate it from the sickly "isms" of the present day as neither a ghastly Methodism with its eye turned ever on its navel, nor a mere Dilettantism, a galvanized spasmodic Puseyism, but a faith whose contrast with such foolishness can strike one dumb.

Faith is not the only lesson the modern state can learn from the Middle Ages. It can also learn the lesson of leadership, which is faith's corollary. Without religion, Carlyle concluded, inaction and sham stifle every hope of government. With it, men can find the leaders or heroes for whom all things are possible. In contrast to the modern do-nothing state, the feudal one seemed to him rugged and stalwart, "full earnestness, of a rude God's truth" (X, 244), and led by a never-idle aristocracy. Listen to the repetition of the word "alive" in this passage in which Carlyle describes the functions of the state. It forms a bitter commentary on the breakdown of government between the decline of the manor and parish and the rise of the municipality as instruments of social welfare: "How much is still alive in England; how much has not yet come into life! A Feudal Aristocracy is still alive, in the prime of life; superintending the cultivation of the land, and less consciously the distribution of the produce of the land, the adjustment of the quarrels of the land; judging, soldiering, adjusting; everywhere governing the people" (X, 65).

Using the view of the Middle Ages found in all the English medievalists, particularly Cobbett and Southey, Carlyle reminds his readers that all classes prospered under such personalized rule. The aristocracy had the reaping of the land in return for ruling it; and the peasant, though he no doubt "got cuffs as often as pork parings" (X, 246) was at least far better off than the modern workman rotting in the workhouse or slaughtering his children for the burial fee. Surely, Carlyle claims, this was a far juster society than that of today, in which a corn-lawing, game-preserving aristocracy had the reaping without the ruling and the peasantry had only the name of freedom in place of the far more valuable reality of security and leadership. Referring to characters from Scott's *Ivanhoe*, as he does several other times in the book to form a common reference point for his reader, Carlyle sums up this view in a memorable passage:

> Gurth, born thrall of Cedric the Saxon, has been greatly pitied by Dryasdust and others. Gurth, with the brass collar round his neck, tending Cedric's pigs in the glades of the wood, is not what I call an exemplar of human felicity: but Gurth, with the sky above him, with the free air and tinted boscage and umbrage round him, and in him at least the certainty of supper and social lodging when he came home; Gurth to me seems happy, in comparison with many a Lancashire and Buckinghamshire man of these days, not born thrall of anybody! Gurth's brass collar did not gall him: Cedric *deserved* to be his master. The pigs were Cedric's, but Gurth too would get his parings of them. Gurth had the inexpressible satisfaction of feeling himself related indissolubly, though in a rude brass-collar way, to his fellow mortals in this Earth. He had superiors, inferiors, equals.—Gurth is now "emancipated" long since; has what we call "Liberty." Liberty, I am told, is a divine thing. Liberty when it becomes the "Liberty to die by starvation" is not so divine!
> Liberty? the true liberty of a man, you would say, consisted in his finding out, or being forced to find out the right path, and to walk thereon. To learn, or be taught, what work he actually was able for; and then by permission, persuasion, and even compulsion, to set about doing of the same. (X, 211–12)

By denying the importance of liberty, Carlyle also denies the responsibility of the common man. Indeed, his whole conception of the hero, which was to grow more important in his thinking in the years after he wrote *Past and Present*, implies the inadequacy of most men to cope with the conditions of existence. In this he seems to ally himself with other medievalists such as Scott and Southey. There is, however, one great difference. For Carlyle, as a rule, heroism is innate, dependent on spiritual nature not on hereditary status. His Abbot Samson rises from the masses as do many of the men he celebrates in *Heroes and Hero Worship*. Only later in his career does Carlyle tend to associate heroism and noble birth. In his only other

146

medieval production, *The Early Kings of Norway* (1875), the eighty-year-old sage ends his book with the assertion that while dictatorship has many faults, democracy has "little possibility of any virtue."[28]

After showing, primarily in Books II and III of *Past and Present*, the ways in which the Middle Ages were superior to the modern, Carlyle goes on in Book IV to apply the lessons of the past to the present and future. Artistically this section is much less successful. His satiric figures—Pandarus Dogdraught, Sir Jabesh Windbag, the Duke of Windlestraw—are far less convincing than the historical heroes he took from Jocelin. Lacking a clear narrative thread, he lapses, as he does so often, into repetition and dogmatism. In spite of its faults, however, the last half of the book is extremely interesting to the modern reader. It not only applies medieval concepts to nineteenth-century problems but makes suggestions still valid in the twentieth.

Essentially, Carlyle is looking here, as always, for a hero to lead society out of its wasteland, and he finds leadership possible in two groups, the aristocrats and the industrialists. His treatment of the aristocrat is perhaps the less original of the two. It is one of the last expressions in English literature of a new feudalism based on the return of large landholders to their historical role of ruling the nation. Nevertheless, Carlyle's program for landholders is not as purely manorial as Scott's or Cobbett's. Living in the age of reform, he thinks, instead, of parliamentary action. The first step, he suggests, is that the landowners give up their corn laws, thus giving England a ten-year breathing space of new prosperity in which to solve her other problems. After that they can participate, again through Parliament be it noted, in a series of projects and reforms that will restore the English government, though in a new form, to her medieval function of serving the people's welfare.

The landed classes, however, were not to carry out these reforms alone. Carlyle's most original contribution to the development of

---

[28] Carlyle, *Works*, III, 308. The lack of any medieval writings between 1843 and 1875 is probably explained by Carlyle's preoccupation with the periods of Oliver Cromwell and Frederick the Great, in both of which he looked for medievalist values.

English medievalism is in adapting the idea of the paternal leadership of society to an industrial age. He makes the manufacturers and business-men take on responsibilities previously reserved for the landed aristoc-racy. All the previous medievalists, most of them born a generation before Carlyle, had had an emotional belief in England as an agricultural country; their medievalism was essentially a mode of advocating a return to the land. Carlyle alone fully appreciated the inevitability of industrialism. Unlike his predecessors, he did not think it possible to diminish the importance of commerce and industry and make a neofeudal agriculture serve as the basis of a national economy. As Carlyle put it, "the Gospel of Richard Arkwright once promulgated, no monk of the old sort is any longer possible in this world"—nor any Landlord Edmund either. The future lay not in an impossible revival of St. Edmund's Abbey, but, however dreadful now, with the flame-mountains, "flaming with steam fires and useful labor" of Lancashire, Yorkshire, and counties and nations to come (X, 57).

With obvious indebtedness to Saint-Simon, though offering far greater detail, Carlyle tries to promulgate a new gospel for the guidance of the industrialists, who will be responsible for the laboring millions of England. "This that they call 'Organizing of Labour,'" Carlyle writes, "is, if well understood, the Problem of the whole Future" (X, 257). With his usual flair for names, Carlyle invents a typical industrialist, Plugson of Undershot, and lectures for his benefit. Much is wrong with Plugson, Carlyle insists. He is possessed by mammonism, thinks money-making the great aim of life, and fears financial failure like the terrors of hell. So intent is he upon wealth-getting that he has forgotten all other ties to mankind except that of cash payment, and in order to extract the last cent of profit from his mills keeps that cash payment to a minimum, letting his workers choke in thick cotton-fuzz and copperas fumes. Buccaneer like, he addresses his workers: "Noble-spinners, this is the Hundred Thousand we have gained, wherein I mean to dwell and plant vineyards; the hundred thousand is mine; the three and sixpence daily [is] yours" (X, 193).

For all that, Carlyle finds hope in Plugson. At least he is a worker and work, however mammonish, helps man communicate with nature, each completed job showing more clearly the next thing to do. Just as the buccaneer and pirate gave way to the medieval lord (a rude fellow perhaps, but one willing to defend his land and stand by his retainers in plenty or want), so the modern Captain of Industry must also give way to a better leader who will be attached to his workers by kindly feelings as well as the cash-nexus. Echoing the ideal of knighthood defined in such medieval works as *Piers Plowman* or the *Prose Lancelot*, Carlyle proposes a "chivalry of labor" in which the industrialists shall govern their men with wisdom and kindness. The suggestions, however, in spite of their feudal inspiration, are completely forward looking, similar to some of the more liberal developments in present-day capitalism.

One of his ideas is permanence of contract, an acknowledgment of the fact that while "men cannot now be bound to men by brass collars" (X, 250), they also cannot be constantly in danger of unemployment and need whenever the market drops or cheaper labor becomes available. If they were bound together for a sizable length of time, the workman would wish to see his master's interests prosper and the master his workmen's. The one would put his best efforts into his job, while the other would make sure by adequate wages and conditions of work that the men he was bound to retain would be healthy and willing. Carlyle even suggests, though very tentatively, that the two classes might be merged to a degree by some form of what we would call profit-sharing or stock bonuses so that industry might "become in practical result what in essential fact and justice it ever is, a joint enterprise" (X, 282).

But for all this modernism Carlyle's underlying motif is always feudalism. How "reconcile Despotism with Freedom?" he asks. "Is that such a mystery? Do you not already know the way? It is to make your Despotism *just*." The Middle Ages were essentially a military organization and their symbol might be "arms and the man." Carlyle thinks that the industrial ages might be similarly militarized under the banner of "tools and the man." Working together, the industrialists, the landed aristocrats, and the "natural aristocrats" (men of genius) might through parliamentary action create "an army ninety-thousand strong, maintained and fully equipt in continual real action and battle against Human Starvation, against Chaos, Necessity [and] Stupidity." There is no question in his mind that to accomplish this end, unbridled laissez faire must be replaced by state control: "Legislative interference, and interferences not a few, are indispensable" (X, 263–64). His age already had factory inspectors, why could it not also have mine inspectors, furrowfield inspectors, sanitary regulations, an education bill, a teaching service, and an effective emigration service? Hierarchical and paternalistic, these schemes show the influence of Carlyle's idealized Middle Ages upon his conception of an industrialized Utopia.

All this seems very far from the earlier agrarian medievalism and yet Carlyle's feudalization of industry is simply the next step in the tradition. All humanitarians realized that the condition of England demanded change. Those who were conservatives, as all medievalists tended to be, saw in the medieval ideal of the guided society a rough sketch of the changes to be made. Religion, a deep spiritual faith, was one of the values it offered both the English and Continental medievalists—the same faith that was being sought in Romantic poetry. Paternalism was another advantage. Man was a "poor, bare, forked, animal" according to the conservatives' fearful yet pitying view. The Middle Ages provided him with adequate food and shelter and, more important, with the ties and traditions that by making him content would eliminate the danger of revolt.

Carlyle's contribution to English medievalism was first to make the contrast between modern and medieval England sharper and more horrifying than it had ever been. He could do this partly because the current condition of England had grown worse over the years and partly because he knew how to etch forever on our memories the image of the St. Ives workers and the Stockport mother. His Middle Ages, shared a vividness equalled only by Scott's. Carlyle gave new direction to the practical application of medievalism, transferring its field of action from agriculture, which was no longer the center of English life, to manufacturing, in which its lessons could be extremely valuable. Plugson of Undershot's most direct descendants, perhaps, are the Tory Disraeli's Millbank and the Socialist Shaw's Undershaft—a combination that is a good symbol of Carlyle's paradoxical Tory-radicalism. Plugson's influence and that of other aspects of Carlyle's medievalism are to be found throughout the literature of the Victorian age and, indirectly at least, in much of the social legislation of the past hundred and more years.

5

Medievalism in Action:
Young England and Disraeli

IN MANY WAYS medievalism, as it developed during the nineteenth century, was a program of resistance; and though the terminology kept changing, it always resisted the same thing. In Scott or in Burke the force being resisted was called utilitarianism or calculation, and the opposing force was denominated chivalry. The undesirable historic tendency was seen to rely on sheer rationality and materialism—the Machiavellianism of a Louis XI or the barbarous philosophy of the Jacobins. The medieval or chivalric, by contrast, provided man with images and illusions with which to conceal and limit his natural acquisitiveness. The customs and traditions of the feudal age were seen as symbols on which man could focus his moral imagination and which enabled him to love, venerate, and admire the institutions of his society. The Lakists, too, used the Middle Ages as a counterweight to the individualism of their age, seeing in the ordered past a symbolic and sometimes a practical solution to the problems of a tortured and rebellious era. And the same ideas continue very clearly in Carlyle, with his explicit use of the medieval-modern contrast—or, as he terms it, the difference between Mammonism and Hero Worship. Even Cobbett, who at first glance would not seem to fit into this scheme, is actually countering what he calls "Old England" against the materialism and social ruthlessness of the "Thing"—or the manipulative capitalism of his age.

The common factor in all these figures and in all the terms and images they use to describe their ideas is very plain. Medieval society is seen to be built upon imagination and emotion; modern society upon a shallow rationalism. As a result one society is said to bind men together by ties of loyalty and generosity, the other to force men apart through the spread of self-interest. One provides order and leadership, the other only a devil-take-the-hindmost democracy. Whether the Middle Ages are examined politically, socially, or morally, an emphasis on emotion and tradition—the heart rather than the head—is always central to the medievalist tradition. The Middle Ages thus stand for absolute as opposed to purely relative values, for a concept best phrased as "nobility." Even so unlikely a figure as John Stuart Mill, who usually derided medievalism, acknowledged the power of such symbolism when he wrote that the old romances were to be praised for "keeping alive the chivalrous spirit . . . giving to the aspirations of the young and susceptible a noble direction, and keeping present to the mind an exalted standard of worth." [1]

In the 1830s and 1840s the term which was usually contrasted with medievalism or chivalry was "liberalism" or "liberal opinions." Generally speaking, liberal opinions consisted in a belief in reason and education, in physical science and material progress as the keys to human development. More specifically, they meant Erastianism, or state dominance, in religion, and a Whiggish or reforming tone in politics. In all areas its ethic was based on the utilitarian test of happiness and measurable achievement. To be traditional or venerable was no justification for either an institution or belief.

One area in which medievalism was deliberately used as a counterforce to liberalism was in religion. The Oxford movement has been defined as medievalism in religion, and certainly much of its content lay in a renewed concern for the Middle Ages. Hurrell Froude's *Remains*, for instance, one of the significant documents of the movement, shows a consistent fascination not only with the medieval church—its austerities, its miracles, its saints' lives—but with the medieval relationship between secular and religious government. A good portion of the *Remains* is devoted to a full-length study of Becket's quarrels

[1] Quoted in Walter E. Houghton, *The Victorian Frame of Mind, 1830–1870* (New Haven: Yale University Press, 1957), p. 317.

with Henry II—a study unquestionably inspired by such contemporary religious controversies as the suppression of the Irish sees. One of Froude's poems, "Farewell to Feudalism," contributed to *Lyra Apostolica* goes even further in idealizing the Middle Ages:

> 'Tis sad to watch Time's desolating hand
>   Doom noblest things to premature decay:
>   The Feudal court, the Patriarchal sway
> Of kings, the cheerful homage of a land
> Unskilled in treason, every social band
>   That taught to rule with sweetness, and obey
>   With dignity, swept one by one away,
> While proud Empirics rule in fell command.[2]

Froude's use of empiricism, or the liberal-utilitarian ethic, as the special foe of feudalism is significant, for it shows once again the special appeal of medievalism.

Edward Pusey, too, was powerfully drawn to the medieval church, whose ceremonialism seemed to him best able to evoke the sense of awe and reverence so necessary to devotion. It is interesting to see him using the mystery and half-lights of the Gothic church—the chancel's shadows and the dappling colors of the stained-glass windows —to describe the appeal of the past, since this is just what the eighteenth-century poets had done. Pusey became particularly interested in medieval writers after 1841 and 1842 when his translations of various Continental works of devotion stimulated him to encourage a revival of monasticism and such other medieval observances as vows, confessionals, and sisterhoods. His concern with these customs and with the revived use of crosses, candlesticks, alms dishes, altar cloths, vestments, and other appurtenances of devotion earned for the movement the often derisory title of Puseyism. But the essential seriousness of his medievalism cannot be denied; for his underlying aim, like that of all the Tractarians, was to counteract the growing rationalism within the Church and to make the Anglican religion once again a mystery and a faith.

[2] *Lyra Apostolica*, ed. H. C. Beeching (London: Methuen, n.d.), p. 170.

And yet, despite the Tractarians' interest in the Middle Ages, it would be a mistake to overestimate the medievalism of the Oxford movement. Cardinal Newman's comment that Froude was "powerfully drawn to the Medieval Church, but not to the Primitive" is a clue that such staunch medievalism was exceptional.[3] A study of the Tracts and of Newman's writings prior to his conversion shows a far greater concern with the theology of the fourth or seventeenth centuries than with that of the Middle Ages. Unlike the Continental writers of the Catholic revival, who often referred to Aquinas, the Anglican revivalists, because they feared being charged with Catholicism, relied on Patristic or Caroline theologians to set them right. In their concern to purify the English church, they remained fearful of Rome. While they admired the hierarchical order of the Middle Ages and the supremacy and unity of the medieval Catholic church, they were nonetheless ambivalent about the centuries before the Reformation.

A far more programmatic and explicit medievalism than that espoused by the Tractarians is to be found in the writings and activities of a number of Catholic figures, of whom the most outstanding was Kenelm Digby, a Cambridge graduate and a convert to the Church of Rome. Digby's chief work, *The Broad Stone of Honour; or the True Sense and Practice of Chivalry* (1822–27) is a five-volume, unconditionally eulogistic compendium of facts, anecdotes, and legends of the Middle Ages, as full of matter as Robert Burton's *Anatomy of Melancholy*, which it resembles in structure. Digby defines chivalry as "conversant with all that is beautiful and sublime in the intellectual world" and claims that it belongs to all generous and heroic minds throughout the ages.[4] As might be expected from a Roman Catholic writer who had absorbed the doctrines of Schlegel, de Maistre, and de Bonald, Digby was convinced that the Middle Ages were superior to modern times because of their religious faith. Materialism, he preached, was divisive. It made men concentrate on their own self-interest rather than

[3] John Henry Cardinal Newman, *Apologia Pro Vita Sua*, ed. A. Dwight Culler (Boston: Houghton Mifflin, 1956), p. 44.

[4] Kenelm Henry Digby, *The Broad Stone of Honour; or the True Sense and Practice of Chivalry*, 4 vols. (London, 1846), I, 86.

on attempts to govern themselves and their nation according to the precepts of God. In the Middle Ages, he wrote, "the clergy did not preach on keeping accounts and the way to succeed in life, upon attention to business and the comfort of having lived decently, and of having a good character, but they preached . . . on the commands of the decalogue, on the laws of the Church, on the mysteries of faith, on deadly sin" (II, 316). Seen in this way, the medieval Church was an obvious counterbalance to the growing secularism and Erastianism of the age.

Digby also praised the social system of the Middle Ages, reiterating the ideas found in other contemporary medievalists. Objecting to Adam Smith's economics, which he thought treated men as mere cattle employed for the good of the state, Digby preferred the patriarchal kindness of the Middle Ages, when all men were parts of one family, when great and low dined together at a single board, when all classes joined together in sports on the village green, and when the Church gave charity with kindness and tact. Angrily he asks if it is

> for the rich of the nineteenth century to talk of the inhumanity of the Middle Ages? To give alms, with them, is to encourage idleness: he is hungry, he is naked? let him work; but he is old? there are employments for all; but he is a child? do not teach him to beg; it is a mother of a large family? perhaps she does not tell the truth. We have institutions on a new system. Yes, truly, and woe to the unhappy who are doomed to receive relief from them! In order that the children of pleasure may not be incommoded by the sight of poverty, the poor are shut up within high walls, and condemned to confinement for the crime of being poor and miserable; thus secluded from the enjoyment of nature, an odious board of governors takes care that they should be provided with what is sufficient to support life, and then they have to endure the countenances of ferocious barbarians, who are the officers to administer this horrible humanity! (III, 87–88)

Digby also shares the anti-industrialism common to most early nineteenth-century medievalists. He reminds his readers that in days when the smoke curled above thatched roofs and the countryside was dotted with flocks and herds, there were "no lawyers, no rich manufacturers to stimulate the passions of a peaceable and innocent people, no speculations ending in ruin and suicide, or success and the license of hell" (I, 93–94).

Several other Roman Catholics shared Digby's dream of reviving the religion and traditions of medieval England. Ambrose Phillipps De Lisle anticipated the Oxford movement in his ritualism and was interested for a time in the possibility of reuniting the churches of England and Rome. Phillipps was probably acquainted with the charitable and pious Lord Shrewsbury. Faithful to the spirit of his medieval forebears, Shrewsbury was in many ways the perfect new feudalist. He contributed toward churches, endowed a hospital on the model of Leycester Hospital in Warwick, and provided work without question at road building on his estate for unemployed individuals who cared to apply for it.

Still another Catholic new feudalist was Aubrey de Vere, a friend of Tennyson and himself a poet. De Vere's attitude toward the tenants on his estate was clearly paternalistic. He exerted himself to provide food and clothing for his people and even attempted to start a lace-making center in his vicinity in order to provide them with employment. His attitude toward the medieval ideal is best summed up in his own statement that the Middle Ages still survive among us in their "instincts of honor and affection."[5] By the middle of the nineteenth century, when he made this statement, a great number of educated Englishmen would have agreed with him.

II

It is perhaps no accident that the alternate title to Hurrell Froude's "Farewell to Feudalism" is "Farewell to Toryism," for Toryism throughout the century clung, consciously or unconsciously, to its medieval roots. The "New Toryism" of the 1840s, like the contemporaneously developing, Oxford movement, was quite deliberately retrogressive, seeing in a return to ancient principles a bulwark against

[5] S. M. Paraclita Reilly, *Aubrey de Vere: Victorian Observer* (Lincoln: University of Nebraska Press, 1953), p. 154.

corrosive liberalism. Faced with increasing pressures for economic and political change, the New Tories "advocated a return to order, discipline, and obedience, the preservation of established institutions, and a deeper reverence for ancient ways."[6] Although they were influenced in these views by the whole stream of medievalism from Scott onward, the immediate impetus for their beliefs came from the Anglican and Catholic revivals.

The New Toryism, however, represented a split within the party. The Tories had been traditionally allied with Church and Crown, but they had begun to show certain divisive tendencies during and after the 1830s. Under the guidance of Sir Robert Peel a sizeable portion of the party had begun to see its future in a rapprochement with the new mercantile and industrial classes. Peel's "Tamworth Manifesto" specifically outlined his desire to appeal to the industrial classes, and his parliamentary policies, right down to the repeal of the Corn Laws, showed that he was moving the Tory party in a "liberal" direction. The opposing forces within the Tory party, led first by Young England and then, more effectively, by Disraeli, objected to Peel's divergence from their traditional party allegiances and posited instead a new political philosophy—one might well say, a new feudalism—that attempted to forge a bond between the landed aristocracy and the laboring masses. This tendency within the Tory party, though never wholly successful and perhaps not wholly sincere, continued right through the century, reappearing in the 1880s as Randolph Churchill's "Tory democracy"—"democratic because the welfare of the poeple is its supreme end; . . . Tory because the institutions of the country are the means by which the end is to be maintained."[7]

It is easy enough to give a textbook definition of Young England. Except for Disraeli, it was a party of well-born, predominantly noble, young men, who acted fairly concertedly in Parliament between 1842 and 1845. The core of the party consisted of Lord John Manners

[6] Joseph Ellis Baker, *The Novel and the Oxford Movement* (New York: Russell and Russell, 1965), p. 1.

[7] Quoted in Janet Henderson Robb, *The Primrose League, 1883–1906* (New York: Columbia University Press, 1942), p. 24.

(later duke of Rutland), George Smythe (later Lord Strangford), and Alexander Baillie-Cochrane (later Lord Lamington). Among its more outspoken associates in Parliament were Peter Borthwick and William Busfield Ferrand; outside of Parliament its aides included John Walters of the *Times* and Richard Monckton Milnes. The most brilliant figure associated with it was, of course, Disraeli. Young England's program included improving the condition of the poor, restoring the harmony of all classes, raising the prestige of the throne, and popularizing a respect for England's ancient institutions.

Any serious study of Young England, however, must take into account many historical and cultural influences, for the movement was symptomatic of its time. It was marked, for instance, by the lingering romanticism that persisted throughout the Victorian age. As Baillie-Cochrane recalled it a half-century later, Young England belonged to a period when "golden youth might be seen with their shirt-collars turned down living on biscuits and soda water à la Byron." [8] It was characterized, too, by a certain dandyism. The white-waistcoats of Lord John Manners and his friends were almost as much discussed in society as Disraeli's rings and ruffles.

But for all their frivolity, the Byronic pose and the dandyism were part of a deeply serious romanticism that attempted to add color and ceremony to life at a time when drabness and utility were threatening to dry up the sources of feeling. To quote Baillie-Cochrane's retrospections again, Young England's very extravagances

> quickened the susceptibilities and sympathies. Young politicians felt kindly toward the poor and suffering, and strove to improve their condition, not by giving them votes, but by ministering to their wants and enjoyments. What Ruskin calls the two essential instincts of humanity, "the love of order and the love of kindness" in their relations to the people, were the first principles of the Young England party.[9]

The development of Young England is most easily traced in the

[8] Alexander Baillie-Cochrane, "In the Days of the Dandies, III: The Young England Party," in *Blackwood's Edinburgh Magazine*, CXLVI (March, 1890), 314.

[9] *Ibid.*

career of Lord John Manners, the Don Quixote of the new chivalry. Born on the estate of Belvoir, which had been in possession of the Manners family since 1508 and in existence since Norman times, when Robert de Todeni build a castle on its hill and a priory for four Black Monks at its foot, he was perhaps predisposed by birth to a fondness for the Middle Ages and a belief in his own destiny. Even at Eton and Cambridge he was convinced of the importance of an aristocracy in assuring national well-being and hoped to sit in Parliament alongside his friend George Smythe. His attitudes found confirmation in his reading. He and his friends in the Young England party read almost the complete roster of English medievalists: Hurd, Scott, Burke, Hallam, Turner, Coleridge, Wordsworth, Southey, Cobbett, and Carlyle. More influential was their reading of Kenelm Digby's *The Broad Stone of Honour*, which has been called "the breviary of Young England."[10] The book helped develop their image of the Middle Ages and gave them a heroic ideal for which they could work as young aristocrats. On the threshold of what they hoped would be great careers, Manners and Smythe found Digby's views hopeful and also bracing; for if *The Broad Stone of Honour* gave them dreams, it also gave them responsibilities. "Princes and nobles," Digby wrote, "were elevated solely for the purpose of ministering to the wants of their inferiors."[11]

The Anglo-Catholic revival also attracted Young England's interest. Both Manners and Smythe were close friends of Frederick Faber and through Faber were made aware of Newman and other members of the Oxford movement. Unquestionably, Faber shared their ideals of chivalry and encouraged their belief in a reborn Church of England, free from its current lethargy and materialism. In August 1838 a fortnight after he first heard Faber, Manners recorded in his journal what may be the genesis of the Young England movement: that he and Smythe had "virtually pledged [themselves] to attempt to restore what? I hardly know—but still it is a glorious attempt . . . and all,

[10] Charles Whibley, *Lord John Manners and His Friends*, 2 vols. (London and Edinburgh: Blackwoods, 1925), I, 133.
[11] Digby, *Broad Stone of Honour*, I, 240.

or nearly all the enthusiasm of the young spirits of Britain is with us."[12]

Inspired by Digby and Faber and possibly by what he had heard or read of Coleridge, Lord John Manners adapted the religious ideals of the Roman and Anglican revivals to the political and social needs of the Hungry Forties. His poem *England's Trust* (1841) is best remembered for the tactless couplet,

> Let wealth and learning, laws and commerce die,
> But leave us still our old Nobility,[13]

that haunted him throughout his political career. But the poem's real significance lies in its blending, in serviceable though uninspired verse, of a High Church conviction of the value of religion, with the Tory-Radical, medievalist belief in the alliance between rich and poor.

"Is it not true," he asks in a note to the poem, "that many of the worst evils from which we are now suffering, have arisen from our ignorant contempt of the rules of the Church?" (43). But, unlike Faber, he does not mean rubrics or rituals here, but rather the over-all fabric of religion by which in medieval times "Mother Church" and "Sister State" were closely knit together. Then, under the moral guidance of the clergy, all classes were united:

> Each knew his place—king, peasant, peer, or priest—
> The greatest owned connexion with the least;
> From rank to rank the generous feeling ran,
> And linked society as man to man.
>
> (16)

Pilgrim and stranger, master and servant, he continues in the true medieval vein, all sat together then at a common board and worshipped together in the great churches and cathedrals, unmarred as yet by disfiguring pews and undivided by post-Reformation sectarianism. By keeping her doors open at all times to all men, the Church afforded everyday solace to even her meanest worshippers, while her feasts

[12] Whibley, *Lord John Manners*, I, 66.
[13] Lord John Manners, *England's Trust and Other Poems* (London, 1841), p. 24.

and festivals broke up the monotony of a life of labor with special days of rest and pleasure. Describing the charitable role of the medieval Church, he stresses her all-inclusiveness:

> The daily beadsman [waited] for his bread
> Where good and bad were all, unquestioned, fed.
> For then it was not to our rulers known
> That God was mindful of the first alone;
> The monks still practised their dear Lord's command
> And rained their charity throughout the land.
>
> (15)

In contrast to the lenity and harmony of the Middle Ages, Lord John claims that his own "liberal and enlightened times" are harsh and divisive. A "yawning gulf" now separates the "noble's castle from the village green," and class opposes class with a hatred he fears may turn into revolt.

> Gone are the days and gone the ties that then
> Bound peers and gentry to their fellow men
> Now in their place behold the modern slave,
> Doomed from the very cradle to the grave,
> To tread his lonely path of care and toil
> Bound, in sad truth, and bowed down to the soil;
> He dies, and leaves his sons their heritage—
> Work for their prime, the workhouse for their age.
>
> (16)

In *England's Trust* Lord John devotes little space to the means of reform. The revival of the church as a social force and the resumption of the ancient baronial relationship between master and man are all he has to suggest. His next work, however, *A Plea for National Holy-Days* (1842), explains somewhat more fully the ways in which the harmony of all classes can be restored and places his ideas in a broad social context. Like Cobbett, whose phraseology he occasionally borrows, Lord John is concerned with the physical decline of the English yeoman and with the loss of joy characteristic of Victorian England. Taking issue with those philanthropists who "imagine that a course of astronomy or a lecture in geology is all the recreation of mind or body that a man who works sixty hours a week requires," he demands a "revival of NATIONAL HOLY-DAYS and RECREATIONS."[14] It is not debating societies that will bring back the health, vigor, and loyalty of old England, when all classes played together on the village green and the apprentice could challenge the master's son at the broadjump, but the games and holidays of former times. For, with "scarce a May pole . . . left in England, or a holy day observed," these ancient ties have been split apart and "the banks of the mighty river of pent-up sin and misery are beginning to give way and men shrink from contemplating the impending deluge."[15]

Maypoles and village sports, of course, are fit subjects for humor. The Ullathorne games in *Barchester Towers*, to cite one example, seem a deliberate parody of his ideas, and even Lord John's friend Disraeli finds time in *Coningsby* to poke fun at his enthusiasms. But for all their surface foolishness, Lord John's recommendations had a deeper significance—just as his dandyism had—for he was placing the Romantic regret for the loss of joy in a social framework and reminding his audience, as Matthew Arnold was to do a quarter-century later in *Culture and Anarchy*, of the boring seriousness, the deadly Philistinism that was beginning to oppress Victorian England.

The completed medieval creed of Young England, however, rests on a broader base than that suggested by Lord John's works alone. Neither he nor his companions were so naïve as to believe that a purely rural program could relieve the distresses of a heavily industrialized nation. Or, if he and Smythe did think so as young men, they changed their minds after making a tour in 1841 of the manufacturing districts of Lancashire. Much of what Lord John describes in his letters and journal reads like the pages of *Past and Present*, *Hard Times*, or *North and South:* old women who sell their last blanket for fourpence to avoid starvation; cottages without food, fire, or furniture; Stockport deserted and dolorous with the tolling of its church bells. Like Carlyle, Dickens, and Mrs. Gaskell, he believed that the only hope for an

[14] Lord John Manners, *A Plea for National Holy-Days* (London, 1842), p. 1.
[15] *Ibid.*, p. 19.

alienated and impoverished proletariat lay in humanitarian masters.

During his visit to the Grant brothers, whom Dickens fictionalized as the kindly Cheerybles of *Nicholas Nickleby*, Lord John saw one example of what a good master-workman relationship might be and, as we might expect, interpreted his findings in a medieval light. He anticipates *Past and Present* in recognizing the similarity between the medieval baron and the modern millowner. He describes a certain Mr. Bashall as a "modern feudal lord," who uses his "absolute dominion over his men" to their mutual advantage. This enlightened manufacturer rents his workmen well-built, well-ventilated cottages for far less than they would otherwise have to pay; gives them twenty holidays in the year; and closes his spacious factory at night so that it can be properly aired.[16] Indeed, Lord John maintains, as long as proper legislative control can be maintained over such matters as unemployment, hours, and work conditions, "so complete a feudal system as that of the mills" is not a bad thing at all.[17]

Several of Lord John's letters after he entered Parliament in 1841 show how deeply these neofeudal ideas had penetrated his thinking and how seriously, like such predecessors as Scott and Southey, he feared revolt. Writing to Lord Lyttleton in 1842, he hopes that the current unrest will open "the eyes of our governors and rich people to the tremendous volcano on which they are dawdling; the mists are rapidly rolling away, and the alternative will soon present itself—a democracy or a feudalism"—democracy which he thinks is leveling, divisive, and anarchic, or feudalism which is based on the union of all classes under the guidance of the best.[18] As he writes in still another letter of that year:

> In a word let society take a more feudal appearance than it presents now, that's my vision; it may be a wrong one; but . . . I believe the Whig one of giving the people the political power and prating to them of the rights of man, the glories of science, and the merits of political economy is wrong.[19]

[16] Whibley, *Lord John Manners*, I, 100.
[17] *Ibid.*, p. 106.   [18] *Ibid.*, p. 137.   [19] *Ibid.*

As it appears in the pages of *Hansard*'s, much of Young England's parliamentary activity during the three years the party was in existence may be described as "applied medievalism." In religion there was much sympathy for the degraded condition of the Church of Rome and much hope for renewed activity by the Church of England, a political extension of the Oxford movement. Lord John, for instance, wished the Anglican clergy to maintain control over the education of the poor lest "all the feelings of home and family affection, upon which the well-being of the community mainly depended, be eradicated";[20] another member argued the comfort to the poor of keeping the churches and cathedrals open throughout the week; and even Disraeli advocated a return to the parochial distribution of alms.

The new Poor Law compelled their universal scorn. The workhouse test was cruel and oppressive. "It had the effect of weakening the feelings of responsibility on one hand, and of attachment and respect on the other."[21] Far inferior to the system that had prevailed before the Reformation, it was breeding a perilous disaffection and disloyalty among the once-loyal masses. The same humanitarian concern for the welfare of the lower orders also brought almost all of Young England, except George Smythe, into alliance with Lord Ashley in his attempt to limit to ten the working hours of women and youths in factories.[22]

[20] 76 *Hansard Parliamentary Debates* (3rd ser.) 769 (1844).

[21] 66 *ibid.* 1217 (1843).

[22] One of Lord John's speeches on the subject is worth quoting as an example of Cobbett's persistent influence in the field of social welfare, since Lord John's argument in 1844 is almost the same as Cobbett's in 1833.

Cobbett	Manners
We have this night discovered that the shipping, the land, and the Bank . . . are all worth nothing compared to the labour of three hundred thousand little girls in Lancashire . . . from whose labour if we only deduct two hours a day, away go . . . the resources, the power and the glory of England.	It was saying to this country—it was affirming in the face of all England—that the whole secret of our vast manufacturing lay in the one hour before sunrise, and in the one hour after sunset, which we snatched from the poor people of England.

An idea that the Young Englanders shared with Cobbett, though they might also have derived it from Southey, was a belief in the allotment system, or the granting of small plots of land to the laboring poor. According to its backers, the scheme had a twofold benefit: it would encourage the poor man's self-respect and loyalty and it would bring him back in some degree to the comfort he had formerly enjoyed in times when all men had rights of commonage, turfage, and goosage. Strenuously advocated by the impetuous William Busfield Ferrand, who had once startled the entire House by dramatically tearing to shreds a piece of cloth adulterated with "devil's dust," the allotment idea also attracted the attention of Lord John Manners and Disraeli.

Nor were the ideas of Lord John's *A Plea for National Holy-Days* forgotten in Parliament. Maypoles and village games could not be legislated, but other amusements could be guaranteed by law. Not only did the Young Englanders urge that museums and other places of wholesome entertainment be opened to the poor but that they be opened on *Sundays*—a deliberate defiance of the Sabbatarianism that had been overtaking England since the Reformation and a gesture toward reviving the Merry England of old. As always, when paternalism and *noblesse oblige* could give comfort to the poor and keep them peaceable at the same time, Young England was more than willing to act.

To conclude this brief Parliamentary history of Young England, it remains to be said that its members consistently upheld the rights of the queen, whom they saw as a symbol of unity for the entire nation, and that they finally split apart on the vexed question of the Corn Laws, Lord John standing by Disraeli in favor of them, Alexander Baillie-Cochrane and George Smythe defecting to Peel. The impact of

---

The ten-hour issue also caused Karl Marx to engage in some of his strongest statements in *Das Kapital*. Discussing the question of the ten-hour day, he writes: "But this dreadful 'last hour,' about which you have invented more than have the millenarians about the day of judgment, is 'all bosh.' If it goes it will cost neither you your profit, nor the boys and girls whom you employ their 'purity of mind.' Whenever *your* 'last hour' strikes in earnest, think on the Oxford Professor [Nassau Senior, opponent of shorter working hours]."

Young England, however, should not be measured by the brevity of its duration. As Robert Blake writes in his biography of Disraeli, the Young Englanders must "be regarded as symbols and examples that lend an imaginative glow to the dull course of party politics; showing that there are other ways to fame than conformism, diligence, and calculation; showing that a gesture, however absurd it may seem to contemporaries, may sometimes live longer than many Blue Books."[23]

III

Now, if we have any relics of the feudal system, I regret that not more of it remains. . . . Now, what is the fundamental principle of the feudal system, gentlemen? It is that the tenure of all property shall be the performance of its duties. Why, when the Conqueror carved out the parts of his land, and introduced the feudal system, he said to the recipient, "You shall have the judgment upon it, but you shall feed the poor; you shall endow the Church; you shall defend the land in the case of war, and you shall execute justice and maintain truth to the poor for nothing." . . . The principle of the feudal system . . . was the noblest principle, the grandest, the most magnificent that was ever conceived by sage or ever produced by patriot.[24]

The ideas in this passage belong generally to Young England. But only one member could have had the boldness to praise the Middle Ages so openly on the hustings to a predominantly middle-class audience which, in spite of fifty years of a medieval revival among the educated classes, probably still clung to old-fashioned notions of the Dark Ages of popery and superstition. That member was of course Disraeli, the "alien patriot," whose ties with the past, though not hereditary like Lord John's, were as consistently expressed and more closely reasoned.

[23] Robert Blake, *Disraeli* (New York: Doubleday, 1968), p. 162.

[24] Benjamin Disraeli, earl of Beaconsfield, *Selected Speeches of the Late Right Honourable, the Earl of Beaconsfield*, ed. T. E. Kebbel, 2 vols. (London, 1882), I, 50.

The speech, in fact, is as clear as it is bold. It is perhaps the best explanation to be found in any medievalist writing of the moral claims of the past on the present. Scott, Southey, Cobbett, and Carlyle, all knew that it was the property owner's duty to protect the poor, but they explained it as a form of semivoluntary *noblesse oblige*. It is Disraeli who explicitly states that the very possession of property automatically involves obligations to the poor—to those, that is, who contribute toward creating that wealth without themselves possessing it. In so doing, he gives a logical basis for applying the principles of feudalism, not simply to hereditary lords and landowners, but to any property owner, including finally the state itself.

The medievally derived concept that wealth entails duties is not a random idea in Disraeli. Some of its more striking expressions can be found as early as 1839, when he said that "great duties can alone confer great station,"[25] and as late as 1870, when he wrote that "the feudal system may have worn out, but its main principle, that the tenure of property should be the fulfillment of duty, is the essence of good government."[26] As always, Disraeli's degree of sincerity here is difficult to determine, but the idea that privilege entails duties does appear regularly in both his speeches and his novels.

Yet for all his intensity and consistency in uttering it, this idea of *quid pro quo* (duty in return for wealth) does not completely convey the quality of Disraeli's social philosophy or of the medievalism that pervaded it. Although he wished to place the relations of class to class on a logical or legal basis, he also realized that the nation was formed by emotional ties as well and that the state was an entirely new entity, different from the mere aggregate of persons that composed it. Viewing all purely utilitarian schemes of government with the same disfavor that Burke felt for the *philosophes*, he believed that the most important qualities of the state were imagination, tradition, loyalty, and individual

[25] William Flavelle Monypenny and George Earl Buckle, *The Life of Benjamin Disraeli, Earl of Beaconsfield*, 6 vols. (London and New York: Macmillan, 1911–1920), II, 82.
[26] Benjamin Disraeli, *The Works of Benjamin Disraeli, Earl of Beaconsfield*, Empire edition, 20 vols. (London and New York: M. Walter Dunne, 1904), XVII, xix.

heroism. These ideas appear as early as 1834 in a dreadful poem called *The Revolutionary Epick*, in which Magros, the spirit of feudalism, debates with Lyridon, the spirit of federalism; and they are more explicitly stated in both *The Vindication of the English Constitution* (1835) and *The Spirit of Whiggism* (1836). Their most dramatic and interesting presentation occurs in two novels of the next decade: *Coningsby* (1844) and *Sybil* (1845). Part of what is sometimes called the Young England trilogy, these books are the stories of young men coming to know and then seeking to reform nineteenth-century English society.

Of these novels, *Coningsby, or the New Generation,* is the most closely related to the Young England movement. Its chief character, Harry Coningsby, is said to be George Smythe; Lord Henry Sydney is Sir John Manners; Lord Buckhurst is Alexander Baillie-Cochrane; Eustace Lyle is Ambrose De Lisle; and Oswald Millbank is perhaps John Walters of the *Times*. It is not, however, as a *roman à clef* that the novel has any modern significance. What is important is the novel's concern with the class structure of Victorian England and the way in which the wealthier classes do or do not fulfill their obligations. As the story of Coningsby's initiation into life, the book offers a brilliantly defined portrait of English upper-class society in the 1830s and 1840s. Beginning with a nostalgic portrait of Eton school days, by a man who never went to a public school, the novel carries its hero into the worlds of fashion, chivalry, and manufacture. The contrasts that Coningsby sees between the useful and the useless aristocrats and the worthy and unworthy manufacturers serve the same purpose as the contrasts between medieval and modern times in *Past and Present* since they illustrate the same differences between a benevolently cohesive and heartlessly atomistic society.

Vanity Fair, or the great world of fashion and politics, is appropriately presided over by Coningsby's grandfather, Lord Monmouth, who, like Thackeray's Lord Steyne, is modeled on the famous voluptuary, the third marquis of Hertford. Surrounded always by a glittering society, whose manners, though not its morals, are splendid, the marquis lives among flatterers and dies among courtesans. He represents in almost every respect the most serious faults of the English aristocracy: its frivolity, its wastefulness, its mendacity, and worst of all its absenteeism. Especially after the Reform Bill deprives him of *twelve* seats in the Commons, Lord Monmouth is determined to live as little as possible in England and returns to his native land only when his vote is urgently needed by his party. He has no interest in his tenants; does not "trouble himself at all" about the new Poor Law; and thinks the Reform Bill is the result not of deep-rooted dissatisfaction with English society but of a personal quarrel between Wellington and Lord Grey. His sole interest in politics is to turn his coronet into a ducal one.

To manage his affairs for him in his absence, Monmouth makes use of some of the worst elements in English political life. His agent, Nicholas Rigby, said to be a caricature of John Wilson Croker, is just the man to write a "slashing article" or manipulate an election. A creature of party rather than principle, Rigby usually appears on the scene accompanied by his political Rosencrantz and Guildenstern, Tadpole and Taper—bureaucrats without bureaus, £1,200 a year men in search of a job. The four of them—Monmouth, Rigby, Tadpole, and Taper—represent the moribund Toryism of which Disraeli thought Peel to be the head and which he described as a party that "discards prescription, shrinks from principle, disavows progress; [and] having rejected all respect for antiquity ... offers no redress for the present, and makes no preparation for the future" (XII, 133).

If in the Vanity Fair of his uncle's castle, Coningsby meets only those who deny the feudal principle of responsible wealth and think they can have their pleasure for nothing, he meets far different ideas at Beaumanoir, the hereditary estate of his friend Lord Henry Sydney. Here, in a setting calculated to suggest John Manners's Belvoir, which Disraeli was proud to have visited, characters are enshrined who represent Disraeli's views of the best possible English aristocracy. The duke himself, Lord Henry's father, is an almost perfect landlord, prompted to his excellence perhaps "by the ancient blood in his veins." Disraeli describes him as public-spirited, "munificent, tender, and bounteous to the poor," and lavishly hospitable to all (XII, 111).

Though firm in supporting the Corn Laws, he never refuses a lease. Only in backing the new Poor Law, with its heartless substitution of a central board of guardians for traditional parish administration, does the duke mar the perfection of his record in maintaining the unity of the classes.

Other members of the duke's family also show Coningsby the importance of a resident aristocracy to what Disraeli calls the "parochial constitution" of the country—a constitution which he claims is more important, more ancient, and more universal than the political one. The duchess and her daughters work practically toward achieving a superior peasantry by their frequent visits to the surrounding neighborhood and show, in so doing, that the "ancient feudal feeling that lingers in these sequestered haunts is an instrument, which, when skillfully wielded, may be productive of vast social benefit" (XII, 198). Lord Henry's assistance to the peasantry is more philosophical and consists in defending their rights on every possible occasion. His views are remarkably similar to those of Lord John Manners:

> He [Lord Henry] assured his father that it would never be well for England until . . . the peasantry was restored to its pristine condition; not merely in physical comfort, for that must vary according to the economical circumstances of the time, like that of every class; but to its condition in all those moral attributes which make a recognized rank in a nation; and which, in a great degree, are independent of economics, manners, customs, ceremonies, rights, and privileges.
>
> "Henry thinks," said Lord Everingham, "that the people are to be fed by dancing round a May-pole."
>
> "But will the people be more fed because they do not dance round a May-pole?" urged Lord Henry. (XII, 179)

All that is good at Beaumanoir, then, is associated with England's past, with the feudal and parochial society of the Middle Ages. On the neighboring estate of St. Geneviève, Coningsby encounters an even more determined effort to bring back the medieval—or rather the Roman Catholic—past. Eustace Lyle, who figures in all keys to *Coningsby* as Ambrose Phillipps De Lisle, though he might just as easily be Lord Shrewsbury, is a Catholic noble of ancient family. His aim is to bring back, if he can, as many of the old English customs as will enable the lower classes to realize that "property is their protector and their friend" (XII, 193). Thus, not only is out-of-door relief still given at St. Geneviève even after the passage of the new Poor Law, but it is accompanied by a ringing of church bells and a ceremonious procession of villagers, bearing certificates from their rectors and Mr. Lyle's almoner, to the postern gate of his Gothic-revival castle.

The Christmas festivities at St. Geneviève's rival those at Chainmail Hall. A Yule log blazes in the wide hearth of the castle and in every hearth in Mr. Lyle's domain. The buttery hatch is open all week from noon to eve, offering supplies of beef, ale, and white bread to every comer, and there are additional gifts of a red cloak for every woman and a warm coat for every man. Commenting on the scene he has created, Disraeli states that all this medievalism in action

> was a fresh argument in favour of Lord Henry's principle, that a mere mechanical mitigation of the material necessities of the humbler classes, a mitigation which must inevitably be limited, can never alone avail sufficiently to ameliorate their condition; that their condition is not merely a "knife and fork question," to use the coarse and shallow phrase of the utilitarian school ... that you must cultivate the heart as well as seek to content the belly; and that the surest means to elevate the character of the people is to appeal to their affections. (XIII, 176)

Nevertheless, Disraeli does not think that the revival of ancient customs is the complete answer to the condition of England question. England has progressed too far on the road to industrialization to make it possible or desirable to return to the agrarian past. As Sidonia tells Coningsby, "the Age of Ruins is past" and a good portion of the future belongs to manufactures and manufacturers (XII, 154). Inspired perhaps by Manners's and Smythe's tour of Lancashire in 1841, Disraeli sends Coningsby off to the industrial North to complete his acquaintance with English society.

Disraeli's portrait of factory life is surprisingly naïve, or perhaps simply one-sided. The factories Coningsby sees, in defiance of all that blue books and experience might have taught his author, have more windows than "Italian palaces" and chambers vaster than those in "Arabian fables." Disraeli expresses fear in *Coningsby* that this manufacturing wealth "was rapidly developing classes whose power was imperfectly recognised in the constitutional scheme, and whose duties in the social system seem altogether omitted" (XII, 207). To show what these duties might be he presents a manufacturer who is as worthy an examplar of the new feudalism as Lord John's Mr. Bashall. Indeed, Oswald Millbank, bears a striking resemblance to Bashall in his building of cottages, attention to ventilation, and general care for "the moral and physical well-being of his people" (XII, 216). It is from Millbank that Coningsby first hears the Carlylean idea, which Disraeli seems to adopt, of the importance of an aristocracy of talent, as well as one of birth.

Although not a very carefully drawn character, Millbank is important to the denouement of the novel. Coningsby's marriage to his daughter Edith seems a symbolic wedding of "Norman manners" and "Saxon industry," and Millbank himself acts as a *deus ex machina* to allow Coningsby to take his seat in Parliament after his grandfather disinherits him. The novel concludes with the fulfillment of all wishes: Coningsby married, and with his Eton friends, Sydney and Buckhurst, on the threshold of a parliamentary career in which he hopes to achieve the aims of Young England. He hopes "to establish great principles which may maintain the realm and secure the happiness of the people ... [to] see authority once more honoured; a solemn reverence again the habit of our lives; ... [and] property acknowledging, as in the old days of faith, that labour is his twin brother, and that the essence of all tenure is the performance of duty" (XIII, 139).

In *Sybil, or the Two Nations*, Disraeli's next novel, the social portraiture is far more inclusive, and the structure is dramatic rather than discursive. Time ceases to be, as in *Coningsby*, a mere continuum in which action occurs and becomes an urgent force. The darkening shadows of a swiftly changing England hang over the individual fortunes of characters who are in themselves symbols of the changing

173

nation. Beginning in 1837, when the coronation of the young queen seemed to inaugurate bright hopes for the future, the novel moves on to the growing hard times of the late thirties and early forties. Historic events serve to develop the plot. The characters are involved first in the peaceful beginnings of the Chartist movement, then in the rejection of the Charter, and finally in the outbreaks of violence at Birmingham and in the agricultural districts that marked the opening of the Hungry Forties. Quite as much as Carlyle does in *Chartism* or the opening chapters of *Past and Present*, Disraeli conveys a sense of increasing suffering and impending revolt. The tacked-on happy ending, which Disraeli found necessary for all his novels, must have scarcely comforted an audience increasingly worried by the famines and unrest of 1845.

Disraeli's picture in *Sybil* of the aristocracy's role in these events is less optimistic than that in *Coningsby*. Apart from Sir Vavasour Firebrace, a ridiculous baronet of ancient lineage, all the families Disraeli describes are of recent creation. The Egremonts, currently headed by the earl of Marney, owe their ennoblement to the zeal of an ancestor, in presenting Henry VIII with tasteful plunder from the great religious houses; the Mowbrays owe theirs to John Warren, a London waiter, who somehow turned a fortune in India. Perhaps because they lack a sense of tradition, these modern-day nobles also lack a sense of responsibility. The Mowbrays are only indolent, usually unconcerned about the workers in Mowbray Town, but occasionally brought to acknowledge their duties by their High Church vicar, who represents the possibilities of a revived Church of England. Lord Marney, on the other hand, is downright villainous. Stripped of his title, he would make an excellent superintendent in a Dickens workhouse, for his personal harshness and coldness predispose him to the most literal applications of political economy:

> I wish the people were as well off in every part of the country as they are on my estate. They get here their eight shillings a week, always at least seven, and every hand is at this moment in employ, except a parcel of scoundrels, . . . who would prefer wood-stealing and poaching

if you gave them double the wages. The rate of wages is nothing: certainty is the thing; and every man at Marney may be sure of his seven shillings a week for at least nine months in the year; and for the other three, they can go to the House ... it is heated with hot air, and has every comfort. .... The poor are well off ... they have no cares, no anxieties; they have always a resource, they have always the House. People without cares do not require so much food as those whose life entails anxieties. (XIV, 214–16)

Among the aristocrats, only Charles Egremont, Lord Marney's brother and the hero of the novel, has any real understanding of the condition of England or the part the nobility should take in its improvement. It is mainly through his eyes that we see the difference between the lives of the "two nations ... The Rich and the Poor" and through his political program, similar to that of Young England, that we gain some hope for the future.

Disraeli's portrayals of the lives of the rich and the lives of the poor are starkly contrasted. Scenes of splendor in Lord Marney's mansion are followed by a description of Marney Town itself: narrow, crowded, its badly built cottages drafty and wet, its ditches full of the sewage and filth that make death and disease the common companions of its wretched inhabitants. As part of his attempt to depict England's forgotten nation of the poor, Disraeli introduces a series of minor characters from industries typical of England about 1840. A poverty-stricken hand-loom worker symbolizes in his misery the fate of traditional artisans in a machine age, while a group of spinners in their prosperity and succeeding destitution represent the possibilities and pitfalls of an industrial society. Seen at work and at leisure, in tommy shops and trade-union meetings, are miners and locksmiths, shopkeepers and barkeepers, factory foremen and farm tenants—all struggling somehow to comprehend and gain their rights in a struggle that grows more desperate as time goes on.

Disraeli's conclusions about the relationship between master and man are for the most part quite dismal. In the mines or in the caricatured factory of Shuffle and Screw, it seems a hideous compound of cruelty and avarice. Fines are imposed for trivial offenses, wages are paid in useless tommy, women are harnessed like horses, and children are confined in solitary darkness. "Atween the poor man and the gentleman there never was no connection," says one of the miners, "and that's the wital mischief of this country" (XIV, 206)—a judgment that seems only too charitable in the light of the horrors Disraeli describes. Only at Trafford's mill, as at Millbank's in *Coningsby*, are master and man bound by ties other than the cash nexus and the owner aware of the "baronial principle" of paternalistic rule.

Even though most of the masters he presents are bad ones, Disraeli still finds hope in a society where "mastership" is acknowledged. He rejects as meaningless theory the egalitarian and socialistic principles put forth in *Sybil* by the writer Stephen Morley, which ignore man's need for warmth and leadership. Even more horrible to him is the situation of the workers of Wodgate, a town of almost surrealistic hideousness, which he describes as having sprung up as a result of the Industrial Revolution, with neither parochial nor manorial ties, nor indeed any form of law at all except a primitive master-apprentice relationship. Here physical violence rules: the master workmen batter the heads and pull the ears of their apprentices, and the apprentices endure their tortures stoically in the knowledge that they, too, will one day be masters. The town is utterly godless. Even the professed Christians among them are so debased that they believe in "our Lord and Saviour Pontius Pilate . . . and in Moses, Goliath, and the rest of the Apostles" (XIV, 238).

Lacking the guidance of either state or church, Wodgate remains autonomous—a parody, Disraeli may wish us to believe, of democracy. He has, at any rate, no pity for the Wodgate poor. When the agricultural insurrection breaks out at the end of the novel, they are the purely destructive force, and they alone perish, destroyed by their savage stupidity, in the flaming wine cellars of Mowbray Castle—a melodramatic symbol of the fate of those who would undermine or bypass the hierarchic structure of society.

At the other end of the moral scale from the bestial inhabitants of Wodgate as representatives of the people are the almost angelic Sybil

Gerard and her father, Walter. Whereas all the other characters in the novel are recognizable social types, Sybil symbolizes an idea. As Monypenny puts it, "she stands for the people, for the nation of the poor for pity of their suffering, for their hopes of redemption."[27] She is also sibyllic—a prophetess of the future. Although the final recognition of her legal right to be countess of Mowbray may have some symbolic meaning, this conclusion is probably a mere plot device. Her real inheritance is to the estate of the poor as it existed in the Middle Ages when both the Nobility and the Church were devoted to securing man's needs in a far more personal and meaningful way than that achieved by any modern device of parliamentary representation. Sybil, who is a Roman Catholic and convent bred, feels deeply the decay of the English people between the Catholic Middle Ages and the well-nigh atheistical present:

> When I remember what the English people once was; the truest, the freest, and the bravest, the best-natured and the best-looking, the happiest and most religious race upon the surface of this globe; and think of them now, with all their crimes and all their slavish sufferings, their soured spirits and their stunted forms; their lives without enjoyment, and their deaths without hope, I may well feel for them, even if I were not the daughter of their blood. (XIV, 177)

For all her importance as the symbolic focus of the novel, Sybil has few speeches, a rather fortunate silence since her diction belongs to the unhand-me-unmannerly-churl school of rhetoric. The task of expounding a political philosophy, therefore, falls to her father, the Chartist leader, Walter Gerard. For his character Disraeli claimed to have studied the writings of Feargus O'Connor, but his social philosophy sounds far more like that of William Cobbett.

Like Cobbett, Gerard is convinced that pre-Reformation Englishmen were far more prosperous than their nineteenth-century counterparts. They were better fed, better clothed, and better lodged. Like Cobbett, too, who believed that the medieval laborer drank water only for penance and could "earn the price of a fat goose and a half for a

---

[27] Monypenny, *Life of Disraeli*, II, 256.

day's work," [28] Disraeli's Gerard found proof in the acts of Parliament regulating prices and wages from the Plantagenets to the Tudors "that the wages of those days brought as much sustenance and comfort as a reasonable man could desire" (XIV, 246). Although he is not as picturesque as Cobbett in describing the material superiority of the medieval man, he is more violent in asserting his superior freedom and morality. Gerard insists that

> There is more serfdom in England now than at any time since the Conquest. I speak of what passes under my eyes daily when I say that those who labour can as little choose or change their masters now as when they were born thralls. There are great bodies of the working classes of this country nearer the condition of brutes than they have been at any time since the Conquest. Indeed I see nothing to distinguish them from brutes except that their morals are inferior. Incest and infanticide are as common among them as among the lower animals. (XIV, 245)

Gerard sees the degradation of the poor as particularly tragic. He shares with Cobbett a pre-Marxist conviction that the impoverishment of the many has been accompanied by the increasing wealth of the few. The origin of Disraeli's phrase the "two nations" has been variously ascribed to Rousseau and Carlyle. But the idea may well have come from Cobbett, whose assertion that there are now "but two classes of people in a community, masters and slaves, a very few enjoying the extreme of luxury and millions doomed to the extreme of misery," [29] is strikingly similar to Disraeli's contention that the country is divided into "two classes, masters and slaves," with no "resting-place between luxury and misery" (XIV, 87).

Gerard also seems indebted to Cobbett for seeing the origin of this schism in the destruction of the Roman Catholic church during the Reformation. Speaking through Gerard, Disraeli describes the monasteries in Cobbett's phrase as "deathless landlords," who having

[28] William Cobbett, *History of the Protestant Reformation in England and Ireland* (London, 1829), I, letter xiv, para. 260.
[29] *Ibid.*, I, v, 149.

no personal greed to satisfy could afford to grant the long leases at low rentals that made the yeoman class the backbone of English society. Disraeli's wording here in describing the monks is so similar to Cobbett's that it seems as if he wrote part of *Sybil* with *A History of the Protestant Reformation* open in front of him:

Cobbett	Disraeli
a body of men . . . having wisdom to guide the inexperienced, and wealth to relieve their distress.	a body of individuals . . . with wisdom to guide the inexperienced, with wealth to relieve the suffering, and often with power to protect the oppressed.[30]

Both men also agree that the monastics' generosity created not only a class but a culture, since the monks cared not only for their present tenants but for posterity as well. They created the best part of English civilization with their cathedrals and colleges—buildings for which Disraeli, like Cobbett, does not think treadmills and workhouses a proper substitute.

Even in trivial points—such as the value of monasteries in absorbing the younger sons of great families or the greater population of parts of England in the Middle Ages—Disraeli seems to borrow from *A History of the Protestant Reformation*. But it is not simply through Gerard, whose sayings might partly be discounted as mere dramatic propriety, that Disraeli shows his debt to Cobbett. Not Gerard but Disraeli himself describes Marney Abbey, with cattle browsing among its ruins, in a passage whose ideas and images might find parallels in several parts of Cobbett's history:

> Over a space of not less than ten acres might still be observed the fragments of the great Abbey . . . moss-grown and mouldering memorials that told where once rose the offices, and spread the terraced gardens, of the old proprietors; here might still be traced the dwelling of the lord abbot; and there, still more distinctly, because built on a greater

[30] Disraeli, *Works*, XIV, 88. Cobbett, *Protestant Reformation*, I, v, 152.

scale and of materials still more intended for perpetuity, the capacious hospital, a name that did not then denote the dwelling of disease, but a place where all the rights of hospitality were practised; where the traveller, from the proud baron to the lonely pilgrim, asked the shelter and the succour that never were denied, and at whose gate, called the Portal of the Poor, the peasants on the Abbey lands, if in want, might appeal each morn and night for raiment and for food. (XIV, 80–81)

That Disraeli borrowed from Cobbett without acknowledgment (although he does compare him at one point in the novel with Shakespeare) does not undermine the value of his medievalism. It simply points out the affinities of Disraeli's aristocratic Tory-Radicalism with the democratic Tory-Radicalism of Cobbett, Michael Sadler, and Richard Oastler. Like *Coningsby*, the novel ends on a hope of social betterment with which any nineteenth-century humanitarian would have found it impossible to argue. Egremont, the voice of Young England, declares that in the future, as in the past, the rights of labor will be sacred and the purpose of government will be to assure the "greater social felicity of the millions." This will not, however, be achieved by a "levelling principle." Rather, as Egremont says, "it will seek to ensure equality, not by levelling the few, but by elevating the many" (XV, 5).

IV

How far, one asks, did Disraeli's own social program carry out the ideals enunciated in *Coningsby* and *Sybil?* The answer for the period when he was allied with Young England in Parliament is somewhat ambiguous, since he took little part in advocating the Ten Hours Bill, surely a crucial test of social attitude, and was occasionally too involved in minor issues of foreign policy and finance to engage in all of Young England's skirmishes. Most of Disraeli's political acts until the late 1840s are explicable as part of his long and bitter struggle to gain control of his party, just as the succeeding quarter-century is marked by his efforts to maneuver that party into real control of Parliament.

A series of acts beginning in 1874, the first year of his long prime ministership, show, however, that once Disraeli gained effective power, he did turn his party toward social reform. But the existence of the reforms is probably more owing to circumstances and necessity than to any long-held Tory-Radical philosophy. Robert Blake, Disraeli's recent biographer, acknowledges that the legislation passed by Disraeli's government during the 1870s constitutes "the biggest installment of social reform passed by any one government in the nineteenth century." But he quite wisely claims that "it is an exaggeration to regard them as the product of a fundamentally different political philosophy from that of the Liberals, or to see in them the fulfillment of some concept of paternalistic Tory democracy which had been adumbrated by Disraeli in opposition to Peel during the 1840s and now had reached fruition."[31] Certainly, there is little evidence that Disraeli in the intervening decades had been actively working to promote the ideals of Young England. And yet, whatever the causes, much of the legislation passed during his prime ministership seems specifically designed to remedy evils described thirty years earlier in *Sybil*. An Artisans' Dwelling Bill, one of the first items in Disraeli's program, sought to make impossible such housing conditions as he had pictured in his description of Marney Town by providing local authorities with the power to replace unsanitary buildings with new public housing for the poor. The Employee and Workmen Bill remedied some of the injustices in labor-management relations by making breach of contract by the workers a civil offense, as it was for the employer, instead of a criminal one, as it had formerly been. Together with another law which changed the old regulations of "conspiracy" in regard to labor disputes, the act made possible a whole new range of trade-union activities.

Sanitas sanitatum, omnia sanitas—still other enactments bore out Disraeli's slogan. The Public Health Act of 1875, for example, reorganized the whole sanitary code. The Sale of Food and Drugs Act of 1875 and the Rivers Pollution Act of 1876 protected the public against contamination and filth. The Consolidations Act of 1878,

[31] Blake, *Disraeli*, p. 531.

though not specifically concerned with sanitation, improved the health of industrial workmen by a review and codification of all previous factory legislation.

Not only the medievalism of Young England but that of Southey and Cobbett can be seen in the series of laws Disraeli proposed concerning agriculture and landholding. By one such act agricultural tenants were compensated for improvements they had made which were not exhausted by the end of their leases—a bit of justice Cobbett would have heartily applauded. And, more revolutionary, by another act the centuries-old tendency toward enclosure was finally ended by a law forbidding any further encroachment on the public domain unless it was of general benefit. The use of the commons as public playgrounds was also encouraged, though not perhaps for the sort of games Lord John Manners would have suggested. A complementary piece of legislation secured the Epping Forest area near London to the public forever as a small relic of England's departed woodlands.

In many ways Disraeli's legislative program of the seventies expresses in practical political terms what the medievalists of the preceding three-quarters of a century had been asking for. It is paternalistic, concerned with the welfare of the poor and dedicated to the preservation of at least some relics of England's preindustrial past. In contrast to the "liberal" (in the nineteenth-century sense of the word) assumption of the economic man, functioning best without interference, it presupposes a less responsible creature who must be nurtured in the kindly matrix of state and church.

The realization of these medievalist goals, however, came from an unexpected agency. With the exception of Carlyle, Disraeli, and Manners, who managed to include the new managerial class in their scheme, all the other new feudalists had seen the paternalistic care of the masses emanating from the landed gentry. But Disraeli's program showed that while paternalism was necessary, its source was not the landowner, nor even the manufacturer, but the state. It was the state that built houses; the state that regulated factories; the state that supervised commerce, enforced sanitation, protected the woodlands and waterways; the state, even, that regulated the workings of the Church.

In one sense, then, the function of medievalism was finished by the 1870s. It had been a transitional philosophy, clothing in imaginative and emotionally appealing language a necessary new concept of the functions of government. It had shown clearly the power of literature and scholarship to shape history. Paradoxically, though it always opposed the spread of republicanism, it was perhaps more responsible than has been realized for the attitudes that have led to the paternalistic form of government that characterizes most modern democracies.

This is not to say that the political and economic role of the medieval ideal abruptly ceased. Ruskin and Morris—both of whom despised Disraeli—continued to augment and expand the ideas of the earlier medievalists, and finally, at least in Morris's case, to relate them to revolutionary socialism. Even in the twentieth century, in fact, the medieval ideal continued to shape some views of society. Guild socialism, various forms of agrarianism, and some Catholic worker movements are among its most notable manifestations. But the real importance of medievalism in the late nineteenth century lies in its return to elements deeper than the political. There is an upsurge in medievalist writings of elements that are best called Romantic—elements, that is, which idealize the natural and the beautiful, the spontaneous and the joyous, the harmonious and the permanent. Ruskin and Morris both use their visions of the Middle Ages to oppose the increasing materialism and alienation of modern life; Henry Adams in *Mont-Saint-Michel and Chartres* shows the hopelessness of their attempt.

6

Art and Society: Ruskin and Morris

No ASPECT of medievalism is more complex or pervasive than the Gothic Revival in architecture and in art. It started early and ended late, and, while frequently absurd, often showed both seriousness and beauty. Like the other manifestations of medievalism, it began as a quest for feeling and concluded as a search for meaning. But unlike the medievalism expressed in literature, architectural medievalism never really questioned the organization of society. Even as the theorists of the Gothic Revival increasingly argued that the decay of art and architecture since the Middle Ages was a sign of social deterioration, the practitioners of the art went right on using fashionably medieval ornament on churches, banks, and railway stations, without ever questioning its integrity. The success of these practitioners was overwhelming. As Sir Kenneth Clark writes in his admirable study, *The Gothic Revival*, the renewed taste for the medieval "changed the face of England, building and restoring churches all over the country-side, and filling our towns with Gothic banks and groceries, Gothic lodging-houses and insurance companies, Gothic everything from a town-hall down to a slum public house. . . . There cannot be a main street in England quite untouched by the Revival." [1]

Because the actual creation of such architecture was usually, though not universally, divorced from the theoretical medievalism, the Gothic Revival need not be studied here in detail. Its origins were, as might be expected, in the picturesque, in the eighteenth-century desire for emotion and terror that produced the Graveyard school. The nostalgic

[1] Sir Kenneth Clark, *The Gothic Revival*, rev. and enlarged ed. (New York: Scribner's, 1950), p. 294.

184

melancholy that caused Thomas Gent to regret the "awful Ruins" of Kirkstall Abbey had led, even as early as the seventeenth century, to a cherishing of medieval buildings. Ned Ward, author of the *London Spy*, admired Henry VII's gothically ornamented chapel as a work "so far exceeding human excellence that a man would think it was knit together by the fingers of angels, pursuant to the directions of the Omnipotence"; and even the sober Defoe praised the spires of Lichfield Cathedral as "so beautiful no pen can describe them."[2]

Although a minor but uninterrupted tradition of medieval craftsmanship continued in isolated villages and townships almost down into modern times, the first consciously medieval creations were the Gothic "ruins" that began ornamenting rich men's gardens at the beginning of the eighteenth century. The ruins were meant to give a park or garden a pleasurably romantic gloom. They show in their landscape setting the same attempt to couple nature and the past that was characterizing the poetry of the time and the same attempt to use the faraway in time and place as a stimulus to emotion. It may seem foolish to take a sham ruin made of plaster or canvas very seriously. But the gentlemen and ladies who retired to such structures were presumably helped by them to meditate more sensitively on change, morality, and time. The false past, almost as well as the true past, could teach a sense of the sublime.

Just as the purely emotional aspects of the medieval revival in poetry were, almost from the start, accompanied by a scholarly interest in historical detail, so architecture, too, valued accuracy. Gentlemen antiquaries traveled all over England, furiously studying, measuring, and debating the nation's ancient buildings. Journals for the period are filled with acrimonious debates over the origins of the Gothic arch, and quarrels over nomenclature became almost venomous. The architect Batty Langley's Gothic summerhouses, designed during the 1740s, seemed ridiculous even to some of his contemporaries. But they were based, according to Langley, upon a twenty-year study of the

[2] B. Sprague Allen, *Tides in English Taste (1619–1800)*, 2 vols. (Cambridge: Harvard University Press, 1937), II, 52, 62.

"lost orders" of Saxon architecture. Horace Walpole's famed Strawberry Hill, which began to be gothicized in 1750, also exhibits this paradoxical craving for the imaginative and the scholarly. The chimney in the "Holbein Chamber" was supposedly copied from the altarpiece of Rouen Cathedral (though Walpole himself claimed it came from a tomb at Canterbury), and almost all his other designs had similar claims on authenticity. Still, the effect of the house, much of it executed in plaster, papier-mâché, and lithodipra, was more romantic than pedantic, consistent with the spirit that had led Walpole to write *The Castle of Otranto*. Interestingly enough, at least one modern critic sees in Strawberry Hill a foreshadowing of the emphasis on old English hospitality that is a continuing theme in nineteenth-century medievalism:

> The type of architecture which Strawberry Hill was supposed to represent did appeal to the English for reasons—we can call them sentimental if we wish—that were rooted in a respect for the traditions and customs associated with the hospitable old mansions of their forefathers. They felt that the formal splendor of the house of Renaissance design was not a native growth but characteristic of a style that had been imported without regard to its adaptation to English conditions. The older Gothic architecture, on the other hand, belonged to England and was a symbol of her past.[3]

In this connection it is perhaps significant that Henry Beckford's pseudo-Gothic Fonthill, which, with its eight miles of walls and 226-foot tower was the grandest of all eighteenth-century imitations, served partly to give five hundred workmen poor relief.

Another aspect of the Gothic Revival was the dynastic element. The great Gothic house of Abbotsford was Scott's claim to stability, a kind of spurious antiquity to bestow upon his descendants, and Abbotsford is merely a dramatic example of the widespread use of Gothic for everything from cottages to castles. When the authentically ancient peers of Arundel, Wilton, and Knowsley consented to live in homes built or rebuilt in Gothic manner, it is no wonder that the

---

[3] *Ibid.*, II, 81.

parvenus sought to do likewise. The home of Tennyson's uncle, Charles Tennyson-D'Eyncourt, provides a wonderful example of the self-made ancestral mansion. No sooner had his claim to the D'Eyncourt name been validated, than he set about building a vast, baronial edifice, into whose designs were worked the escutcheons of the D'Eyncourts, Lovels, Beaumonts, Marmions, Grays, Plantagenets, Lancasters, and Bardolphs—to all of whom he claimed relationship.[4]

However, in spite of sentimentality, pedantry, and snobbishness, Gothic architecture continued to develop. More than three-quarters of the churches erected under the Church Building Act of 1818 were Gothic in design, even though their builders carefully avoided any architectural features, such as altars or transepts, that might smack of Catholicism. Probably the main reason that Gothic was chosen for these structures was that it could be built relatively cheaply. But the 1818 act had primarily been passed to combat the rising infidelity and Jacobinism of the cities with a sufficiency of places to worship; and "Gothic" must have suggested to its backers the same sense of security and stability that "feudal" was currently conveying to Wordsworth and Southey.

And yet, even as these eminently Protestant and conservative churches continued to be built, a major figure, Augustus Welby Pugin, was attempting to use Gothic architecture as an argument for returning England to the Catholic fold and for questioning the whole structure of English society. Pugin is chiefly famous today as the real architect of the Houses of Parliament, an achievement for which he received practically no credit during his lifetime, when he was usually recalled as the author of *Contrasts; or a Parallel between the Noble Edifices of the Middle Ages and the corresponding buildings of the Present Day, showing the Present Decay of Taste* (1836). The book is one of the clearest statements ever made of the medieval ideal. Reminiscent of Cobbett and Southey, it anticipates the ideas and methods of Carlyle's *Past and Present*, with its juxtaposed portraits of medieval and modern life, except that the portraits are visual rather than verbal. The book

[4] For a detailed description of the D'Eyncourt mansion, see *Gentleman's Magazine* (Sept., 1861), 328–330.

is composed entirely of a series of facing plates, showing the same scenes of buildings in the fifteenth century and in the nineteenth. The pictures are intended to demonstrate the superiority of medieval life and art. They might, indeed, serve to illustrate almost any of the new-feudalist texts.

One of Pugin's most effective pairs of plates is his "Contrasted Conduits." In the medieval picture he shows a well-dressed, graceful youth, drinking from a Gothic fountain, richly ornamented with heraldic and religious devices. In the nineteenth-century picture he shows a Dickensian scene of an official brandishing a cat-o'-nine-tails to keep a shabby urchin away from an ugly padlocked pump. Another plate, entitled "Contrasted Residences of the Poor," must have been especially topical since *Contrasts* was published only two years after the passage of the new Poor Law of 1834. In the medieval picture a magnificent Gothic abbey is shown surrounded by small insets of typical medieval scenes. In one a poor pensioner is shown clad in his seemly robe and badge; in another he is being edified by a sermon delivered from a Gothic pulpit; and in the last he is being given a noble Christian burial. Not so the modern workhouse! A grim panopticon dominates that picture. The poor pensioner is now clad in rags; moral edification is administered by locks and chains; and when he dies, his corpse is offered up for dissection. As for the diet of the two ages—the medieval poor man is given beef, mutton, bacon, ale, milk, porridge, wheat bread, and cheese, whereas his modern successor subsists on bread, gruel, oatmeal, and potatoes.

Pugin is convinced that only a spiritual renovation of England can recreate the ideal society of the Middle Ages. Himself a Roman Catholic —"jangled into a change of religion," Ruskin angrily insisted, "by the chimes of a belfry" [5]—Pugin became convinced that only a revival of the old beliefs of England could restore her former moral greatness and that only moral greatness could produce great architecture. In such works as the *True Principles of Pointed or Christian Architecture* . . .

[5] John Ruskin, *The Works of John Ruskin*, ed. E. T. Cook and Alexander Wedderburn, Library edition, 39 vols. (London and New York: George Allen and Longmans Green, 1903–1912), IX, 438.

(1841) and *An Apology for the Revival of Christian Architecture in England* (1843), Pugin continued to attack English architecture and, through architecture, the moral tone of England. He claimed that English life was at a low ebb when "every linen-draper's shop apes . . . the palace of the Caesars . . . [and] every paltry town has a cigar divan with something stuck out to look Turkish." [6] He derides as equally absurd the craze for spiky and crocketed furniture and fenders. Pugin once said that one was lucky to escape without injury from a Gothic parlor.

For the creators of architecture, Pugin prescribed a stern and pious course of conduct:

> The student of Christian architecture should also imbue his mind with the mysteries of his Faith, the history of the Church, the lives of those glorious Saints and Martyrs that it has produced in all ages, especially those who by birth or mission, are connected with the remains of ancient piety in this land. He should also be well-acquainted with the annals of his country,—its constitutions, laws, privileges, and dignities,—the liturgy and rubrics of the Church,—customs and ceremonies,—topographical antiquities, local peculiarities and natural resources . . . [If this were done,] we should have structures whose arrangement and detail would be in accordance with our Faith, customs, and natural traditions. [7]

To Pugin it went without saying that such a student would have to be a Roman Catholic. "What! an Englishman and a Protestant!" he wrote in his *Apology*. "Oh, worse than parricide to sever those holy ties that bind him to the past." [8]

At the same time that Pugin was advocating a return to the purity of medieval Catholicism, a parallel tendency in the Church of England, as we have seen, was attempting to restore a more pristine faith to the

[6] Augustus Welby Pugin, *The True Principles of Pointed or Christian Architecture* (London, 1853), p. 48.

[7] Augustus Welby Pugin, *An Apology for the Revival of Christian Architecture in England* (London, 1853), p. 21.

[8] *Ibid.*, p. 50.

Anglican religion. By a curious coincidence the impact of the Anglican revival in architecture manifested itself most strongly at Cambridge rather than Oxford. The Cambridge Camden Society was founded in 1839 to "promote the study of Ecclesiastical Architecture and Antiquities, and the restoration of mutilated Architectural Remains."[9] In some ways the movement seems an outgrowth of the demand for archaeological correctness which had been symptomatic of the early phases of the Gothic Revival, but certain of its demands are similar to Pugin's. Like Pugin, its practitioners demanded integrity in materials, and, like Pugin, they believed that the greatness of a building depended on the greatness of its builders. It was the "deeply religious habits of the builders of old," their "Hours, the cloisters, the discipline, the obedience," which spelled the success of their buildings, while "the worldliness, vanity, dissipation, and patronage of our own architecture issues in unvarying and hopeless failure."[10] Hence, the Anglican revivalists insisted that bricklayers forgo swearing and that masons live lives of simple piety. Hence, too, they were frequently accused of Catholic leanings—accusations that they successfully withstood.

So successful were all these campaigns on behalf of Gothic architecture that by the second half of the century Gothic was the dominant mode. Such figures as Gilbert Scott, William Butterfield, and George Edmund Street reigned over English architecture, and parallel figures existed on the Continent and in America. Perhaps the most significant single sign of the Gothic triumph over all rival architectural modes was the publication of Sir Charles Eastlake's *A History of the Gothic Revival* in 1872. Even though critical of specific architects and buildings, Eastlake nonetheless thinks the whole movement well worth studying. He takes as axiomatic what had become the central and most meaningful tenet of the revival: that the spirit of the age is all-important to the value of the building. In his discussion of some illustrations of England's ancient mansions, he blends his idea of architecture as representing the spirit of the age with a familiar, almost Scott-like description of medieval life. "There was feasting in the hall and tilting in the court-

[9] Quoted in Clark, *Gothic Revival*, p. 212.
[10] Quoted in *ibid.*, p. 218.

yard," he writes. "The yule log crackled on the hearth, and mummers beguiled the dullness of a winter's evening." Landlords remained on their estates all the year round, and all the "adjuncts and incidents of social life, dress, pastimes, manners, and what not, formed part of the picturesque whole of which we, in these prosaic and lack-lustre days . . . can form no conception."[11]

Eastlake's joint role as historian of both art and architecture serves as a reminder that the Gothic Revival also manifested itself in painting. Although medievalist painting is usually thought to have begun in England with the founding of the Pre-Raphaelite Brotherhood in 1848 and thus to have started almost one hundred years after the Gothic Revival, medievalism in the arts actually had a very long genealogy.

The earliest sources of the medieval ideal in painting are to be found among the writings of the German Romantics, particularly among the works of Wilhelm Wackenroder and Friedrich von Schlegel. Wackenroder's *Herzergiessungen eines Kunstliebenden Klosterbruder* (1797) is a series of conversations with an imaginary monk, which praises medieval art and society and suggests that art and life can only flourish when linked with a living religious tradition. The book was designed to oppose the rationalism of the Enlightenment and had wide influence, as did his *Phantasien über Kunst* (1799). Even more influential in the revival of medieval art was Schlegel's *Gemälde beschriebungen aus Paris und den Niederlanden*. It influenced such early neomedieval painters as Philipp Otto Runge, Caspar David Friedrich, and Alfred Rethel. Their work, in turn, anticipated that of the so-called Nazarene Brotherhood, whose chief members were Peter von Cornelius and Johann Friedrich Overbeck.

It is interesting to look at the Nazarene Brotherhood since it typifies in many ways the general intellectual atmosphere of the medieval revival on the Continent. First calling themselves the St. Luke Brotherhood, because St. Luke had been the patron saint of the medieval artists' guilds, the members of this early group undertook in the first years of the nineteenth century to reintroduce into painting the noble

[11] Sir Charles Eastlake, *A History of the Gothic Revival* (London, 1872), p. 237.

spirit of the medieval artist, whom they imagined to have sacrificed his individuality to his communal tasks. They praised the Middle Ages as a period when the dignity of man was still fully apparent and aimed to restore the joyous innocence of early Italian painting. They claimed that their art was devoted to truth and nature.

After Peter Cornelius, who was a Roman Catholic, became associated with the St. Luke's Brotherhood, the name of the group was changed to the *Nazarenes* and the emphasis became more monastic and more cloistered. There is no question that these Continental painters affected the Pre-Raphaelites, but because of this association with Catholicism, both the Pre-Raphaelites and Ruskin, for all their indebtedness, tended to disown them. Holman Hunt, for example, was careful as late as 1905 to disinfect himself from charges of "Over-beckism," which he regarded as a "deadly blight on the fair blossom of advancing taste." Nevertheless, in spite of his hostility to the movement, Hunt recognized that medievalism in English painting was to be traced "through the original example of Overbeck through Madox Brown to Rossetti."[12] And it is certainly true that Ford Madox Brown, although never a member of the Pre-Raphaelite Brotherhood, was deeply affected by meeting Cornelius and Overbeck during his travels abroad and that his painting in the early forties, before he met Rossetti, shows the influence of their medievalism.

The Pre-Raphaelites were subject to English influences, too. Much earlier in the century, William Dyce and John Frederick Lewes were painting with a Pre-Raphaelite devotion to detail, and Daniel Maclise, whom Rossetti greatly admired, had executed a number of paintings on chivalric subjects. Nor were the Italian primitive painters unknown in England before the Nazarenes taught the Pre-Raphaelites to praise them. Even in the eighteenth century connoisseurs in England had been collecting the works of such painters as Giotto and Cimabue, and a book of drawings based on Giotto's work, published in 1808, had been reprinted in 1811, 1825, and 1843. In 1836 a committee had recommended that the nation should buy medieval Italian art for its

[12] William Holman Hunt, *Pre-Raphaelitism and the Pre-Raphaelite Brotherhood* (New York: Macmillan, 1905), II, 334.

collections, and it was partly owing to the availability of such works that the Pre-Raphaelites were able to form their judgment of the painting they espoused. A highly influential book was Lord Lindsay's *Sketches of the History of Christian Art*, whose praise for such figures as Giotto and Cimabue caused Ruskin to revise his opinion of the Italian primitives. Lord Lindsay, it should be noted, derived his ideas from Overbeck.

The actual founding of the Pre-Raphaelite Brotherhood took place in 1848. The nucleus of the group was John Everett Millais, Holman Hunt, Thomas Woolner, and Dante Gabriel Rossetti, who, despising the frivolity and conventionality of contemporary art, "wanted to show forth what was in them in the way of solid and fresh thought or invention, personal observation, and the intimate study of and strict adherence to nature." [13] Joining with James Collinson, Frederick George Stephens, and William Michael Rossetti, the original four became a band of seven, which chose the name Pre-Raphaelite out of banter, defiance, and a belief that the art of the Middle Ages provided a greater truth to nature than had been seen since the days of Raphael. In this assertion, as in the pronouncements of the Nazarenes, the familiar elements of Romanticism and medievalism lie mingled: the belief in the superior creativity of simpler folk and the corollary notion that the current age is crass and sterile.

In actual practice, however, how medieval were the Pre-Raphaelite paintings? A random list of some of the medieval or quasi-medieval titles over the years by the more important members of the brotherhood shows a fairly wide range of subjects. Rossetti gives *Ecce Ancilla Domini*, *King Arthur and the Weeping Queens*, *The Wedding of St. George and the Princess Sabra*, *Dante's Dream at the Time of the Death of Beatrice*, and *King Arthur's Tomb*. Hunt shows designs for the Moxon Edition of Tennyson, as do all the Pre-Raphaelites, and should perhaps be credited for the rather medieval atmosphere of *The Light of the World*. Millais has the quasi-medieval, or is it proto-Renaissance, *Lorenzo in the House of Isabella* and *The Eve of St.*

[13] William M. Rossetti (ed.), *Praeraphaelite Diaries and Letters* (London, 1900), p. 205.

Agnes—a sign, by the way, of the brotherhood's continuing interest in Keats.

In all these works, however, certain aspects of medievalism are lacking. In spite of their intensive and prolonged association with Ruskin, whose work was one of their inspirations, the brotherhood never really conceived of medieval society as an ideal. Although a recent critic has seen a special significance in Rossetti's medievalism because of his belief in eternal suffering and damnation, most Pre-Raphaelite uses of the Middle Ages are essentially decorative unless one thinks that the choice of medieval rather than modern subjects for so many of their works is in itself a criticism of contemporary society. Their writings and statements praised the medieval painters as faithful to the truth, but they did not use their paintings, as Pugin had used his drawings, to show the superiority of medieval life. Their topics are Arthurian, Dantesque, chivalric; but the values they reveal are esthetic rather than social.

It is only in the paintings on contemporary subjects that the Pre-Raphaelites manifest any overt sense of social consciousness. Ruskin claims that the very furniture in Holman Hunt's *The Awakened Conscience* criticizes the materialistic values of the parvenu class. But Ford Madox Brown's *Work*, with its moiling multitude in the background and portraits of Carlyle and Frederick Denison Maurice in the foreground, implies an ever broader criticism. In fact, it is only in Brown that one is likely to run across social criticism such as this, which he wrote after visiting a country estate: "What an accumulation of wealth and impotence! ... Is it for this that a people toils and wears out its myriad lives? For such a heaping up of bad taste, such gilding of hideousness, for such exposure of imbecility .... Oh how much more beautiful would six model labourers' cottages be, built by a man of skill for £100 each! As Carlyle says, 'Enough to make not only the angels, but the very jackasses weep.'" [14] But, then, Brown was not really a Pre-Raphaelite, and one searches in vain for similar statements among the brethren.

[14] *Ruskin: Rossetti: Pre-Raphaelitism: Papers 1854 to 1862*, arr. and ed. William Michael Rossetti (New York, 1899), p. 41.

II

Of all the writers of the medieval revival, Ruskin is in many ways the most profound. There is no question that he was influenced by the medieval tradition. He begins his autobiography by calling himself a Tory of Sir Walter Scott's school; praises Southey's *Colloquies;* and dedicates *Munera Pulveris* to Carlyle, "who alone of our masters of literature has written, without thought of himself, what he knew to be needful for the people of his time to hear." [15] Ruskin was also influenced by and was himself an influence upon the medieval revival in the arts. And yet the most significant aspects of Ruskin's thought go beyond almost anything the previous medievalism had expressed and have no real influence, either. Although Morris and a number of lesser figures followed him superficially, only the American Henry Adams wrestled with the real implications of Ruskin's medievalism—its almost metaphysical vision of an ordered universe—and all Adams's work goes to show the impossibility of such coherence.

Medievalism, as we have seen, has two major aspects in the eighteenth and nineteenth centuries. One is its naturalism—its identification with nature and the past and thus with simpler and truer modes of feeling and expression and nobler and more heroic codes of action. The other is its feudalism—its harmonious and stable social structure which reconciled freedom and order by giving each man an allotted place in society and an allotted leader to follow. The bridge between these two aspects of medievalism is chivalry, which made the spontaneous generosity of the natural man the guiding principle of man in society and which compensated for human frailty by having the strong protect the weak. Although the medievalists wished to revive this ancient generosity and kindliness at all levels of society, it is from the aristocracy—usually of the land though sometimes of industry—that chivalry, altruism, or what Ruskin comes to call *largesse* are primarily expected. Opposed to the medievalist belief in the power of chivalry as a binding force,

---

[15] Ruskin, *Works*, XVII, 145; John Ruskin, *The Diaries of John Ruskin, 1835–1847*, sel. and ed. Joan Evans and John Howard Whitehouse (Oxford: The Clarendon Press, 1956), p. 252; Ruskin, *Works*, XVII, 146.

as we have seen, is utilitarianism, which posits a natural and beneficent selfishness as the root motive of man and society. Viewed through the simplifying eye of medievalism, the political and economic manifestations of utilitarianism are seen to be democracy and laissez faire, and its practical results are an industrialization and urbanization that have destroyed the natural and venerable appearance of the nation and the natural and venerable ties between social classes. The two forces, medievalism and utilitarianism, remain opposed throughout the century and sum up the most basic contradictions of the age.

None of the new feudalists seems to have consciously recognized the relationship between the idealization of nature and the idealization of the Middle Ages, although several of them achieved at least a fragmentary comprehension of this underlying assumption. Scott, in particular, closely allies his medievalism and his primitivism, although he is consistently aware of the potentiality for violence and bestiality in purely natural man. Carlyle, too, sees the rebirth of faith in nature —in what he calls "natural supernaturalism"—as the only hope for man in society. He believes that his simple and heroic Abbot Samson must be born again into our industrial world if we are to have peace and order. But nowhere in Scott and Carlyle—and certainly not in such figures as Cobbett, Southey, or Disraeli—do we find an explicit statement of the relationship between the natural order and the medieval state. Ruskin alone consistently bases his medievalism on a belief in nature and nature's God, not without an acknowledgment of mountain gloom as well as mountain glory, but with a full and explicit recognition of the relationship between nature, art, and man.

The basis of Ruskin's philosophy—and he must be considered as a philosophic rather than pragmatic medievalist—can be found in his statement in the preface to the first edition of *Modern Painters* (1843), written when he was twenty-four, that he would "declare and demonstrate, wherever they exist, the essence and the authority of the Beautiful and the True" (III, 4). Although Ruskin eventually sloughed off the evangelical religious beliefs on which this assertion was based, he never wholly lost faith in the inner order of nature nor in the capacity of the faithful, patient man to find it, however much concealed by a selfish and debased society. Art was for him the record of this insight into nature, the expression of noble and meaningful truths. Children and primitive artists could express these truths unerringly, for they maintained an uncorrupted eye, whose truthful vision far outweighed any awkwardnesses of technique. Thus, he writes, with what sounds like a belated Romanticism, that "childhood often holds a truth with its feeble fingers, which the grasp of manhood cannot retain, which it is the pride of utmost age to recover" (III, 31). To such primitivism as this medievalism is, of course, a corollary. As he elsewhere phrases it, "the early efforts of Cimabue and Giotto are the burning messages of prophecy, delivered by the stammering lips of infants (III, 90).

The power of Giotto and the whole Gothic school of art and architecture to express truths that most artists are striving all their lives to find points up the relationship that Ruskin sees between society and nature. Nature he finds eminently hospitable to man. As he writes in his diary, "I looked at the slope of distant grass on the hill; and then at the waving heads near me. What a gift of God that is, I thought; who could have dreamed of such soft green, continual, tender clothing for the dark earth, the food of cattle and man."[16] Modern society, according to Ruskin, debars man from this view. It has lost sight of nature and can produce no art. It can imitate but it cannot create. And in this impotence at creation, in this falsity of taste—nowhere more apparent than in the britannia-ware meretriciousness of contemporary English art—lies the sign and stigma of human failure. As he wrote in a very early essay, composed when he was only sixteen, English architecture is now a mere burlesque of style, in which parish paupers smoke their pipes and drink their beer under Gothic arches and statuary and nice old English gentlemen peep from the windows of Swiss chalets. Only a return to nature and an elevation of the national mind will purify such architecture. The creators of buildings must be "natural in all that they do, and . . . look for the beauty of the material creation . . . not in the chanceful and changing disposition of artificial

[16] John Ruskin, *The Diaries of John Ruskin, 1848–1873*, sel. and ed. Joan Evans and John Howard Whitehouse (Oxford: The Clarendon Press, 1958), p. 382.

decoration, but in the manifestation of the pure and animating spirit which keeps it from the coldness of the grave" (I, 168).

In spite of the references to the Middle Ages in his earlier writings, Ruskin's first extensively medievalist work is the second volume of *Modern Painters* (1846). His reading of Lord Lindsay's volume on Christian art and of Alexis François Rio's *De la poèsie Chrétienne* had persuaded him to look again at primitive Italian painting. The result was a Nazarene-like enthusiasm for the simplicity, purity, and innocence of the early masters and his first persistent use of the medieval-modern contrast. The early Italian primitives, he claimed, despised or were ignorant of any theories of composition and painted directly from nature, knowing instinctively it was divine.

> [They] indicated by perfect similarity of action and gesture on one hand, and by the infinite and truthful variation of expression on the other, the most sublime strength, because the most absorbing unity, of multitudinous passion that ever human heart conceived. Hence, in the cloister of St. Marks', the intense, fixed statue-like silence of ineffable adoration upon the spirits in prison at the feet of Christ, side by side, the hands lifted, and the knees bowed, and the lips trembling together; and in St. Domenico of Fiesole, that whirlwind rush of the angels and the redeemed souls round Him at His resurrection, in which we hear the blast of the horizontal trumpets mixed with the dying clangour of their ingathered wings. The same feeling occurs throughout the works of the serious men . . . and it is well to compare it with the vileness and falseness of all that succeeded. (IV, 100–01)

Modern artists, however, have turned from the contemplation of natural and therefore God-made things, to the study of purely human objects. Ruskin claims their deterioration is symbolized by the fall of Raphael, who, in the middle of his painting career, "betrayed the faith he had received from his father and his master, and substituted for the radiant sky of the Madonna del Cardellino, the chamber-wall of the Madonna della Seggiola" (IV, 85). Raphael's turning from landscapes to interiors, from the natural to the artificial, foreshadows for

Ruskin the failure of all later art and society—a failure of vision and moral perception that his writings attempt to rectify.

The Seven Lamps of Architecture (1849) continues the idea of fidelity to nature and the inner truth it represents and once again finds these values in medieval art. Its first two aphorisms restate the primacy of the moral law: "*We may always know what is right,*" and "*All practical laws are the exponents of moral ones*" (VIII, 20, 22). But the book develops much more fully the relationship between art, morality, and social order, and thus serves as a link to Ruskin's later writing. Four of Ruskin's seven lamps—or illuminating ideas—help clarify his developing medievalism. They are the lamps of sacrifice, memory, life, and obedience—all distinctively Ruskinian and yet all linked to the ideas of chivalry and *noblesse oblige* implicit in earlier medievalist writings.

The lamp of sacrifice is presented as the direct opposite of the modern spirit of utilitarianism. Like Burke's idea of chivalry, it is opposed to calculations and economics. Or, to use another familiar example, it is the generous altruism of a Quentin Durward as opposed to the mechanical thriftiness of a Louis XI. Here is how Ruskin defines it:

> it is a spirit . . . which of two marbles, equally beautiful, applicable, and durable, would choose the more costly, because it was so, and of two kinds of decoration, equally effective, would choose the more elaborate because it was so, in order that it might in the same compass present more cost and more thought. It is therefore more unreasoning and enthusiastic, and perhaps less negatively defined, as the opposite of the prevalent feeling of modern times, which desires to produce the largest results at the least cost. (VIII, 30)

"Sacrifice" must not, however, be confused with mere ostentation. Such expenditure is always for a cause or a truth, never for the enhancement of self. The conception is also suggestive—though very different in tone—of the attacks on capitalism, and particularly on the profit motive, that Karl Marx was contemporaneously working out in *The Communist Manifesto* and *Das Kapital*.

The lamp of memory is also important in showing how Ruskin's medievalism developed, for it is here that he first fully records the idea that architecture is the visible and moving record of earlier and more heroic times. Like his predecessors, all the way back to the Graveyard Poets, Ruskin responds to the emotional power of history. But, more important, he sees and expresses the value of preserving the past as an object lesson or inspiration to mankind, since it is an embodiment of the higher values of an age that was closer to God—a living sermon carved in stone:

> For, indeed, the greatest glory of a building is not in its stones, nor in its gold. Its glory is in its Age, and in that deep sense of voicefulness, of stern watching, of mysterious sympathy, nay, even of approval or condemnation, which we feel in walls that have long been washed by the passing waves of humanity. It is in their lasting witness against men, in their quiet contrast with the transitional character of all things, in the strength which, through the lapse of seasons and times, and the decline and birth of dynasties, and the changing of the face of the earth, and of the limits of the sea, maintains its sculptured shapeliness for a time insuperable, connects forgotten and following ages with each other, and half constitutes the identity, as it concentrates the sympathy of nations: it is in that golden stain of time that we are to look for the real light and colour, and preciousness of architecture; and it is not until a building has assumed this character, till it has been entrusted with fame, and hallowed by the deeds of men, till its walls have been witnesses of suffering, and its pillars rise out of the shadows of death, that its existence, more lasting as it is, than that of the natural objects of the world around it, can be gifted with even so much as these possess, of language and life. (VIII, 233–34)

Other authors had seen the past as monitor and guide to struggling modernism. None, however, saw the past so fully alive as Ruskin did and none, apparently, saw the logical necessity of creating a present worthy in its turn of becoming another people's past. The sense of continuity is strong in Ruskin, a fit correlative to his sense of natural order. Antiquity and nature thus are one.

Also important for an understanding of Ruskin's later thought are the distinctions he makes in *Seven Lamps* between the lamp of life and that of obedience. At first glance the ideas seem contradictory. The lamp of life tells Ruskin that "all things are noble in proportion to their fullness of life" (VIII, 190) and that architecture depends for its power on allowing the ordinary laborer to express his joy and freedom in his work, as he did in the Middle Ages. The lamp of obedience, however, suggests the need for discipline and restraint. In a passage foreshadowing his later work, Ruskin moves from a discussion of the lamp of obedience to a thundering attack upon liberty:

> how false is the conception, how frantic the pursuit, of that treacherous phantom which men call Liberty: most treacherous, indeed, of all phantoms; for the feeblest ray of reason might surely show us, that not only its attainment, but its being, was impossible. There is no such thing in the universe. There can never be. The stars have it not; the earth has it not; and we men have the mockery and semblance of it only for our heaviest punishment. (VIII, 248–49)

However, the oppositions between life and obedience are only apparent, for to recognize and do God's work is to be truly free. Ruskin writes in his diary that "the more the man is an inspired instrument and the less there is of himself and of toil and trouble in what he does, the more divine it is, and so we should always in our work stop short at that which we do pleasurably; not that we may not work hard, but work in joy and not in hesitation, nor despondency, and because we feel a necessity of working, not because we force ourselves to work." [17] Great art is for him the expression of man's delight, not in his own work, but in God's. By making labor pleasurable in this way, Ruskin synthesizes, in a manner typical of his thinking, the Romantic conception of joy and the Victorian belief in work. Creativity and obedience, spontaneity and diligence are reconciled here, as they usually are in his better work. A willing self-discipline based on a consent to natural law makes a meaningful existence possible, and the Middle Ages serves as the inspiration for such a life.

Ruskin's most famous book, *The Stones of Venice* (1851–53),

[17] Ruskin, *Diaries, 1848–1873*, p. 366.

continues and develops these ideas of freedom and order. The book traces the history of Venice through her Byzantine, Gothic, and Renaissance periods, but the core of the book is the distinction between Gothic and Renaissance, or, in essence, between medieval and modern. Venice is a touchstone, and in the decline of her architecture Ruskin perceives the decline of postmedieval society.

Primarily Ruskin conceives of the Middle Ages as a period of faith. Despite his frequently absurd anti-Catholic strictures, he is more concerned with the question of whether a man believes than what a man believes. The greatest difference, he proclaims in Carlylean tones, is between "the calculating, smiling, self-sustained, self-governed man, and the believing, weeping, wondering, struggling, Heaven-governed man;—between the men who say in their hearts 'there is' no God,' and those who acknowledge a God at every step." As in St. Edmundsbury, the contrast is between medieval faith and modern unbelief. "That is indeed the difference which we shall find . . . between the builders of this day and the builders on that sand island long ago" (X, 67).

So intertwined were faith and architecture in the Middle Ages, Ruskin says, that no separation was made between ecclesiastic and domestic architecture. All was Gothic; for Gothic is the perfectly functional style and hence dominant in a period when worship was too sincere to require false ornamentation. Far from thinking, as many writers such as Coleridge had insisted, that the Gothic arch symbolized aspiration, Ruskin felt that it was merely an unmysteriously useful architectural form, the product of healthy minds and strong emotions. More important, because Gothic architecture was so full of faith and so honest, it was able to accept imperfections. Ruskin says that it is the essence of Christian architecture in an age of faith to prefer the intention to the deed and to prefer a high aim to a low achievement. Thus the excellence of Gothic architecture is that it will "receive the results of the labour of inferior minds; and out of fragments full of imperfection . . . indulgently raise up a stately and unaccusable whole" (X, 190). Christian architecture, like feudal chivalry, is thus an outlet for human strength and compassionate to human weakness.

Because of this fundamental Christian *caritas*, this chivalric mercifulness, medieval society did not, as modern society does, turn the workman into a machine. In his celebrated section on "Savageness" in "The Nature of the Gothic," Ruskin insists that medieval society allowed man joy and freedom in his work. He claims that the high polish and perfection of contemporary English architecture are actually signs that our society has degraded the worker into a machine:

> Alas! if read rightly, these perfectnesses are signs of a slavery in our England a thousand times more bitter and more degrading than that of the scourged African, or helot Greek. Men may be beaten, chained, tormented, yoked like cattle, slaughtered like summer flies, and yet remain in one sense, and the best sense, free. But to smother their souls within them, to blight and hew into rotting pollards the suckling branches of their human intelligence, to make the flesh and skin which, after the worm's work on it, is to see God, into leathern thongs to yoke machinery with,—this is to be slave-masters indeed; and there might be more freedom in England, though her feudal lords' lightest words were worth men's lives, and though the blood of the vexed husbandman dropped in the furrows of her fields, than there is while the animation of her multitudes is sent like fuel to feed the factory smoke, and the strength of them is given daily to be wasted into the fineness of a web, or racked into the exactness of a line. (X, 193)

Emphasizing the way in which modern society has separated itself into two nations, not merely rich and poor, but man and machine, Ruskin casts about for a solution to his problem. In *The Stones of Venice*, however, his solutions are limited: all men should embrace some form of handwork and think it no degradation to do so; but there must always be masters and men. His proposition is chiefly negative, mere boycott, or *sacrifice*, as he significantly calls it. One should never encourage the manufacture of luxury items in which invention has no share and never desire an exact finish or a work which is totally imitative. Moreover, Gothic architecture should be universally adopted for all forms of building, since by allowing for imperfection, it allows for human freedom.

In contrast to the virtues of medieval society, Renaissance and therefore modern society are chiefly at fault for what Ruskin calls

Pride of Science, which seems to include all that is at enmity with joy. He states that "the desperate evil of the whole Renaissance system is . . . that knowledge is thought the one and the only good, and it is never inquired whether men are vivified by it or paralyzed." Learning is not mere repetition, but the joy of continued discovery. No wonder, says Ruskin, that men have been turning recently to the past and to works of the imagination. "The essence of modern romance is simply the return of the heart and fancy to the things in which they necessarily take pleasure" (XI, 224). A lover of Scott himself, he thinks these are the reasons Scott's works have been so popular.

Taken as a whole, then, Ruskin's medievalism in the forties and fifties is essentially a criticism of modern life for its lack of joy and loss of closeness to nature. It is a vision that darkens in succeeding volumes of *Modern Painters*. In the last volume, for example, Ruskin compares the birthplaces of the fifteenth-century painter Giorgione and the nineteenth-century's Joseph Mallord William Turner in one of the bleakest statements ever made of the medieval-modern contrast. Giorgione's Castelfranco is a "city of marble . . . a golden city, paved with emerald." Turner's London is the product of the "present work of men," mean, aimless, unsightly, with "thin-walled, lath-divided, narrow-garreted houses of clay; booths of a darksome Vanity Fair, busily base" (VII, 374, 385). The real shift in Ruskin's thought, however, can be seen in *A Joy Forever*, two aptly titled lectures on the "political economy of art" which he delivered in Manchester in 1857. Although Ruskin had attacked conventional laissez faire economy as early as 1841 in his children's story, *The King of the Golden River*, here in the very locus of the Manchester school he really first begins his campaign for a managed economy. "Let alone," laissez faire, he says, is the principle of death. Government must become paternalistic. It must check men's follies and relieve their distresses, repress dishonesty, and manage wealth. The masses have a right to this kind of protection. They have "a right to ask that none of their distresses should be unrelieved, none of their weaknesses unwatched; and that no grief, or nakedness, or peril should exist for them, against which the father's hand was not outstretched, or the father's shield uplifted."

In return, they must give obedience to their superiors, and allow them a "father's authority to check the childishness of national fancy, and direct the waywardness of national energy" (XVI, 27).

These ideas, which are extensions of earlier ideas in Goethe, Burke, Scott, Southey, and Carlyle, are carried over into the more famous *Unto This Last* of 1860, which combines them with Ruskin's earlier ideas about fullness of life as a value. His basic premise in this book is that the political economists have defined wealth falsely. Wealth is not useless, ugly products or accumulated gold; that is "illth." There is no wealth but life, and life is the power of love, joy, and admiration. Given this assumption, he goes on to show that the creation of such wealth requires an essentially paternalistic state, in which the production and distribution of wealth is carefully supervised. His definition of political economy is therefore quite the opposite from that of the Manchester school. Where they advocate as much economic freedom as possible for master and workmen alike, Ruskin sees the need for an economy carefully regulated by the state. Ruskin also emphasizes the need for a meaningful relationship between master and man. Like previous medievalists, he stresses the importance of the "affections" and insists that every employer should treat his workmen as if they were his own sons: "the only means which the master has of doing justice to the men employed by him is to ask himself sternly whether he is dealing with such subordinate as he would with his own son" (XVII, 41–42). According to Ruskin, this human paternalism is a mirror of the basic paternalism of the natural order.

The final and most explicit application of Ruskin's medieval principles is to be found in *Fors Clavigera* (1871–84). Though often marred by the mental instability of his later years, the book makes absolutely clear that what Ruskin saw as the underlying difference between medieval and modern times was that one era remembered God and was altruistic, while the other forgot Him and was selfish:

> The utter and inmost secret is that you have been fighting these three hundred years for what you could *get* instead of what you could *give*. You were ravenous enough in rapine in the olden times; but you lived

fearlessly and innocently by it, because, essentially, you wanted money and food to give,—not to consume; to maintain your followers with, not to swallow yourselves. Your chivalry was founded, invariably, by knights who were content all their lives with horses and armour and daily bread. Your kings, of true power, never desired for themselves more, down to the last of them Friedrich. What they *did* desire was strength of manhood round them, and, in their own hands, the power of largesse. (XXVIII, 157–58)

Largesse, or what we have been calling chivalry, the protection of the weak by the strong, is Ruskin's central virtue, as it was implicitly that of all the other medievalists. It must be born again in England if the nation is to survive.

Ruskin's concept of the state in *Fors Clavigera* is hierarchic, ranging from kings, nobles, and landed gentry through manufacturers and craftsmen, with each class depending on the one above it. He sees the inspiration for such relationships in the medieval ideal of chivalry: "For all English gentlemen this is the part of the tale of the race of man which is the most essential for them to know. They must be proud that it is also the greatest part. All that hitherto has been achieved of best,— all that has been in noble preparation instituted,—is begun in the period, and rooted in the conception, of Chivalry." Significantly enough, he realizes that this ideal is only an ideal, a myth, a mental construct. But for him, as for the other writers in the medievalist tradition, the myth is intensely valid. As Ruskin phrases it, "The things that actually happened were of small consequence—the thoughts that were developed are of infinite consequence" (XXII, 270–71).

His praise for the Middle Ages, as it runs through the many years of *Fors*, is lavish and varied, but his chief plea for the restoration of medieval values is to be found in his plans for St. George's Guild. As he develops his thesis, it appears that he is really continuing the idea of sacrifice from *The Seven Lamps of Architecture* and the conception of chivalry in other earlier works. He wants all the gentlemen of England to set aside a portion of their incomes as a "national store," which will be used to better the condition of England. Unfortunately, the aristocracy of England has been idle for a long time. In a passage that recalls some of Carlyle's sarcasms, he writes that "during the last eight hundred years, the upper classes of Europe have been one large Picnic Party. Most of them have been religious also; and in sitting down, by companies, on the green grass, in parks, gardens, and the like, have considered themselves commanded into that position by Divine authority, and fed with bread from Heaven, of which they duly considered it proper to bestow the fragments in support, and the tithes in tuition, of the poor" (XXVII, 145). In contrast to the "Christian feudalism" of the Middle Ages, he argues, our age can only show "atheistic liberalism." It is therefore his "chief hope," says Ruskin, "to bring back for good instead of evil, the organization of the feudal system" (XXVII, 264).

What Ruskin therefore proposes is the formation of a St. George's Guild dedicated to the wise creating and bestowing instead of the wise stealing of money. He says he will begin, and does so, by buying land and settling on it as many young and healthy families as the land will support who are willing to work on it with their own hands. He will select those families on recommendation of landlords who know their people best and will send him cheerful, honest people. His conception is in many ways monastic, dedicated to the redemption of waste lands and the repurification of English air and water. He thinks it possible that the redemption of Godless and lordless England will come from "cloistered companies." As the idea of St. George's Guild spreads, Ruskin believes that society will become composed of self-sufficient units, producing most of what they need by hand and relying very little on trade or commerce. As in the Middle Ages the artisans will be divided into guilds and the medieval principles of hierarchy will be fully reorganized.

As Frederic Harrison wisely complains, Ruskin is always vague when one most wants him to be concrete, and *Fors* is no exception. How he plans to reconcile the small isolated units with a national reorganization is unclear. What is clear, however, is that the central idea, here in Ruskin's penultimate major work, is obedience rather than liberty. (Two very late works *The Bible of Amiens* and *The Pleasures of England* slightly reverse this tendency.) All of *Fors* is permeated with the Carlylean conception of hero worship. The feudal system, he writes, "begins in the existence of a Master," or Mister, and a Mistress and goes on through the masters of masters and mistresses of mistresses to the final authority of God Himself (XXVIII, 737–39). The purpose of education, as organized under St. George's Guild, is to inculcate instant obedience. As in *The Seven Lamps of Architecture*, Ruskin sees no distinction between obedience and happiness since they both express man's consent to the natural order of the universe. He writes that true justice "consists mainly in granting to every human being due aid in the development of such faculties as it possesses for action and enjoyment; primarily, for useful action, because all enjoyment worth having . . . must in some way arise . . . either in happy energy, or rightly complacent and exulting rest" (XXVII, 147–48). Given such a conception of the universe, freedom, as Ruskin had said long ago, is meaningless, except for the freedom to do right. He therefore insists that the children of St. George's Guild, as patterns to the rest of the world, be trained to the "habit of instant, finely accurate, and totally unreasoning obedience to their fathers, mothers, and tutors," who must in their turn offer the "same precise and unquestioning submission . . . to the officers set over them" (XXVIII, 20).

In actual practice St. George's Guild was a tragicomedy. As reported in the Masters Records and Reports over the years, it was a total failure—the unhappy fusion of an archaic idea with an unbalanced mind. *Fors* is essentially a reversion to the early medievalism of Scott and Southey, which relied on the landed gentry to accept again their former responsibilities. However, neither Scott nor Southey, nor indeed any of the previous medievalists had ever attempted to make so literal a translation of theory into practice as Ruskin did. As a result, their theories remained meaningful, for they only suggested broad lines of advance; Ruskin's practicalities, however, became absurd, by reducing the ideal to the level of the banal.

As a philosophical statement *Fors* is a fascinating document, however. It brings to a focus almost all the elements of previous medievalist writings and goes beyond them to show the underlying assumptions on which the movement rested. There is the desire to help the poor and the chivalrous insistence that it is the responsibility of the rich and the wellborn to do so. There is also the elitist assumption that the poor cannot help themselves, that they are children who must be guided by wiser fathers. And there is the agrarian bias so common to earlier medievalism. What is different here, though, from any previous medievalist writings, with the partial exception of Carlyle's, is the extent to which the social structure serves as a metaphor for the larger order of the universe, which is also hierarchical, paternal, and benevolent—at least to those who obey its laws.

Both in time and space medieval architecture and society serve as emblems and reminders to Ruskin, even in his darker moments, of the higher order that man must seek. By surviving and transcending time, the ancient buildings of Europe remind man of what is permanently valuable in the universe. In their complexity and richness of structure they testify to both life and freedom. This freedom, however, is never anarchic, for the existence of universal law shows Ruskin the need for obedience. Less insistent in earlier works, this emphasis on obedience is reinforced in *Fors* by his developing fear of the masses.

In all Ruskin's writing, then, medievalism verges on metaphysics. His most obvious disciple, William Morris, borrows many of his ideas but, rejecting Ruskin's philosophical bias, grafts them on to a democratic socialism. Only in the works of Henry Adams are Ruskin's basic questions raised again.

III

As we have seen, many of the earlier medievalists came from medieval backgrounds. Born in 1834, William Morris came too late to witness the last remnants of the Middle Ages, and yet his family home, a modern structure but surrounded by a narrow moat, shows how some vestiges of ancient ways were being kept up in the middle of the nineteenth century. As J. W. Mackail describes the Morris household in his biography of Morris, "At some points there were links with the habits of medieval England. Woodford Hall brewed its own beer and made its own butter, as much as a matter of course as it baked its own

bread. Just as in the fourteenth century, there was a meal at high prime
... when the children had cake and cheese and a glass of small ale.
Many of the old festivals were observed: Twelfth Night especially
was one of the great days of the year, and the Masque of St. George
was always then presented with unconscious elaboration." [18] Morris
himself was given a small suit of armor to wear when riding in the
park and, having learned to read at the age of four, had gone through
the family's entire set of the Waverley Novels by the time he was seven.

Over and over, Morris's early and pleasant experiences were with
rural and therefore in many ways archaic English life. While his father
tried at Woodford Hall to maintain the illusion of old England (and
perhaps thus compensate for his parvenu wealth), the young Morris
was developing a far more authentic sense of the nation's sylvan past
through his explorations of neighboring Epping Forest. Riding among
its shadowy rows of birch trees, clad in his miniature armor, he could
imagine himself reliving his favorite scenes from Scott. Queen Elizabeth's lodge at Chingford Hatch in the forest was linked in his mind,
he said later, with *The Antiquary*, and other places he rode through
must have had similar associations with Scott's historical scenes.
"Nature and History," Morris asserted in one of his essays, were, or
at least ought to be, the two great teachers of mankind. His yoking
together of nature and the past in this way and his unwavering identification of both these forces with the Middle Ages places him squarely
in the tradition of such nostalgic medievalists as Scott, Cobbett,
Wordsworth, and Southey, all of whom had bestowed upon their
medievalism the hallowing associations of nature and rural life and
all of whom had resisted the onslaughts of industrialism. A child of
medievalism's later days, however, Morris also inherited the ideas of
Carlyle and Ruskin, and his mature medievalism, clearly influenced by
these writings, marks a new attempt to reconcile the Middle Ages
with modern times. Alone of our authors, Morris is both a medievalist
and a socialist. But, despite his revolutionary philosophy, the pastoral-
historical element should never be forgotten since it accounts for both

[18] J. W. Mackail, *The Life of William Morris* (New York: Longmans Green,
1922), I, 9.

the tone and content of his medievalism. His medieval visions and programs must thus always be seen against a half-remembered, half-created background of an England beautiful in its fields and woods and splendid and fresh in its homes and churches.

If Morris's childhood experiences made him susceptible to the beauty of the past and of nature, his years at Oxford (1853–55) deepened this sense and began showing him the inadequacy of the present. At preparatory school he had assimilated the contents of a library rich in volumes on architecture and archaeology. At Oxford he continued to read medieval chronicles, taking great delight in the *Morte d'Arthur*, which he read in the Southey edition and which became for him and his friend Edward Burne-Jones an object of veneration, according to one memorialist, a world of "mystical religion and noble chivalry of action . . . of lost history and romance."[19] Ruskin's *The Stones of Venice* and, in an almost equal degree, *Modern Painters* were also sacred volumes and provided a moral focus for his medievalism. As he later wrote in the preface to the edition of "The Nature of the Gothic," which he lovingly printed at the Kelmscott Press, "To my mind this chapter is . . . one of the very few necessary and inevitable utterances of this century. To some of us when we first read it now many years ago, it seemed to point out a new road on which the world should travel."[20] What he learned from Ruskin was reinforced by his reading of *Past and Present*, which Morris and his friends discussed at length. Other medievalist readings included *Tracts for the Times*, works by Kenelm Digby, and Charlotte Yonge's highly popular, Anglo-Catholic and Young Englandish novel *The Heir of Redclyffe*.

The reading of Ruskin and Carlyle, in conjunction with writers of the Catholic and Anglo-Catholic revivals, led Morris and Burne-Jones to think for a time of founding some kind of monastic order. Burne-Jones wrote to a friend in 1853 that he had been celebrating May Day by pouring water on passers-by from a garret window and memorizing Tennyson's "Sir Galahad," since Galahad was to be the patron saint

[19] Georgiana Burne-Jones, *Memorials of Edward Burne-Jones*, 2 vols. (London: Macmillan, 1904), I, 116.
[20] Mackail, *Life of Morris*, II, 289.

of the order. A few months later he wrote, in a manner reminiscent of Lord John Manners's youthful proposals, to enlist a friend "in the crusade and holy warfare against the age." And he spoke elsewhere of belonging to a "glorious little company of martyrs."[21] Although the ideal of monasticism, to which Morris at one point thought he would devote his fortune, faded before other attractions, it may have been revived by Morris's association with the architect George Edmund Street, with whom he studied for a time. One of the soundest architects of the Gothic Revival, Street had himself once proposed a brotherhood of artists patterned after that of the Nazarenes. It is possible to see in Street's notion of a brotherhood of artists the origin of Morris's later fascination with medieval craft guilds—an idea that, like many medievalist beliefs, seems to have sprung from a multiplicity of roots.

Morris's and Burne-Jones's association with Rossetti, whom they met in 1856, formed the nucleus of what is sometimes known as the second Pre-Raphaelite Brotherhood. Their most famous activity was the ill-starred venture of the Oxford frescoes. Rossetti had been asked to undertake the frescoes for the new building of the Oxford Union Society, which was being built in Gothic style. Finding uncongenial such suggested topics as "Newton Gathering Pebbles on the Shores of the Ocean of Truth," he invited Morris, Burne-Jones, and several other young men to work with him on a series of Arthurian themes. How the paintings faded almost before they were finished, owing to the painters' technical shortcomings, is a measure of the group's naïveté at that time and of its ignorance of painting techniques— inadequacies that Morris, for one, would later remedy in his studies of medieval handicrafts. The topics of the paintings show that under Rossetti's influence the group's medievalism did not have the social consciousness that Morris would later achieve. *How Sir Palomydes Loved La Belle Iseult with Exceeding Great Love Out of Measure, and How She Loved Not Him but Sir Tristram; Launcelot Found in Guenevere's Chamber; The Three Knights of the Sangrail; Nimue Luring Merlin;* and *The Death of Arthur*—none of the titles suggests

[21] Quoted in Philip Henderson, *William Morris: His Life, Work, and Friends* (New York: McGraw-Hill, 1967), pp. 22–23.

any of the social concerns that Morris and Burne-Jones had been studying in Carlyle and Ruskin but rather a medievalism that is purely esthetic.

Morris's contributions to the *Oxford and Cambridge Magazine*, founded by the second Pre-Raphaelite Brotherhood in 1856, also show his esthetic bent at this time. One of the most characteristic pieces is a little short story showing the beauty of medieval life—a beauty so intense that it is almost painful. "The Story of an Unknown Church" is set in a beautiful landscape of poplars, red poppies, and blue cornflowers, and the church itself is richly ornamented with flowing fountains, carved conduits, and gilded spires. Remembering its splendor, the master mason who is Morris's narrator sees it against the changing background of nature:

> I do not remember very much about the land where my church was; I have quite forgotten the name of it, but I know it was very beautiful, and even now, while I am thinking of it, comes a flood of old memories, and I almost seem to see it again ... that old beautiful land! Only dimly do I see it in spring and summer and winter, but I see it in autumntide clearly now; yes, clearer, clearer, oh! so bright and glorious! yet it was beautiful too in spring, when the brown earth began to grow green: beautiful in summer, when the blue sky looked so much bluer, if you could hem a piece of it in between the new white carving; beautiful in the solemn starry nights, so solemn that it almost reached agony—the awe and joy one had in their great beauty.[22]

Other early writings combine this sense of beauty with a concern for social justice. "Svend and his Brethren" tells of a land of great material prosperity, whose rulers have conquered other lands to increase their own riches and have turned the people they have subjugated into serfs, who are driven like cattle but worse fed and worse housed. And yet, Morris adds in Carlylean accents, the rulers were even worse off than their serfs, for they were the slaves of their own misdoing. "'They could do everything but justice and truth and mercy; therefore

[22] William Morris, *The Collected Works of William Morris*, 24 vols. (New York: Russell and Russell, 1966), I, 149.

God's judgment hung over their heads, not fallen yet, but sure to fall one time or another" (I, 227). How a group of brave mountaineers eventually triumphed over these tyrannous kings is a story that not only suggests the theme of such works as *A Dream of John Ball* that Morris was to write thirty years later, but shows how early Morris turned to the notion of revolution as a solution to social ills.

Morris's first volume of poetry, published in 1858, although almost completely medieval in content, is far from presenting the Middle Ages as an ideal. Several of his poems imitate Browning; most show a curious mingling of beauty and anguish, or, as one critic has phrased it, the decorative and the violent. The title poem, "The Defence of Guenevere," with which the book opens, establishes this strange combination right from the start. Beautiful though she is, Guenevere is a beauty caught in anguish—her wet hair streaming backward, her hand on her burning cheek, her body twisted passionately. She sees herself snared in a trap of excruciating choice that forces her to decide between heaven and hell, yet gives her no clue as to the answer. Shame and remorse are her only portion during the action of the poem, and even the remembered kisses of her lover suggest painful yearning rather than fulfillment.

The brilliant primary colors in which this poem and others in the volume are painted underline the intensity of Morris's medievalizing imagination and his simultaneous attraction to both strength and loveliness. It is perhaps too much to see any anticipation of Morris's later revolutionary fervor in such lines as

> "Swerve to the left, son Roger," he said,
>   "When you catch his eyes through the helmet slit,
> Swerve to the left, then out at his head,
>   And the Lord God give you joy of it."
>
> (I, 96)

Nevertheless, such physical brutality can be found in many of Morris's works, right down to his later socialist lyrics, and any full evaluation of his medievalism must take into account the contrarieties of his imagination, its fascination with force as well as beauty and its need to reconcile this primitive vitality with a sense of brotherhood and order.

Perhaps the most important aspect of Morris's early medievalism lies in the founding and practices of Morris, Marshall, and Faulkner, the firm that originated in his need to supply himself with well-designed furnishings for his house. Morris and Company bears the same relation to the doctrines that Morris had inherited from Ruskin that Disraeli's political activities bear to the program of Young England. It is an apparent carrying out and a modification of theory in actual practice. Ruskin had called for a revival of the Gothic; Morris's designs were usually medieval. Ruskin had called for the reuniting of the artist and the artisan; Morris was never happier then when he was dyeing or weaving. Ruskin had called for the elimination of machinery; the whole career of Morris and Company is a flight from the urban and the industrial. And yet, it will not do to oversimplify, for the firm realized neither the profundities of Ruskin's thought or even its more superficial aims.

According to the prospectus of the firm, issued in 1861, the company's aim was to create "work of genuine and beautiful character," which would satisfy "the luxury of taste rather than the luxury of costliness."[23] Although the firm's most famous production was to be its wallpapers, initial manufactures included mural decoration, carvings, stained glass, metal work, and furniture. The first three of these productions depended to a large degree for their success on the Anglo-Catholic revival, which had created a whole new market for medievally oriented ornaments. Embroidered altar cloths were also a subsidiary Morris product, again closely associated with ritualism. According to Philip Henderson, the fortunes of the company dated to the acclamation its furniture, stained glass, and tapestries received in the Medieval Court of the International Exhibition at South Kensington in 1862, for which the firm was accorded two medals.[24] Nevertheless, despite the firm's medieval proclivities, Morris and Company was far from doctrinaire in its use of medieval techniques and materials. The famed Morris chair was simply a traditional Sussex design of relatively recent

[23] Quoted in Henderson, *William Morris*, p. 67.
[24] *Ibid.*, p. 70.

provenance, and the firm's catalogs listed a number of Queen Anne tables and cabinets. Even the seemingly medieval items of furniture and design were only loosely imitative, though Morris throughout his manufacturing career was perfecting his knowledge of medieval crafts and designs by studying the collections and acquisitions of the newly founded South Kensington Museum. As always, medievalism in action lacked the purity of medievalism in theory.

Nor could Morris really maintain in his company the form of economic organization in which he gradually came to believe. Although Morris tried in later years to institute a form of profit-sharing among his key workers, most of whom were local people, he did so only half-heartedly, fearing that such palliative measures simply helped one or two more workingmen become capitalists instead of destroying the whole class system altogether. His wages and working conditions were high, but not as high as his ultimate aims. He could not achieve egalitarianism in the division of labor, either. Morris soon discovered that not every worker had the gift for free and joyous carving that Ruskin had described. He himself, for example, never learned to do animal shapes properly and had to have them done for him. Nor could the Morris and Company designs really revitalize English art from the roots. They were created by a rich man for the use of other rich men. Only secondarily did Morris's creativity recharge and reform the existing order, and it did this by improving the taste of the very machine-made goods that he and Ruskin despised.

The real significance of Morris and Company in terms of Morris's later development was not so much in what it produced or what it achieved as in what it taught Morris about himself and the uses to which he could put his energies. The anecdotes that have come down about Morris's activities in the firm emphasize his participation in the company's creations. Were there wallpapers to design? Morris designed them. Altar cloths to embroider? Morris embroidered them. Tapestries to weave? Morris wove them. Fabrics to dye? Morris not only dyed them but discovered new colors and new fixatives as well, turning himself blue to the elbows for some weeks in his experiments with indigo. His industry was incredible and unceasing.

Whatever the causes of Morris's activity—whether in the contradictions of his exuberant personality or the frustrations of his marriage —his happiness in artisanship was one of the central realities of his life. Undertaken for the firm or performed solely for himself, his pleasure in handicrafts made vivid for him the lessons of Carlyle and Ruskin. "Produce! Produce!" Carlyle had said, "Were it but the pitifullest infinitesimal fraction of the Product, produce it in God's name . . . Whatsoever thy hand findeth to do, do it with thy whole might. Work while it is called today; for the Night cometh wherein no man can work." [25] Ruskin, too, asserted the necessity for work and its relationship to the underlying order of the universe. He claimed, as we have seen, that modern life had separated thought from labor and turned England's once-free craftsmen into wretched and servile laborers. What Carlyle and Ruskin wrote, Morris lived. There is no understanding the medievally oriented future he projected without the realization that joyous labor is at its heart. More important than the destruction of the class structure, the assurance of comfort for all, and the restoration of a natural existence that characterize Morris's socialism is his demand for an existence made meaningful through work and art—through work, that is, not separated from either physical or creative satisfaction. Setting up three criteria for useful work— "hope of rest, hope of product, hope of pleasure in the work itself"— he comes increasingly to claim that modern life has robbed the worker of all three (XXIII, 99). It has made man's life a cyclic misery in which he toils to live that he may live to toil.

Perhaps the first step toward Morris's mature realization of what the Middle Ages had meant to the common man and what the future could be again came during the journey he took to Iceland in 1871. With his attraction to the vigorous and the violent, Morris was understandably drawn to the stern dramatism of Icelandic scenery and the stoical hardihood of its people. Significantly for his later views, he wrote that the one lesson he had learned from the classless Icelandic society, and that he had learned thoroughly he hoped, was "that the

[25] Thomas Carlyle, *Works of Thomas Carlyle*, Edinburgh edition, 30 vols. (New York: Scribners, 1903–1904), XVII, 104.

most grinding poverty is a trifling evil compared with the inequality of classes."[26] He retained to the end of his life his respect for the sturdy Icelandic peasant, who held on to his personal and economic independence in the face of adverse conditions—a kind of latter-day "hard primitive." Also Icelandic or Scandinavian in origin was the idea of the *Ragnarok*, or day of judgment, when good will triumph over evil in great battle and a new order will be founded. This idea of judgment day, which he encountered in his study of the sagas, found its way into his major literary works of the seventies, his translation of *Sigurd the Volsung*, and it may have provided the imaginative framework for the socialist ideal of revolution.

Two seemingly unrelated issues in which Morris became involved in the mid-1870s also prepared the way for his eventual adherence to a medievalistic socialism. One was Anti-Scrape, or the Society for the Protection of Ancient Buildings. On the surface, the organization, which was founded to combat the destruction of ancient churches and buildings in the name of restoration, was purely esthetic in intent. Morris had been horrified in September 1876 by the sight of a church in Oxfordshire being torn down for improvements and had immediately begun to make plans for action. The sight of another church, half a year later, undergoing similar depredations led to the formation of SPAB (called Anti-Scrape because of its protests against the scraping clean of old stonework). Philosophically, the organization followed the doctrines of Ruskin and Pugin since it denied the capacity of a mechanical era to restore the handwork of an earlier age. Morris defended the doctrines of Anti-Scrape by explaining that the earlier architecture had been great because it was the joyous product of the people themselves and that it could only be damaged by self-conscious and studied restoration. In speaking out against such indefatigable restorers as the English Gilbert Scott and the French Viollet-le-Duc, Morris firmly reasserted the doctrine of organic growth. He decried the "fatal practice of 'restoration,' which in a period of forty years has done more damage to our ancient buildings than the preceding three cen-

[26] Quoted in Paul Thompson, *The Work of William Morris* (New York: Viking, 1967), p. 29.

turies of revolutionary violence, sordid greed (utilitarianism, so called), and pedantic contempt" (XXII, 320). Anti-Scrape was also important in showing Morris national treasures being treated as private commodities, with no realization of their significance for the people as a whole. In protesting against this one manifestation of his society, Morris came gradually to protest that society as a whole.

Morris was also shocked into revolution by England's foreign policy in the 1870s. He was bolted out of his previous political complacency by the news that England was about to go to war with Russia in support of Turkey. His letter to the Liberal *Daily News*, written on October 24, 1876, expresses his horror at Disraeli's aligning the nation with the "thieves and murderers" of Turkey and his realization that it is the "quiet men [like himself] who usually go about their own business, heeding public matters less than they ought, who must now take action against oppression." [27] As a member of the Eastern Question Association formed to oppose Disraeli's policies, Morris came to know many radical labor leaders and through them came to see the connection between war and capitalism. As he wrote in a later essay, "That is how we live now with foreign nations, prepared to ruin them without war if possible, with it if necessary, let alone meantime the disgraceful exploiting of savage tribes and barbarous peoples on whom we force at once our shoddy wares and our hypocrisy at the cannon's mouth" (XXIII, 7).

In 1883 Morris enrolled as a member of the Social Democratic Federation, the first of the socialist groups to which he belonged. How much Morris was indebted to Marxism for his ideas, or how much he understood of Marxist economics, has been a matter of some question. He read *Das Kapital* in its French translation and, while sometimes claiming that he was more a socialist of the heart than of the head, made ample use of Marx's historical chapters both in his lectures and the two visionary novels, *A Dream of John Ball* and *News from Nowhere*. Morris could have had little difficulty, work-oriented as he was, in absorbing Marx's labor theory of value nor could he have had any problems in appreciating Marx's diatribes against English working

[27] Quoted in Henderson, *William Morris*, p. 274.

conditions. To the generous Morris, the famed "last hour" economics of Nassau Senior and the classical English school, which saw the manufacturers' profits resting on the final moments of his workmen's exertions, must have seemed as cruel and absurd as it did to Marx. And the Marxist realization of the way in which modern capitalism forced the allegedly free laborer to sell the whole of his productive life, his capacity for work, for the price of life's necessary commodities, certainly finds frequent statement in Morris's later works, motivated in part by a rich man's sense of guilt:

> As I sit at my work at home, which is at Hammersmith, close to the river, I often hear some of that ruffianism go past the window of which a good deal has been said in the papers of late . . . . As I hear the yells and shrieks and all the degradation cast upon the glorious tongue of Shakespeare and Milton, as I see the brutal reckless faces and figures go past me, it rouses the recklessness and brutality in me also, and fierce wrath takes possession of me, till I remember, as I hope I mostly do, that it was my good luck only of being born respectable and rich, that has put me on this side of the window among delightful books and lovely works of art, and not on the other side, in the empty street, the drink-steeped liquor-shops, the foul and degraded lodging. I know by my own feelings and desires what these men want. What would have saved them from this lowest depth of savagery: employment which would foster their self-respect and win the praise and sympathy of their fellows, and dwellings which they could come to with pleasure, surroundings which would sooth and elevate them; reasonable labour, reasonable rest. (XXII, 171–72)

One thing reading Marx probably did for Morris was to turn his attention to the latter part of the Middle Ages, particularly the fourteenth century, which Marx saw as the most prosperous period that labor has ever known and the dividing point between feudalism and capitalism. While well aware of the restrictiveness of the guilds, Marx saw them trying to restrain the development of capitalism during the fourteenth and fifteenth centuries by strictly limiting the number of laborers that could be employed by one master and thus effectively limiting the accumulation of capital. That this movement failed was for Marx a tragic episode in the class struggle. Writing of the demise of the guild system, Marx found, though no friend of the medieval revival, that the laboring classes had lost much at the ending of the Middle Ages: "Hence the historical movement which changes the producers into wage workers, appears on the one hand, as their emancipation from serfdom and from the fetters of the guilds.... But on the other hand, these new freedmen became sellers of themselves only after they had been robbed of all their own means of production, and of all the guarantees of existence afforded by the old feudal arrangements. And the history of this, their expropriation, is written in the annals of mankind in letters of blood and fire."[28] Using Cobbett as one of his references, Marx went on to show how the spoliation of the Church during the Protestant Reformation further led to the development of capitalism and the degradation of the proletariat.

Through Marx and through the so-called Germanic school of historians, the mature Morris began to interest himself in the late Middle Ages rather than in the chivalric period which had occupied his imagination as a young man. He began concerning himself with the issues that were occupying such contemporary medieval historians as Bishop Stubbs, Edward Freeman, and John Richard Green. They included such questions as the primitive democracy of the open-field system, the liberties of the late medieval towns, and the relationship between the craftsman and the guild. It is still possible to see the influence of Ruskin and other earlier medievalists on Morris's work at this time, but his perceptions have been modified by other insights. He still frequently makes the medieval-modern contrast in his writings of the eighties and nineties, but he is beginning to contrast different things than his predecessors. Placing more emphasis than any previous medievalist since James Thomson, perhaps, on the primitive Germanic period, Morris praises the Anglo-Saxons for their hardihood and liberty and claims that the Norman invasion was a tragedy because

[28] Karl Marx, *Capital, A Critique of Political Economy*, ed. Frederick Engels, rev. Ernest Untermann, Modern Library edition (New York: Random House, 1906), p. 786.

it replaced the great northern heritage of English literature with the inferior Romance tradition and, what was worse, substituted the hierarchy of feudalism for the early fellowship of free men. Unlike the other writers in the medievalist tradition, Morris is opposed to feudalism, for, unlike them, he does not believe that men are either irrational or unequal. For him no "illusions" are necessary to sustain society. Comradeship and reason are enough. And no paternal control is necessary since natural man is good.

Morris's comments on history tend to slough over the period from the Norman Conquest to the fourteenth century. But he is very explicit about the fourteenth century. For him, as for Karl Marx, it is the golden age. Coming independently to the same conclusion that Thorold Rogers made in his famous *Six Centuries of Work and Wages* (1884), Morris sees the fourteenth century as a period of rough plenty in which large numbers of serfs first managed to free themselves from bondage to the land and came to the towns as journeymen or free laborers. As the corporations of the towns increased their powers, these laborers associated themselves into guilds. Although Morris thinks there was some rivalry between the more aristocratic trade guilds and the craft guilds, he states that for the most part the history of the guilds is the "history of the people in the middle ages." By the late fourteenth century, he continues, the crafts guilds had won out, not only against their rivals but against the violence and tyranny of the times and the hierarchical spirit of feudality. For a brief moment, as shown in art, architecture, and everyday existence, English life was communal and beautiful. He writes:

> Not seldom I please myself with trying to realize the face of mediaeval England; the many chases and great woods, the stretches of common tillage and common pasture quite unenclosed; the rough husbandry of the tilled parts, the unimproved breeds of cattle, sheep, and swine . . . , the strings of packhorses along the bridle-roads . . . ; the little towns well bechurched, often walled; the villages just where they are now, . . . but better and more populous; their churches, some big and handsome, some small and curious, but all crowded with altars and furniture, and gay with pictures and ornaments; the many religious houses . . . the

beautiful manor houses.... How strange it would be to us if we could be landed in fourteenth-century England. (XXIII, 61–62)

Morris explains the decline of England after the fourteenth century by the rise of the spirit of commercialism. At first, he says, after the Black Death had made labor a vital and valuable commodity, the landlords tried to refeudalize England and turn the yeomen and free laborers back into serfs again. Failing this, they discovered other methods of profit-making. The landlords began to turn the peasants off the land so that they could enclose it for pasture. Thus land, which had once been used to create the useful and varied abundance of the medieval diet was now turned over to a single crop, wool, which meant "money and the breeding of money" (XXIII, 56).

Moreover, instead of the relatively well-treated medieval serf, England began to develop what she still had—a proletariat class working for its masters in a fashion which "exploits him very much more completely than the customs of the manor of the feudal period" exploited the serf (XXIII, 57). It is to saving the proletariat class, working without joy and living without dignity, that Morris's socialism is devoted. For him no half measures will do, whether the palliations of Tory, Whig, or Democrat. Only the revolution can bring release.

In many ways Morris's analysis of the coming of modern society resembles those of the earlier medievalists, who thought that the substitution of commerce for chivalry marked the end of the Middle Ages. In holding such a view he demonstrates how the Romantic recoil against materialism was still operating at the end of the century. His analysis of the change seems closest, in specific details, to that in Southey's *Colloquies*, where Thomas More, as Southey's spokesman, repeats what he had said in his *Utopia* two hundred years before, that the enclosure movement was the chief agent of the change. But it is interesting to note the dissimilarities between Morris's Marxist approach and that of the earlier writers. For all that Morris discusses the plight of the modern worker, he is not particularly interested in his poverty. Economic conditions were sufficiently improved toward the end of the nineteenth century for him to bypass this aspect of

the labor problem. It is the unhappiness of the worker, his dehumaniza-
tion, his dislike for his work, that distresses Morris, just as it had earlier
distressed Ruskin. However, while Ruskin clings to an almost patho-
logical paternalism as a solution, Morris rejects the whole feudal
tradition. He has no fear of revolution. The French Revolution,
Peterloo, Chartism, are merely historical episodes to him, not part
of his experience as they had been for earlier medievalists. His only
experience of revolution, the Paris Commune of 1871, fills him with
hope. Both temperament and experience thus unite to make him seek
something different from what earlier writers had sought in the Middle
Ages—a communal rather than a feudal state, and a society governed
by fellowship rather than fatherhood. For him, medieval life is simple,
primarily pastoral, and very beautiful.

Particularly in that elusive quality, tone, Morris is closer to Cobbett
than to any other medievalist. Even his insistence on handicrafts
more often resembles that of the *Cottage Economy* than *The Stones of
Venice*. It is therefore not surprising to find Mackail writing that
Morris was devoted to Cobbett, with whom he shared many tastes
and prejudices, and whose *Rural Rides* he knew almost by heart. And
May Morris says he used to quote extensively to his children from the
Cottage Economy and *Advice to Young Men*.

Morris's romance, *A Dream of John Ball* (1888), which begins with
a reference to Cobbett's love for "the sweeping Wiltshire downs,"
develops in fictional form the historical thesis of his essays. The
dreamer, who narrates the tale, falls by some magic into Morris's
favorite period, the fourteenth century—and a beautiful time it is.
The fields are still unhedged and the little hamlets are set among rich
tillage, orchards, and copses. The churches are still new, the fresh
dust of their carvings is still visible on the grass; and their white spires
pierce the blue sky or gleam silver in the moonlight. The villagers
are dressed in bright robes or simple black mantles, "rough looking
fellows, tall and stout, very black some of them, and some red-haired,
but most had hair burnt by the sun into the color of tow . . . merry
and good-tempered" (XVI, 219)—traditional hard primitives.

The reason Morris gives for Wat Tyler's rebellion, which is just getting under way as the dreamer arrives on the scene, is that the lords want to turn all men except guildsmen or men on free lands back into villeins again so that they can turn the high cost of labor to their own profit without actually having to work themselves. Interestingly enough, in the light of Lord John Manners's *A Plea for National Holy-Days*, one of the nobles' chief ends is to reduce the number of holy days, a move that strikes at the joy and freedom of the medieval workman. In opposition to this move are Morris's rebellious heroes: Wat, "the valiant tiler of Dartmouth," and John Ball, the strangely prescient apostle of a socialist creed.

Ball's main theme is the importance of fellowship. "Fellowship is heaven," he says, "and lack of fellowship is hell." Although he does not know it, "the proud despiteous rich man . . . is in hell already, because he hath no fellow" (XVI, 230–31). Ball views history from a Marxist viewpoint. The story of the world for him is the eternal quarrel of the rich and poor, and, as the poor grow more numerous and therefore more powerful, the rich grow more frightened and more cruel. Once the poor have gathered courage to rebel, however, all may be well. Ball therefore instructs his followers in the aims of revolution:

> "And how shall it be then when these are gone? What else shall ye lack when ye lack masters? Ye shall not lack for the fields ye have tilled, nor the houses ye have built, nor the cloth ye have woven; all these shall be yours, and whatso ye will of all that the earth beareth; then shall no man mow the deep grass for another, while his own kine lack cow-meat; and he that soweth shall reap, and the reaper shall eat in fellowship the harvest that in fellowship he hath won; and he that buildeth a house shall dwell in it with those that he biddeth of his free will; and the tithe barn shall garner the wheat for all men to eat of when the seasons are untoward, and the rain-drift hideth the sheaves in August; and all shall be without money and without price. Faithfully and merrily then shall all men keep the holidays of the Church in peace of body and joy of heart. And man shall help man, and the saints in heaven shall be glad, because men no more fear each other; and the churl shall be ashamed, and shall hide his churlishness till it be gone,

and he be no more a churl; and fellowship shall be established in heaven and on the earth." (XVI, 237)

Ball tells his followers that only their own weakness can cause their defeat. In a speech which Morris is clearly aiming at contemporary moderates who believe that the problems of society can be solved gradually by parliamentary means, Ball warns against the lords and councilors who, with soft speech, will suggest remedies and reforms, for they will undermine the revolution.

In a series of dialogues with John Ball, the dreamer explains that just such a betrayal will occur and that the revolt will fail of its final aims, precisely because the masses will be cozened into submission. He then goes on to discuss the new forms of serfdom—or wage slavery—that will replace the old. He says that Ball is "'fighting against villeinage which is waning, but they shall fight against usury which is waxing'" (XVI, 274). His descriptions of capitalism give Morris the opportunity to create a satiric situation through the use of Ball as a naïve observer. Ball, for instance, thinks that after his revolution has made those that labor stronger and stronger, "all men shall finally labor and live and be happy and have the goods of the earth without price." But the narrator tells him that the lords of the earth will take over the sources of wealth and compel the poor to serve them to survive. Bell then argues that no man would "sell himself and his children into thralldom uncompelled." But the narrator answers that insufficiency of opportunity will force men to sell their services at ever lower rates until the gap between rich and poor becomes unbridgeable. Ball next wonders why so many slaves do not rise up against their masters. The narrator answers by explaining that the complication of production beyond the means of simple hand-worked tools has forced the worker to sell himself to the "forestallers and regraters" who own the means of production. The priest finally concludes that the dreamer's tale must be true because no man could invent such a tale of folly as the dreamer has told him.

Despite these gloomy prognostications, the book ends with an almost messianic prophecy by the dreamer of the final triumph of labor. He tells John Ball to "'be of good cheer; for the Fellowship of Men shall endure, however many tribulations it may have to wear through.'" In the end, he says, after they have become brave enough to revolt "'men shall have the fruits of the earth and the fruits of their toil thereon, without money and without price'" (XVI, 286).

The dreamer's vision is fulfilled in Morris's Utopian romance, *News from Nowhere* (1890). Here the situation inverts that of *John Ball*. In the earlier work the dreamer falls into the medieval past and uses that past to criticize the future. In *News from Nowhere* the dreamer topples into the future, after the promised revolution has successfully taken place, and his vision of this newly beautiful future accentuates the ugliness and squalor of the present. What makes the book particularly interesting is that Morris's twenty-first-century Utopia closely resembles his conception of fourteenth-century England—without feudalism, however. Machinery has been abolished except for the most unpleasant tasks, and the fields lie open again, unhedged and fertile. Salmon and swans have returned to the clear and sparkling Thames. Men and women wear bright robes or doublets and hose, and the cottages are simply half-timbered or made of stone and thatch.

The chief medieval mythic virtue that Morris gives to his Utopia is joy in work. The boatman who rows the dreamer across the Thames cannot understand why anyone should try to pay him for doing such delightful work. But when he is bored with rowing, he goes upland for a while and helps in the harvesting. This, too, is delightful, for the wheat has ripened under the mellow autumn sun in fields brilliant with poppies and cornflowers. All the houses are beautiful, with bright tiles and carved seats and trestles. Everywhere the dreamer looks, he sees joy in life expressing itself in joyous creation. Death and sin are almost unknown in this idyllic, almost timeless land. Characters live on and on in an atmosphere free from sickness or decay; the one crime that occurs in the story, an accidental manslaughter, brings such tragic remorse to the mind of the murderer that his friends want only to console, not punish, him for his offense.

Utopia has been achieved, of course, through the only possible means—revolution. In conversation with an elderly antiquarian, the dreamer tells of the horrors of nineteenth-century England and learns of the great general strike and revolution that brought it to an end. What John Ball dreamed of has been brought to pass by the means he thought necessary, and men dwell together in fellowship, freedom, and joy.

To criticize Morris's Utopia on practical grounds is pointless. It is like criticizing a myth. Several commentators have discussed Morris's interest in the *Ragnarok*, the great conflict between good and evil after which Balder shall come again. It would probably also be valuable to trace the influence on his thought of the equivalent Christian doctrine of the apocalypse—the great destruction of the earth which shall precede the coming of the New Jerusalem. Although Morris was a professed agnostic in his maturity, it is interesting to speculate how much of a messianic residue was left from his early religious upbringing to be revived by his reading of Marx. Certainly the quest for a land of security and peace is an element in all Morris's writings beginning with *The Earthly Paradise* (1868, 1870), in which he describes the quest for immortality. In his early works the Edenic vision serves as a contrast to the violence and ugliness presented in such poems as "Haystack in the Flood"; in the later works it serves as a counterpoise to the ugliness of society itself.

A few of Morris's other late works are worth mentioning as examples of his continuing belief in the need for a violent purging of society. In *A King's Lesson*, the king of Hungary learns by doing it how hard the peasants' work is. One of his councilors asks him why he does not, then, reorder society on a more equitable basis. His answer is that if he tried to do so his nobles and the other kings would throw him in the madhouse. Morris's moral seems to be that you cannot trust the ruling class to reform itself, that only the worker can change society.

Although Morris denied that they were allegories, several other late works have clear allegorical sentiments. *The House of the Wolfings* and *The Roots of the Mountains* both bear on the theme of freedom and revolt. *The House of the Wolfings*, apparently set in the very early Middle Ages, tells of the revolt of some Germanic tribes against their Roman masters and of the subsequent restoration of their ancient liberties. *The Roots of the Mountains* is more concerned with economics. It tells of the freeing of the serfs of Silverdale by the free men of Burgdale, or—the analogy seems inescapable—of the workers of England by the members of the socialist party.

Because of Morris's idealistic view of human nature he is always drawn to democracy rather than benevolent despotism. In many of his stories the founding or reinstitution of a parliament, or "mote-stead," by freemen is the climax of the story. Here, for example, is the hallowing of the Folk-Mote from *The Roots of the Mountains:* "'Herewith I hallow-in this Folk-Mote of the Men of the Dale, and the Sheepcotes, and the Woodland. . . . Now let not the peace of the Mote be broken. Let not man rise against man. . . . If any man break the Peace of the Holy Mote, let him be a man accursed, a wild beast in the Holy Places, an outcast from home and hearth, from bed and board, from mead and acre" (XV, 279).

In discussing Morris's medieval romances, George Bernard Shaw, with his usual astringency, summed up the reaction of the next generation to Morris's medievalism and perhaps to much of the medieval revival in general. He described the productions of the Kelmscott Press as "all the troubadour romance of chivalry and love," which he said Cervantes had rightly "condemned to the flames as pernicious trash."[29] Shaw's reaction seems typical of the general reaction of the twentieth century, not only against medievalism but against the entire Romantic attitude toward life. And yet, Shaw was far from rejecting the message that lay beneath Morris's medievalism. Politically, he thought, Morris was a "prophet and a saint."[30]

Nor was Shaw the only important twentieth-century figure who admired Morris and his ideas. His impact can be seen on Fabianism in general and on the British Labour party, too. Curiously enough, Ruskin was also an acknowledged patron of the Labourites. Clement Attlee claimed that both Ruskin and Morris affected his viewpoint, and a questionnaire circulated in 1906 among twenty-nine Labourite

[29] George Bernard Shaw, *William Morris as I Knew Him* (New York: Dodd Mead, 1936), p. 33.
[30] *Ibid.*, p. 52.

members of Parliament revealed that *Unto This Last* was among the most influential works they had ever read. How widespread was that influence is shown by the fact that it had sold 100,000 copies by 1910; how far-flung, by the fact that Gandhi claimed that reading it was a turning point in his life. Ruskin's and Morris's views of art and taste in literature did not survive the death of romanticism, but their vision of a joyous and creative society has still not lost its relevance, and perhaps not even its influence.

7

The Failure of the Vision: Adams

PERHAPS THE PERVASIVENESS of medievalism is best symbolized by the fact that even Wemmick, the efficient little law clerk in *Great Expectations*, lived with his Aged P. in a little Gothic house, with a moat, a drawbridge, "the queerest gothic windows . . . and a gothic door almost too small to get in at."[1] Although Dickens seems merely humorous in his descriptions of the "castle," there is a meaning behind the four-foot moat, the sham windows, and the tiny door. Just because it is inexpedient, Gothic architecture becomes a symbol in this book of the human and the emotional, just as Sleary's circus does in *Hard Times*. Wemmick, it may be remembered, has special sentiments to go with his Gothic cottage—"Walworth sentiments" he calls them— and they are far different from the purely utilitarian ones he manifests in Mr. Jaggers's office. Cut off from the harsh world by his little moat, he manifests his underlying goodness of heart in his absurdly tender ministrations to the Aged P. and his romantic attentions to Miss Skiffins.

Although Dickens twists the Gothic revival here to suit his own particular purposes, its very ability to be so twisted points out its essential linkage with the broad range of antiutilitarian thinking. This study has mainly concentrated on the use of the Middle Ages as an ideal, but medieval materials were also used for entertainment and escape. The Gothic novel continued to be popular throughout the century, and the historical novel, derived from Scott, was a persistent

[1] Charles Dickens, *The New Oxford Illustrated Dickens*, 21 vols. (London: Oxford University Press, 1963), XIII, 195.

literary form, practiced by such diverse authors as Ainsworth, Bulwer-Lytton, and Kingsley. Kingsley's *Hereward the Wake*, it might be noted, fuses hard primitivism with muscular Christianity—an odd combination that once again points up the pervasiveness of medievalism. If one broadens, as one must, the definition of medievalism to include an interest in archaic customs, then William Barnes's poetry, Thomas Hardy's novels, and many other works which either describe or allude to England's past would have to be included. Even into the twentieth century such regional literary movements as the Irish Renaissance, whose use of Celtic folklore in part depended on earlier scholarship, continued as offshoots of the medieval revival.

Another aspect of the revival, which has been studied in such books as Maynadier's *The Arthur of the English Poets*,[2] is the continued use of Arthurian material. Tennyson's *Idylls of the King* is, of course, the chief work of that genre; and it is consequently important to see why, since it idealizes Arthur, it is nevertheless still not a manifestation of the medieval ideal. The main reason is that Tennyson's Camelot is not medieval, but symbolic. In spite of its superficial trappings, Arthur's kingdom is really of no specific time or place. If anything, it is simply Victorian England in costume, just as Arthur sometimes seems to be Hallam, or even Christ himself, in chain mail. What Tennyson wants to present are the passions and foibles of men and their strengths; the medieval setting is only a literary device. Nor can it be said that Tennyson does otherwise in his two history plays with medieval subject matter, *Harold* and *Becket*. Neither idealize medieval society. Far from it, they again show it as a microcosmic rendition of the problems of faith and government that beset England, or mankind, in any age.

None of the other medieval poems by major Victorian authors really belong to the medieval ideal, either. Browning's "Childe Roland," Arnold's *Tristram and Iseult*, Swinburne's *Tristram of Lyonesse*, to name only a few, are all set in the Middle Ages; but the medieval

---

[2] See Howard Maynadier, *The Arthur of the English Poets* (Boston: Houghton Mifflin, 1906), pp. 314–348, for a discussion of Arthurian works of the late eighteenth, nineteenth, and early twentieth centuries.

background is only a foil for the author's own attitudes and emotions. Is it not Arnold's Iseult who utters one of the best statements ever made of nineteenth-century despair in her description of

> ... the gradual furnace of the world
> In whose hot air our spirits are upcurl'd
> Until they crumble, or else grow like steel.[3]

And yet Iseult's very outcry against the drabness of life and the inability of man alone to withstand the hostile forces of the universe points straight at the heart of the medieval movement. Trace the medieval movement where one will—in the chivalry of Scott, the religion of Coleridge, the hero worship of Carlyle, the esthetics of Ruskin, the socialism of Morris—and always, in spite of the greatest seeming contradictions, the root is the same. All are implicitly using the Middle Ages as a symbol of a creative universe in which human energy can manifest itself freely, purposefully, generously. For Scott it was a world in which society was bound together by personal loyalty; for Coleridge, a period of meaningful belief; for Carlyle, a time when men could freely give their freedom to a leader; for Morris, a time when free men lived joyously together. For Ruskin, as we have seen, it was very explicitly a period when the organization of society mirrored the structure of nature.

The metaphysical assumption of the medieval revival, then, was that the universe had meaning and could be made to have meaning for man as long as his society was rightly ordered. Such a right ordering, or reordering, of society along lines different from previous laissez faire approaches, did indeed occur. Modified by necessity, the social ideals of medievalism culminated in Tory paternalism, on the one hand, and the semisocialist welfare state on the other. Philosophically, however, the revival did not fare so well. Ruskin attempted a coherent vision; but his vision of life could not withstand the onslaughts of modernity. Materialism, atomism, determinism, all opposed it. Henry Adams's *Mont-Saint-Michel and Chartres* is the culminating work

[3] Matthew Arnold, *The Poetical Works of Matthew Arnold* (London: Oxford University Press, 1961), p. 153.

of the medieval revival; it is also the bitterest proof of its failure. For Adams's book once again tells us that the creative society can only be based on faith; but it shows that even in the Middle Ages, such faith could not exist.

For other reasons, too, *Mont-Saint-Michel and Chartres* is a significant volume with which to close this study. Just as the book itself seems to express the meaning of all preceding medievalism, so Adams's lifelong interest in the Middle Ages seems to have led him, although an American, to recapitulate almost the whole history of the medieval revival. Quite as compactly as his experiences sum up the other beliefs that shaped nineteenth-century thought—transcendentalism, positivism, Darwinism, Marxism—they also embody its medievalism. Thus, a survey of his readings and his friendships not only reintroduces the familiar medievalist figures but introduces some new ones as well.[4]

II

With appropriate symbolism, Adams began drifting toward the Middle Ages in an eighteenth-century environment. He wrote that "the happiest hours in the boy's education were passed in summer lying on a musty heap of Congressional Documents in the old farmhouse at Quincy, reading 'Quentin Durward,' 'Ivanhoe,' and 'The Talisman,' and raiding the garden at intervals for peaches and pears."[5] How much Adams was affected by Scott is hard to say, but, like the rest of his century, he never seems to have escaped the influence of the great romancer. It is significant that in his old age Adams wrote that he wished "Sir Walter Scott were alive to share" his medieval studies with him since "he is my only companion in these fields."[6]

[4] Since Adams is American and committed, almost by birth, to a belief in democracy, the neofeudal aspects of the medieval movement interest him only slightly. In a sense, he helps us see more clearly what the essential meaning of the movement was.

[5] Henry Adams, *The Education of Henry Adams*, Modern Library edition (New York: Random House, 1931), p. 39.

[6] Henry Adams, *Letters of Henry Adams, 1858–1918*, ed. Worthington C. Ford, 2 vols. (Boston: Houghton Mifflin, 1930–1938), I, 615; hereafter cited as Ford, *Letters*.

His youthful readings also included Goethe and Thomas Gray in addition to some volumes of early English ballads and a book of Scandinavian mythology. As a boy he had heard his father read aloud from Tennyson and Longfellow, both of whom made considerable use of medieval material.

Perhaps the first specific influence on Adams's later medievalism was James Russell Lowell, whose Dante course Adams took at Harvard and who remained a lifelong friend. Lowell's conception of the Middle Ages stressed the idea that it was a period of faith. In spite of Ruskin's arguments to the contrary, Lowell stressed the idea that the Gothic arch was a symbol of aspiration. In phrases which suggest the final paragraph of *Mont-Saint-Michel*, he wrote that "the Middle Ages instinctively typified [themselves] in the Gothic cathedral, —no accidental growth but the visible symbol of an inward faith,— which soars forever upward, and yearns toward heaven like a martyr-flame suddenly turned to stone."[7] Lowell's poem, "The Cathedral," which appeared in 1870, reads like a foreshadowing of Adams's descriptions of Chartres. Particularly significant is Lowell's interpretation of the Middle Ages as a time when the uncertainties of modern science had not yet intruded themselves upon a believing universe:

> Is old Religion but a spectre now,
> Haunting the solitude of darkened mind,
> Mocked out of memory by the sceptic day?
> Is there no corner safe from peeping Doubt,
> Since Gutenberg made thought cosmopolite,
> And stretched electric thread from mind to mind?
>
> . . . .
>
> This nineteenth century with its knife and glass
> That made thought physical, and thrust far off
> The Heaven so neighborly with man of old,
> To voids sparse-sown with alienated stars.[8]

[7] James Russell Lowell, *The Writings of James Russell Lowell*, 12 vols. (Boston: Houghton Mifflin, 1892–1899), IV, 234–235.

[8] James Russell Lowell, *The Complete Poetical Works of James Russell Lowell* (Boston: Houghton Mifflin, 1895), p. 354.

Although the neofeudalist view of a medievally paternal state was never important to Adams, he was also too keenly aware of the limitations of democracy not to be interested in it. As his early readings and enthusiasms show, he managed temporarily to dilute his faith in Mill and Tocqueville with a strong draught of Carlyle and Ruskin, adopting their central ideas and discarding all that was of purely English relevance. "Reading in College," an article that Adams wrote as a senior for the *Harvard Magazine*, recommends Carlyle to the attention of his fellow students, and the 1858 catalog of his library shows that he owned a copy of *Past and Present*. The volume, which is preserved in the Adams Collection at the Massachusetts Historical Society, contains a significant marginal penciling next to Carlyle's defense of the soldier. "But he of the red coat," Adams marked for future reference, "is a success and no failure." Other institutions had perished or become ineffectual; mankind had become disorganized and disreputable; but in the army, with its feudal notion of authority and hierarchy, Carlyle saw hope for transforming "multiform ragged losels, runaway apprentices, starved weavers, thievish valets" into "straight-standing, firm-set individuals." The passage that Adams marked is followed by a question with which Carlyle challenged the whole philosophy of laissez faire. Why can there not be, he asked, "an army ninety-thousand strong, maintained and fully equipt, in continual real action and battle against Chaos, Necessity, Stupidity"?[9] Believer in democracy though he was, the young Bostonian seems to have paused to think about this question.

In his undergraduate article, Adams also recommended reading Ruskin and apparently continued to collect his works for many years since his library contains many of his works. These books contain practically no marginal annotations, and Adams, at sixty, derided Ruskin as one of the "preposterous British social conventions." But his admission that he once "read Ruskin and admired"[10] him and the very nature of *Mont-Saint-Michel* show that he never escaped his

[9] Thomas Carlyle, *Past and Present* (London, 1845), p. 350. This is the edition that Adams used.

[10] Ford, *Letters*, II, 3, 468.

influence. Ruskin's belief that a civilization can be judged by its art underlies all Adams's reasonings about the Middle Ages, and his division of Venetian culture into its Byzantine, Gothic, and Renaissance phases anticipates Adams's tripartite use of Romanesque, Transition, and Gothic to trace the rise and fall of medieval culture. Indeed, Ernest Samuels is quite correct in asserting that Ruskin's influence is apparent even in the verbal texture of *Mont-Saint-Michel*.

Many of Adams's basic ideas about the Middle Ages closely resemble Ruskin's. His assertion that "nine churches out of ten actually were dead born after the thirteenth century,"[11] is clearly Ruskinian, as is Adams's belief that the materialistic philosophy of the nineteenth century was an insufficient base for either art or politics. His metaphor that the world had fallen into the hands of the "Jews" is essentially an unattractive version of Ruskin's statement that the world had been taken over by the "Goddess of Getting On." While Ruskin, however, hoped to remake the present by a revivifying contact with the past, Adams had no such hope. Nor did he share Ruskin's belief in a natural order for which feudal society had been a metaphor.

Adams's two years in Germany after his graduation from Harvard in 1858 introduced him to the lingering enchantments of medieval architecture and helped prepare him for contact with the English esthetic movement. "Think me spooney, if you will," wrote Adams, "but last evening as I wandered round ... in these delightful old peaked, tiled, crooked, narrow, stinking lanes I thought that if ever again I enjoy as much happiness as here in Europe ... why then philosophers lie and earth's a paradise." He added that he had "passed the day in a couple of great churches, lying on the altar steps and looking at the glorious stained-glass windows with their magnificent colors and quaint Biblical stories."[12]

During the seven years, from 1861 to 1868, that he spent in England as his father's secretary, Adams managed to meet a number of artists and critics who further refined his medieval sensibilities: Swinburne,

[11] Henry Adams, *Mont-Saint-Michel and Chartres* (Boston: Houghton Mifflin, 1933), p. 103.
[12] Ford, *Letters*, I, 46.

who talked to him of Dante and Villon; Thomas Woolner, who was a member of the Pre-Raphaelite Brotherhood; and Stopford Brooke, whose interests in Anglo-Saxon and Middle English literature may later have stimulated Adams. One of the most interesting of the acquaintances was Sir Francis Palgrave, whom Adams termed "much the greatest of all the historians of early England." [13] Palgrave's essay, "Fine Arts in Florence," written in 1840, had anticipated and very likely influenced some of Ruskin's ideas and may have affected Adams as well. Palgrave argued that architecture formed a "perpetual commentary on the pages of the historian," [14] an idea that Adams was to apply again and again in his writing. His son, Francis Turner Palgrave, editor of *The Golden Treasury*, a brilliant and ferocious critic, was also interested in medievalism, especially as applied to the architecture of the Gothic Revival. Writing in 1898, Adams insisted that it was Turner's rigorous judgment that had formed his tastes in art, just as it had been his college friend Henry Hobson Richardson, student of the indomitable Gothic restorer Viollet-le-Duc, who first taught him about medieval architecture.

Perhaps the most important medieval influence, however, was not a person but a place—Wenlock Abbey, which belonged to his friend Charles Milnes Gaskell. Built in the Middle Ages along the rugged slopes of Wenlock Edge, the abbey seemed to annihilate time. Mrs. Adams described it romantically and nostalgically: "We dine in . . . the old refectory, with a winding stone staircase leading from the kitchen. These rooms open into a low arched corridor which is all mullion windows, and at the end are Henry's and my room which are in the old Norman wing—eight hundred years old . . . I feel as if I were a fifteenth-century dame and newspapers, reform, and bustle nowhere." [15] At Wenlock, Adams admitted, he slipped back into the eighteenth-century appreciation of the picturesque and, like the heroine of *Northanger Abbey*, "yearned for nothing so keenly as to

[13] Adams, *Education*, p. 214.

[14] Sir Francis Palgrave, *The Collected Historical Works of Sir Francis Palgrave*, ed. R. H. Inglis Palgrave, 10 vols. (Cambridge: Cambridge University Press, 1919), X, 368.

[15] Marian Hooper Adams, *The Letters of Mrs. Henry Adams: 1865–1883*, ed. Ward Thoron (Boston: Little Brown, 1936), pp. 17–18.

feel at home in a thirteenth-century Abbey unless it were to haunt a fifteenth-century Prior's house." [16]

Adams's early reading and his English experiences probably gave him the habit of medieval thought, which, like the habit of classical allusion, indicates the degree to which a mind has become steeped in another culture. However, before Adams's medievalism could become more than a superficial mannerism, several other influences had to intervene. First, it was necessary for him to become disillusioned with his own society; second, for him to develop a personal need for the faith that the Middle Ages seemed to offer; and third, for him to acquire real competence in medievalism. The story of Adams's disillusion with his own society can be found in *The Education;* his need for faith, while expressed in such writings as *Esther* and "The Prayer to the Virgin of Chartres," really belongs to the reticences concerning the death of his wife. The third influence, however—the way in which Adams developed his medieval expertise—is important here, for it shows how Adams came to know and use contemporary medieval scholarship.

Much of Adams's knowledge came from his years of teaching at Harvard. Although in keeping with Harvard's interest at the time in attracting able nonacademicians, the appointment is still puzzling, and President Charles Eliot's explanation that no one in America knew more about medieval history than Adams did, still seems about the best. The scientific study of medieval sources was still young on the Continent and had not yet crossed the Atlantic. With an exposure to German method behind him, Adams was at least one generation ahead of his colleagues in approach, if not in knowledge, and no one would supersede him until some of his own students became teachers themselves. Even though he claimed that "the only merit of [his] instruction has been its originality; one hundred youths . . . have learned facts and theories for which in after life they will hunt the authorities in vain," [17] his teachings unquestionably bore fruit. Well into the twentieth century, Harvard records show no dissertations

[16] Adams, *Education*, p. 228.
[17] Henry Adams, *Henry Adams and His Friends: A Collection of His Unpublished Letters*, ed. Harold Dean Cater (Boston: Houghton Mifflin, 1947), p. 54.

in medieval history except those seeming to arise from the basic syllabus that Adams had laid down.[18]

Although Adams later claimed that it was not any recollection of the "dreary Anglo-Saxon law" he taught at Harvard that led him to understand the Cathedral of Chartres, his years as a historian strongly affected his medieval education. For one thing, the mere accumulation of facts slowly taught him to see the Middle Ages as a living era. For another, as Max Baym has pointed out, his rereading of the romantic historian Michelet reinforced that ability to dramatize historical scenes that he had previously observed in Sir Walter Scott. Michelet also strengthened for him the basic medievalist assumption that historical facts can be arranged to show a pattern. This desire had previously been expressed by such historical philosophers as Comte and Saint-Simon, whose conception of historical phases also influenced Adams's later thought. However, in spite of his persistent romanticism, Adams was at least equally influenced by the German school of "scientific historians," whose works he read during the 1870s. Their new canons of history were symbolized by Leopold von Ranke's earlier statement that the historian must tell it like it was—*"wie es eigentlich gewesen ist."* Adams encountered these new attitudes both in the works of German writers on the Middle Ages and in the books of their English disciples, such as Freeman and Stubbs. It was to such writers that Adams turned in his teaching, for the Germanic method, with its emphasis on origins and sources, helped satisfy his desire for a historical approach that would bring the Middle Ages into the mainstream of evolution from the past to the present.

Adams's purposes as a historian are clearly shown in his discussion of the "Anglo-Saxon Courts of Law" in the *Essays in Anglo-Saxon Law* (1876), a venture in co-operative scholarship, in which Adams and three of his students traced the origins of English democracy back to the customs of Germanic and Anglo-Saxon tribes. Although the

---

[18] See *Doctors of Philosophy and Doctors of Science of Harvard University, 1873–1926* (Office of the Registrar of Harvard University), XXIII (Nov. 30, 1926), no. 39.

restrictions of purely historical writing did not allow him to digress, Adams saw in the decentralized Anglo-Saxon hundreds a resemblance to his grandfather's eighteenth-century concept of federated states. And he may well have imagined a parallel between Edward the Confessor, who introduced the "worst maxims of government into England,"[19] and what he himself had been saying recently about Ulysses Simpson Grant. In both the eleventh and nineteenth centuries, the reason for the change was the same: power always rushes toward a common center, all states move toward centralization. Adams realized that this centralization, although it promoted political efficiency, hastened "the decay of . . . democratic institutions, which could only be safe in states so small that the popular assembly could actually include the body of free men."[20] This fear of bigness became more typical of Adams as he grew older. It came to include not only his distrust of the modern, megalithic state but his whole terror of multiplicity—of meaningless, uncontrollable force.

By the time he was forty, then, Adams had followed his century through many of the phases of its medieval vision—feudalism, estheticism, historiography. Nevertheless, he had to augment his information to write *Mont-Saint-Michel*, for the generation after he resigned his professorship in 1877 had been an important one for medieval scholarship. When he began writing in the late 1890s, he prepared himself by intensive reading and note-taking in the newest books on medieval architecture, literature, and philosophy. He familiarized himself with the recently published work in literature of Gaston Paris and Gaultier de Coincy and increased his architectural knowledge by reading such works as the Abbé Bulteau's *Monographie de la Cathédrale de Chartres* and Corroyer's slightly older *Déscription de l'Abbaye du Mont-Saint-Michel*. As Adams himself wrote in 1899, his rooms were "a school of romanesque literature," with volumes strewn about the floor and his dinner guests floundering "in architecture on all the chairs."[21]

[19] Henry Adams, *Essays in Anglo-Saxon Law* (Boston, 1878), p. 52.
[20] *Ibid.*, p. 4.
[21] Ford, *Letters*, II, 246.

Although heavily underscored, none of these architectural volumes was read with anything like the concentration that Adams gave to two books on medieval philosophy, *S. Thomas D'Aquin et la Philosophie Cartésienne*, by Père Eli Maumus, and *De la Philosophie Scholastique*, by Bartelemy Hauréau. The margins of these books (preserved in the Library of the Massachusetts Historical Society) were insufficient for Adams's outlines and arguments, and his penciled marginalia run over the flyleaves and on to separate sheets of paper inserted between the leaves. That Adams, while serious, was not always reverent and obviously dissatisfied with Maumus's inability to satisfy his desire for unity, is shown by some of his remarks in the book on St. Thomas. He comments: "Certainly one admits at once that a want of logic is an imperfection of the mind, whether in Père Maumus or in S. Thomas, but who is responsible for the imperfection of the mind? Surely not Père Maumus? Perhaps his parents? and so on to the first cause."[22] In another place, intolerably distressed by Maumus's want of logic, he simply explodes: "Imbécile! Embryon! Maniaque! Va!"[23]

One of the most important sources for Adams's final formulation of his medievalism in *Mont-Saint-Michel and Chartres* was his brother Brooks Adams's book, *The Law of Civilization and Decay*, which he read in 1893. Brooks saw history as the alternating reigns of two types of men: the imaginative man, the priest, the soldier, the artist; and the economic man, the capitalist, the usurer, the bourgeois. (In other words, the chivalric man and the calculator.) In the first phase woman was dominant; in the second her value fell, for "the monied magnate rarely ruins himself for love."[24] As applied to the Middle Ages, Brooks's theories had a special relevance for Adams, since Brooks had discovered Chartres long before his brother had. In 1896 he wrote to Henry from Normandy: "Of course everything pales before my discovery of the meaning of the Gothic in 1888, which was to me a revelation. My intense excitement when first I began to read Chartres, and Le Mans,

[22] Marginalia in Elisée-Vincent Maumus, *S. Thomas D'Aquin et la Philosophie Cartésienne*, 2 vols. (Paris, 1890), I, 370.

[23] Maumus, *S. Thomas D'Aquin*, II, 64.

[24] Brooks Adams, *The Law of Civilization and Decay* (New York: Knopf, 1951), p. 340.

and all the rest, could never be equalled again by anything."[25] The medieval cathedrals that he "read" were obviously the artifacts of an imaginative society. In medieval Christendom the imaginative man was supreme, and Woman was worshipped in the guise of the Virgin. As it appeared in art, the belief took on for a time the purest form that man had ever known.

Unfortunately, Brooks asserted, the initial purity of the Gothic was soon sullied by the triumph of the economic man. The cathedral became a mere investment, since the burgher, who had succeeded to the power of the priest and the soldier, began to demand that the stained glass for which he paid so dearly contain portraits and perspective rather than saints and symbols. With the ending of the Middle Ages, Brooks Adams feared that art had died forever: "No poetry can bloom in the arid modern soil, the drama has died, and the patrons of art are no longer even conscious of shame at profaning the most sacred of ideals. The ecstatic dream which some twelfth-century monk cut into the stone of the sanctuary, hallowed by the presence of his God, is reproduced to bedizen a warehouse; or the plan of an abbey which Saint Hugh may have consecrated, is adapted to a railway station."[26]

Divested of their economic phraseology, Brooks's theories clearly resemble those of Ruskin with which Adams had long been familiar. In fact, they show that both brothers' books, for all their originality, fit into the mainstream of nineteenth-century medievalism, since what they are doing is contrasting a believing, heroic past with a skeptical, materialistic present. Unlike their predecessors, however, they find no hope in the vision. The earliest medievalists had thought that a reapplication of medieval ideals would bring about a resurgence of the good life and the good society. The Adamses saw only decay. Living on into the twentieth century, Henry Adams claimed that degradation, not progress, was the law of history; just as entropy, not evolution, was the law of science. He thought that the Middle

[25] Thornton Anderson, *Brooks Adams: Constructive Conservative* (Ithaca: Cornell University Press, 1951), p. 44.
[26] Brooks Adams, *Law of Civilization and Decay*, p. 349.

Ages might be used as "the unit from which he might measure motion down to his own time."[27]

III

Adams's historical theory about the Middle Ages as "the point in history when man held the highest idea of himself as a unit in a unified universe" is stated so explicitly and in so many places in his *Education* that it can scarcely be missed or misunderstood. The philosophical position taken up in *Mont-Saint-Michel* is, however, more complicated and, since it is never didactically stated, is easily misinterpreted. One of Adams's biographers, Elizabeth Stevenson, sees the Virgin Mary as the "true center of his study,"[28] and from an emotional standpoint she is undoubtedly correct. Adams, however, characterizes the book differently. He says that "the Virgin and St. Thomas are my vehicles of anarchism."[29] What he means by this—and it is the whole meaning of the book—is that the Middle Ages are part of a complicated and dramatic proof that man cannot live in a universe that is at once rational and free. Using the Middle Ages themselves to deny the basic premise of all medievalism, Adams goes on to show that individualism, freedom, and creativity are logically impossible—and always were.

Adams devotes a major part of the book to showing that the idealization of the Virgin represented medieval man's great effort to be at home in the universe. The ample, unreasoning faith of the Romanesque period—faith represented by the bold placing of Mont-Saint-Michel above the perilous sea—had proved too unsophisticated and perhaps too harsh to last. The full glare of the divine judgment was too strong for men to bear. Hoping for a more personal relation with that mysterious energy called God, they pointed the spires of the churches heavenward toward the Court of Mary the Queen and interposed the warm blues and reds of the stained glass she loved between themselves and

[27] Adams, *Education*, p. 435.
[28] Elizabeth Stevenson, *Henry Adams: A Biography* (New York: Macmillan, 1955), p. 328.
[29] Ford, *Letters*, II, 444.

the cold white radiance of the Godhead. Man wanted to count in the universe, not as an atom, but as an individual. Logic and experience asserted that he was worthless and damned. Knowing that only irrational and infinitely merciful love could save him, he invested the wealth of his world for a hundred years to propitiate not the Trinity— the awful God, the judging Christ, the mysterious Holy Ghost—but the Virgin Mary.

Through iconography, history, legend, and miracle story, Adams tries to portray the comfort the twelfth century found in the Virgin. She is the devoted mother who steps down from her pedestal to retrieve the stone Christ child that another mother had stolen. She is the compassionate queen who stoops to fan a jongleur's forehead. She is the understanding woman who conceals the indiscretions of an erring nun. He even tells us directly what she meant: "Mary concentrated in herself the whole rebellion of man against fate; the whole protest against divine law; the whole contempt for human law as its outcome; the whole unutterable fury of human nature beating itself against the walls of its prison house, and suddenly seized with the hope that in the Virgin man had found a door of escape .... To her, every suppliant was a universe in itself, to be judged apart, on his own merits, by his love for her—by no means on his orthodoxy, or his conventional standing in the Church" (273–74). It is easy to see, then, why the Virgin is a "vehicle of anarchism," although to define anarchy requires a complex series of substitutions. By anarchy is meant love, emotion, individualism. And individualism in turn suggests decentralization— the world of the Anglo-Saxon hundred rather than of the powerful Norman state, the America of the eighteenth rather than the twentieth century. By extension, she is a symbol for Adams of those simpler, kinder worlds that "sensitive and timid natures could regard without a shudder."[30]

Adams was too tough-minded a thinker, however, to rest content with an irrationality, even an inevitable one. Although overshadowed by the section of the book that deals with Mary and the literature and architecture that she inspired, the chapters on scholastic philosophy

[30] Adams, *Education*, p. 505.

are equally important. In his search for a philosophy that would assert both the importance of the individual and the reality of God (by which he meant unity and meaning in life), Adams dismissed the solutions of both William of Champeaux and Peter Abelard. Champeaux, he decided, submerged the individual in the pantheistic flux of God, while Abelard reduced the concept of order to a purely subjective image projected by man against the darkness of the universe. Neither the realism of the one nor the nominalism of the other satisfied man's dual need for freedom and order; for the universe of Champeaux was determinist, while the universe of Abelard was chaotic. Looking for a new synthesis, Adams turned his attention to the scholasticism of St. Thomas, his other "vehicle of anarchism."

According to Adams (and it is important to notice his deliberately mechanistic vocabulary), Aquinas's first step in reasoning about man and God was to say, "'I see motion . . . I infer . . . a motor'" (347). He believed that all the energies in the world could eventually be traced back to God, "an intelligent, fixed prime motor—not a concept or proved by concepts—a concrete fact, proved by the senses of sight and touch." Streaming outward, God's energy creates and sustains at every moment everything existing in the world. "Whatever has form is created, and whatever is created takes form directly from the will of God, which is also his act. The intermediate universals— the secondary causes—vanish as causes; they are at most, sequences or relations; all merge in one universal act of will; instantaneous, infinite, eternal" (351). Nothing whatever intervenes between God and man.

Logical, dynamic, masculine, St. Thomas's world was the opposite of the one envisioned by the worshippers of Mary. The warm hues of her stained glass windows melted into nothing before the irradiating brilliance of his Deity. God flooded the universe, and, though He was scarcely as merciful as the Virgin, He was always present for every man. By eliminating the distance between man and God, Thomas had saved both the existence of Unity and the dignity of the individual. He seemed for a moment, at least, to provide the aging Adams with a philosophy that gave meaning to freedom. But there was a defect in

Aquinas's cathedral of faith (the metaphor is Adams's), and all his elaborate vaulting and buttressing could only lighten the strain. For, if God sustained man at every moment, then how, Adams inquired, could the will ever be free? The mind might pause, accumulate energy, and then act, but the sustaining energy was always God's, the predetermination always his.

No wonder, then, that Adams called the Virgin and St. Thomas his "vehicles of anarchism." Between them they proved that if man were to be free, it must be in an irrational universe such as Mary ruled over; and that if the universe were to be logical, it must be one so permeated with God that man could not be free. Far from using an idealized Middle Ages to prove the significance of man, Adams's used the medieval experience to show that human freedom was only a childish whim and that the past, like the present, showed only the inevitability of determinism.

Even so, however, the medieval view was more cheerful than the modern one, for the progress of knowledge had revealed that Aquinas's hopeful assumption that the prime motor was intelligent, purposive, and benevolent was not necessarily true. The only prime motor that the modern world knew was blind force, symbolized by the dynamo, which Adams addressed in his "The Prayer to the Virgin of Chartres" as a compelling but meaningless power. Modern man might well say with St. Thomas, "'I see motion . . . I infer . . . a motor,'" but his concept of force was purely mechanical. He could not even be sure that man could reduce "all motion to one source or all energies to one law" (347). For St. Thomas's God, the twentieth century could only return a verdict of "not proven."

It is significant that the last page of *Mont-Saint-Michel and Chartres* reintroduces the image so familiar to nineteenth-century medievalism of the Gothic arch as a symbol of aspiration. But unlike his predecessors, he shows, not its strength, but its precariousness. The delicate balance of such architecture, he writes, "the slender nervure, the springing motion of the broken arch, the leap downwards of the flying buttress . . . never let us forget that Faith alone supports it, and that, if Faith fails, Heaven is lost" (377). All through the century men had thought that they might renew that faith through a study of the Middle Ages. But Adams, writing at the end of the tradition, was forced by contemporary science, history, and philosophy to see that using the Middle Ages to prove that man could regain a harmonious and creative existence depended on the belief the universe was fundamentally meaningful. As Adams proved to his own dismay—and the dismay foreshadowed the pessimism of the new century—men may once have believed and acted as if the universe were meant for them. But their beliefs and actions had no basis in logic.

With Adams's fundamental and devastating attack on the concept of an ordered universe, medievalism turns back upon itself, and instead of being the basis for a fundamentally optimistic world view becomes instead the grounds for the bleakest pessimism. Adams not only suggests that Eden cannot be, but that Eden, except for one brief, self-deluding moment, never was. Nothing that Adams said or did could detract from the tremendous influence that the medieval movement had upon men's concepts of the role of the state and the structure of modern society. But medievalism was also a part of a broader movement, expressing in both literary and practical form the hopes of men to live in a world that satisfied their deepest needs for freedom and order, creativity and coherence. For these aspirations, *Mont-Saint-Michel and Chartres* is a beautiful, but tragic, statement of failure.

Bibliography

Adams, Brooks. *The Law of Civilization and Decay.* New York: Alfred A. Knopf, 1951.

Adams, Eleanor N. *Old English Scholarship in England from 1566–1800.* Yale Studies in English, Vol. LV. New Haven: Yale University Press, 1917.

Adams, Henry. *The Education of Henry Adams.* Modern Library. New York: Random House, 1931.

———. *Esther.* New York: Scholars' Facsimiles and Reprints, 1938.

———. *Henry Adams and His Friends: A Collection of his Unpublished Letters.* Edited by Harold Dean Cater. Boston: Houghton Mifflin, 1947.

———. *Letters of Henry Adams, 1858–1918.* Edited by Worthington C. Ford. 2 vols. Boston: Houghton Mifflin, 1930–1938.

———. *Mont-Saint-Michel and Chartres.* Boston: Houghton Mifflin, 1933.

———, ed. *Essays in Anglo-Saxon Law.* Boston: Little Brown, 1878.

Adams, Marian Hooper. *The Letters of Mrs. Henry Adams: 1865–1883.* Edited by Ward Thoron. Boston: Little Brown, 1936.

Akenside, Mark, and Beattie, James. *The Poetical Works of Akenside and Beattie, with a Memoir of Each.* Boston: Houghton Mifflin, [188–].

Allen, B. Sprague. *Tides in English Taste (1619–1800).* 2 vols. Cambridge, Mass.: Harvard University Press, 1937.

Anderson, Thornton. *Brooks Adams: Constructive Conservative.* Ithaca: Cornell University Press, 1951.

Andrews, Keith. *The Nazarenes: A Brotherhood of German Painters in Rome*. Oxford: The Clarendon Press, 1964.

Arnold, Matthew. *The Poetical Works of Matthew Arnold*. London: Oxford University Press, 1961.

Baillie-Cochrane, Alexander. "In the Days of the Dandies, III: The Young England Party," *Blackwood's Edinburgh Magazine*, CXLVI (March, 1890), 313–330.

Barnes, Harry E. *A History of Historical Writing*. Norman, Okla.: University of Oklahoma Press, 1937.

Baym, Max I. "The 1858 Catalog of Henry Adams' Library," *Colophon*, III (Autumn, 1938), 483–489.

————. *The French Education of Henry Adams*. New York: Columbia University Press, 1951.

Beers, Henry A. *A History of English Romanticism in the Eighteenth Century*. New York: Henry Holt, 1899.

————. *A History of English Romanticism in the Nineteenth Century*. New York: Henry Holt, 1901.

Blake, Robert. *Disraeli*. New York: Doubleday, 1968.

Bowles, William Lisle. *Annals and Antiquities of Lacock Abbey in the County of Wilts*. London, 1835.

————. *Parochial History of Bremhill in the County of Wilts*. London, 1828.

————. *Poetical Works*. Edited by George Gilfillan. 2 vols. Edinburgh, 1855.

Brinton, Crane. *English Political Thought in the Nineteenth Century*. London: Ernest Benn, 1933.

————. *The Political Ideas of the English Romanticists*. London: Oxford University Press, 1926.

Bulmer-Thomas, Ivor. *The Growth of the British Party System*. 2nd ed. 2 vols. London: John Baker, 1967.

Burke, Edmund. *The Complete Works of Edmund Burke*. Vols. III and V. London, 1803–1827.

Burne-Jones, Georgiana. *Memorials of Edward Burne-Jones*. 2 vols. London: Macmillan, 1906.

Calder, Grace J. *The Writing of Past and Present: A Study of Carlyle's*

Manuscripts. Yale Studies in English, Vol. 112. New Haven: Yale University Press, 1949.

Cargill, Oscar. "The Mediaevalism of Henry Adams," in *Essays and Studies in Honor of Carleton Brown.* New York: New York University Press, 1940.

Carlyle, Edward Irving. *William Cobbett: A Study of His Life as Shown in His Writings.* London: A. Constable, 1904.

Carlyle, Thomas. *Thomas Carlyle: Letters to His Wife.* Edited by Trudy Bliss. Cambridge, Mass.: Harvard University Press, 1953.

———. *Carlyle's Unfinished History of German Literature.* Edited by Hill Shine. Lexington, Ky.: University of Kentucky Press, 1951.

———. *The Correspondence of Thomas Carlyle and Ralph Waldo Emerson, 1834–1872.* Edited by Charles Eliot Norton. Riverside edition. 2 vols. Boston and New York, 1894.

———. *Early Letters of Thomas Carlyle, 1814–1826.* Edited by Charles Eliot Norton. London, 1886.

———. *Letters of Thomas Carlyle, 1826–1836.* Edited by Charles Eliot Norton. 2 vols. London and New York, 1889.

———. *Letters of Thomas Carlyle to His Youngest Sister.* Edited by Charles Townsend Copeland. Boston and New York, 1899.

———. *New Letters of Thomas Carlyle.* Edited by Alexander Carlyle. 2 vols. London and New York: J. Lane, 1904.

———. *Reminiscences by Thomas Carlyle.* Edited by James Anthony Froude. New York, 1881.

———. *The Works of Thomas Carlyle.* Edinburgh edition. 30 vols. New York: Charles Scribner's Sons, 1903 1904.

Carnall, Geoffrey. *Robert Southey and His Age: The Development of a Conservative Mind.* Oxford: The Clarendon Press, 1960.

Catalogue of the Library of the Late Robert Southey . . . by Messrs. Leigh Sotheby and Company. 1844.

Cazamian, Louis. *Carlyle.* Les grands écrivains étrangers. Paris: Bloud et cie., 1913.

Chadwick, Owen, ed. *The Mind of the Oxford Movement.* Stanford: Stanford University Press, 1960.

Chesterton, G. K. *William Cobbett*. London: Hodder and Stoughton, 1925.

Clapham, J. H. *An Economic History of Modern Britain 1820–1850*. Vol. I. 2nd ed. Cambridge: The University Press, 1950.

Clark, Sir Kenneth. *The Gothic Revival*. Rev. and enlarged ed. New York: Charles Scribner's Sons, 1950.

Cobban, Alfred. *Edmund Burke and the Revolt against the Eighteenth Century*. London: George Allen and Unwin Ltd., 1929.

Cobbett, William. "Address to the Men of Norwich," *Cobbett's Weekly Political Register*, XXXI (Jan. 18, 1817), 80–86.

————. *The Autobiography of William Cobbett*. Edited by William Reitzel. New ed. London: Faber, 1947.

————. *Cobbett's Legacy to Labourers*. London, 1835.

————. *Cobbett's Legacy to Lords*. London, 1863.

————. *Cobbett's Legacy to Parsons*. 6th ed. London, 1835.

————. *Cobbett Selections*. Introduction by A. M. D. Hughes. Oxford: Oxford University Press, 1923.

————. *Cottage Economy*. New ed. London, 1823.

————. *A History of the Protestant Reformation in England and Ireland*. 2 vols. London, 1829.

————. *A History of the Protestant Reformation in England and Ireland*. Edited by Francis Aidan, Cardinal Gasquet. New York, n.d.

————. "Letter to Lord John Russell," *Weekly Political Register*, LII (Oct. 16, 1824), 129–151.

————. *The Opinions of William Cobbett*. Edited by G. D. H. and Margaret Cole. London: The Cobbett Publishing Co., 1944.

————. *Rural Rides*. Edited by G. D. H. and Margaret Cole, 3 vols. London: P. Davies, 1930.

————. *Selections from Cobbett's Political Works*. Edited by John M. Cobbett and James P. Cobbett. 6 vols. London, n.d.

————. "To the British Catholic Association," *Cobbett's Weekly Register*, LII (Oct. 30, 1824), 256–287.

Cole, G. D. H. *The Life of William Cobbett*. 3rd ed. rev. London: Home and Vanthal, 1947.

Coleridge, Samuel Taylor. *Coleridge's Miscellaneous Criticism.* Edited by Thomas Raysor Middleton. London: Constable, 1936.

———. *The Complete Works of Samuel Taylor Coleridge.* Edited by W. G. T. Shedd. 7 vols. New York, 1884.

———. *Letters of Samuel Taylor Coleridge.* Edited by Ernest Hartley Coleridge. 2 vols. Boston and New York, 1895.

———. *Letters.* Selected, with an introduction by Catherine Raine. London: Gray Walls Press, 1950.

Coulton, G. G. *Ten Medieval Studies.* Boston: Beacon Press, 1959.

Cullum, Sir John. *The History and Antiquities of Hawsted and Hardwick.* 2nd ed. London, 1813.

Dawson, Christopher. *The Spirit of the Oxford Movement.* New York: Sheed and Ward, 1933.

Dicey, A. V. *The Statesmanship of Wordsworth.* Oxford: The Clarendon Press, 1917.

Dickens, Charles. *The New Oxford Illustrated Dickens.* Vol. XIII. London: Oxford University Press, 1963.

Digby, Kenelm Henry. *The Broad Stone of Honour, or the True Sense and Practice of Chivalry.* 4 vols. London, 1846.

Disraeli, Benjamin, earl of Beaconsfield. *The Radical Tory: Disraeli's Political Development Illustrated from his Original Writings and Speeches.* Selected and edited by H. W. J. Edwards. Preface by G. M. Young. London: Cape, 1937.

———. *Selected Speeches of the Late Right Honourable, the Earl of Beaconsfield.* Edited by T. E. Kebbel. 2 vols. London, 1882.

———. *The Works of Benjamin Disraeli, Earl of Beaconsfield.* Empire edition. 20 vols. London and New York: M. Walter Dunne, 1904.

Disraeli the Younger [Benjamin Disraeli]. *The Revolutionary Epick.* London, 1834.

Doctors of Philosophy and Doctors of Science of Harvard University, 1873–1926. Office of the Registrar of Harvard University. XXIII (Nov. 30, 1926), no. 39.

Eastlake, Sir Charles. *A History of the Gothic Revival.* London: Longmans Green, 1872.

Eden, Sir Frederick Morton, *The State of the Poor.* 3 vols. London, 1797.

Eggar, J. Alfred. *Remembrances of Life and Customs in Gilbert White's, Cobbett's, and Charles Kingsley's Country.* London: Simpkin, Marshall, Hamilton, Kent and Co., 1924.

Elton, Oliver. *A Survey of English Literature, 1780–1880.* Vol. III. New York: Macmillan, 1920.

Evans, Joan. *John Ruskin.* New York: Oxford University Press, 1954.

Fairchild, Hoxie Neale. *The Romantic Quest.* New York: Columbia University Press, 1931.

Farley, Frank Edgar. *Scandinavian Influences in the English Romantic Movement.* Studies and Notes in Philology and Literature, Vol. IX. Boston: Ginn, 1903.

Fay, C. R. *Great Britain from Adam Smith to the Present Day.* London: Longmans Green, 1928.

Ferrey, Benjamin. *Recollections of A. N. Welby Pugin.* London, 1861.

Fredeman, William E. *Pre-Raphaelitism: A Bibliocritical Study.* Cambridge, Mass.: Harvard University Press, 1965.

Froude, James Anthony. *Thomas Carlyle: A History of the First Forty Years of His Life, 1795–1835.* Vol. II. New York, 1882.

Froude, Richard Hurrell. *Remains of the Reverend Richard Hurrell Froude.* 4 vols. London, 1838–1839.

George, M. Dorothy. *England in Transition: Life and Work in the Eighteenth Century.* Baltimore: Penguin Books, 1965.

Gent, Thomas. *The Antient and Modern History of the Loyal Town of Rippon.* York, 1773.

Gentleman's Magazine (Sept., 1861), pp. 328–330.

The Germ: Thoughts toward Nature in Poetry, Literature, and Art. Portland, Me.: Thomas B. Mosher, 1898.

Gillies, Alexander. *Herder.* Modern Languages Studies. Oxford: B. Blackwell, 1945.

Gooch, George Peabody. *History and Historians in the Nineteenth Century.* 2nd ed. New York: Peter Smith. 1949.

Great Britain. *Hansard's Parliamentary Debates.* 3rd series. Vols. CXVI (1843)–CXXVIII (1845).

Grennan, Margaret Rose. *William Morris: Medievalist and Revolutionary.* New York: King's Crown Press, 1945.

Grierson, H. J. C. *Sir Walter Scott, Bart.* New York: Columbia University Press; London: Constable and Co., 1938.

————, ed. *Sir Walter Scott Today.* London: Constable and Co., 1932.

Gwynn, Denis. *Lord Shrewsbury, Pugin, and the Catholic Revival.* London: Hollis, 1946.

Haferkorn, Reinhard. *Gotik und Ruine in der englischen Dichtung des achtzehnten Jahrhunderts.* Leipziger Beiträge zür englischen Philologie, no. 4. Leipzig: B. Tauschnitz, 1924.

Halévy, Elie. *A History of the English People in the Nineteenth Century.* Translated by E. I. Watkin. 2nd rev. ed. 6 vols. London: E. Benn, 1949–1952.

Hallam, Henry. *View of the State of Europe during the Middle Ages.* New ed. 3 vols. London, 1872.

Haller, William. *The Early Life of Robert Southey, 1774–1803.* New York: Columbia University Press, 1917.

Hammond, J. L., and Hammond, Barbara. *The Village Labourer, 1760–1832.* 4th ed. London: Longmans, Green, and Co., 1927.

Harper, George McLean. *William Wordsworth: His Life, Works, and Influence.* 2 vols. New York: Charles Scribner's Sons, 1916.

Harrold, Charles Frederick. *Carlyle and German Thought: 1819–1834.* Yale Studies in English, Vol. LXXXII. New Haven: Yale University Press, 1934.

Hart, Francis R. *Scott's Novels: The Plotting of Historic Survival.* Charlottesville: University of Virginia Press, 1966.

Henderson, Philip. *William Morris: His Life, Work, and Friends.* New York: McGraw-Hill, 1967.

Herder, Johann Gottfried. *Outlines of a Philosophy of the History of Man.* Translated by T. Churchill. 2 vols. London, 1803.

Herford, C. H. *The Age of Wordsworth.* London: George Bell, 1908.

Hillhouse, James T. *The Waverley Novels and Their Critics.* Minneapolis, Minn.: University of Minnesota, 1936.

Hough, Graham. *The Last Romantics.* London: Gerald Duckworth, 1949.

Houghton, Walter E. *The Victorian Frame of Mind, 1830–1870.*

New Haven: Yale University Press, 1957; London: Oxford University Press, 1957.

Housman, Laurence. "Pre-Raphaelitism in Art and Poetry," in *Essays by Divers Hand, Being the Transactions of the Royal Society of Literature of the United Kingdom*. New Series. Edited by R. W. Macan. Vol. XII. London: Oxford University Press, 1933.

Howitt, William. *The Rural Life of England*. 2nd ed. London, 1840.

Hunt, John Dixon. *The Pre-Raphaelite Imagination*. Lincoln: University of Nebraska Press, 1969.

Hunt, William Holman. *Pre-Raphaelitism and the Pre-Raphaelite Brotherhood*. 2 vols. New York: Macmillan, 1905–1906.

Hurd, Richard. *Hurd's Letters on Chivalry and Romance*. Edited by Edith J. Morley. London: Henry Frowde, 1911.

Ironside, Robin. *Pre-Raphaelite Painters*. With a Descriptive Catalog by John Gere. New York: Phaidon, 1948.

James, William, and Malcolm, Jacob. *General View of the Agriculture of the County of Surrey . . . Drawn up for the Board of Agriculture*. London, 1794.

Kegel, Charles Herbert. "Medieval-Modern Contrasts Used for a Social Purpose in the Work of William Cobbett, Robert Southey, A. Welby Pugin, Thomas Carlyle, John Ruskin, and William Morris." Ph.D. dissertation, Michigan State University, 1955.

Laslett, Peter. *The World We Have Lost: England Before the Industrial Age*. New York: Scribners, 1965.

Lindley, Dwight Newton. "The Saint-Simonians, Carlyle, and Mill: A Study in the History of Ideas." Ph.D. dissertation, Columbia University, 1958.

Lingard, John. *The History of England*. 3rd ed. 14 vols. London, 1825–1831.

Lipson, E. *The Economic History of England*. Vol. II. 5th ed. London: Black, 1931.

Lockhart, John Gibson. *Memoirs of the Life of Sir Walter Scott*. 5 vols. Boston and New York: Houghton, Mifflin and Co., 1902.

Lovejoy, Arthur O. "The First Gothic Revival and the Return to

Nature," *Modern Language Notes*, XLVII (Nov., 1932), 419–446.

Lowell, James Russell. *The Complete Poetical Works of James Russell Lowell*. Boston: Houghton Mifflin, 1895.

———. *The Works of James Russell Lowell*. Boston: Houghton Mifflin, 1892–1899.

Lukács, Georg. *The Historical Novel*. Translated by Hannah Mitchell and Stanley Mitchell. Boston: Beacon Press, 1963.

Lyra Apostolica. Edited by H. C. Beeching. London: Methuen, n.d.

Macaulay, Thomas Babington. *Critical and Historical Essays Contributed to the Edinburgh Review*. 5th ed. Vol. I. London, 1848.

———. *The History of England from the Accession of James II*. Vol. I. Everyman edition. London, n.d.

Mackail, John William. *The Life of William Morris*. 2 vols. in 1. New York: Longmans Green, 1922.

MacLean, Kenneth. *Agrarian Age: A Background for Wordsworth*. Yale Studies in English, Vol. 115. New Haven: Yale University Press, 1950.

Malden, Henry Elliot. *A History of Surrey*. London: E. Stock, 1900.

Manners, Lady John [Janette (Hughan) Manners, duchess of Rutland]. *How the Heir's Coming of Age was Kept at Lamington*. Edinburgh and London, 1886.

Manners, Sir John. *England's Trust and Other Poems*. London, 1841.

———. *A Plea for National Holy-Days*. London, 1842.

Manuel, Frank E. *The New World of Henri Saint-Simon*. Cambridge, Mass.: Harvard University Press, 1956.

Marx, Karl. *Capital, A Critique of Political Economy*. Edited by Frederick Engels. Revised by Ernest Untermann. Modern Library Edition. New York: Random House, 1906.

Maumus, Elisée-Vincent. *S. Thomas D'Aquin et la Philosophie Cartésienne*. 2 vols. Paris, 1890.

Mead, George Herbert. *Movements of Thought in the Nineteenth Century*. Edited by Merritt H. Moore. Chicago: University of Chicago Press, 1936.

Mee, Arthur, ed. *Surrey: London's Southern Neighbour*. London: Hodder and Stoughton, 1938.

Mill, John Stuart. *Autobiography*. The World's Classics. London: Oxford University Press, 1952.

——. *The Spirit of the Age*. Introduction by F. A. von Hayek. Chicago: University of Chicago Press, 1942.

Monypenny, William Flavelle, and Buckle, George Earl. *The Life of Benjamin Disraeli, Earl of Beaconsfield*. 6 vols. New York: Macmillan, 1911–1920.

Morris, William. *The Collected Works of William Morris*. Introduction by May Morris. 24 vols. London: Longmans Green, 1910.

Needler, G. H. *Goethe and Scott*. Toronto: Oxford University Press, 1950.

Neff, Emery. *Carlyle*. New York: W. W. Norton, 1932.

——. *The Poetry of History*. New York: Columbia University Press, 1947.

O'Connor, John J. *The Catholic Revival in England*. New York: Macmillan, 1942.

Ollard, Sidney Leslie. *A Short History of the Oxford Movement*. London: A. R. Mowbray, 1915.

Osborne, John W. *William Cobbett: His Thought and His Times*. New Brunswick: Rutgers University Press, 1966.

Palgrave, Sir Francis. *The Collected Historical Works of Sir Francis Palgrave*. Edited R. H. Inglis Palgrave. 10 vols. Cambridge: Cambridge University Press, 1919–1922.

Patton, Julia. *The English Village: A Literary Study, 1750–1850*. New York: Macmillan, 1919.

Peacock, Thomas Love. *The Works of Thomas Love Peacock*. Edited by H. F. B. Brett-Smith and C. E. Jones. Halliford edition. 10 vols. London: Constable, 1924.

Peardon, Thomas Preston. *The Transition in English Historical Writing, 1760–1830*. New York: Columbia University Press, 1933.

Peckham, Morse, ed. *Romanticism: The Culture of the Nineteenth Century*. New York: George Braziller, 1965.

Pemberton, W. Baring. *William Cobbett*. Penguin edition. Harmondsworth, Middlesex, 1947.

Percy, Thomas. *Reliques of Ancient English Poetry.* Edited by J. V. Pritchard. 3 vols. London, 1857.

Pope-Hennessy, Una. *Sir Walter Scott.* Denver: Alan Swallow, 1949.

Preraphaelite Diaries and Letters. Edited by William Michael Rossetti. London: Hurst and Blackett, 1900.

Pugin, Augustus Welby. *An Apology for the Revival of Christian Architecture in England.* London, 1853.

————. *Contrasts; or a Parallel between the Architecture of the Fifteenth and Nineteenth Centuries.* London, 1836.

————. *The True Principles of Pointed or Christian Architecture: Set Forth in Two Lectures Delivered at St. Mary's Oscott.* London, 1853.

Radcliffe, Ann. *The Mysteries of Udolpho.* 2 vols. Everyman edition. London and New York: J. M. Dent and E. P. Dutton, 1931.

Railo, Eino. *The Haunted Castle: A Study of the Elements of English Romanticism.* New York: Humanities Press, 1964.

Reeve, Clara. *The Progress of Romance and the History of Charoba, Queen of Aegypt.* Colchester edition. 1785. Reproduced with a bibliographical note by Esther M. McGill. New York: Facsimile Text Society, 1930.

Reilly, S. M. Paraclita. *Aubrey de Vere: Victorian Observer.* Lincoln, Neb.: University of Nebraska Press, 1957.

Reiss, H. S., ed. *The Political Thought of the German Romantics, 1793–1815.* Blackwell's Political Texts. New York: Macmillan, 1955.

Robb, Janet Henderson. *The Primrose League, 1883–1906.* New York: Columbia University Press, 1942.

Rosenberg, John D. *The Darkening Glass: A Portrait of Ruskin's Genius.* New York: Columbia University Press, 1961.

Ruggles, Thomas. *The History of the Poor.* 2 vols. London, 1793–1794.

Ruskin, John. *The Diaries of John Ruskin, 1835–1847.* Selected and Edited by Joan Evans and John Howard Whitehouse. Oxford: The Clarendon Press, 1956.

————. *The Diaries of John Ruskin, 1848–1873.* Selected and edited by Joan Evans and John Howard Whitehouse. Oxford: The Clarendon Press, 1958.

————. *The Works of John Ruskin.* Library edition. Edited by E. T. Cook and Alexander Wedderburn. 39 vols. London and New York: George Allen and Longmans Green, 1903–1912.

Ruskin: Rossetti: Pre-Raphaelitism: Papers 1854–1862. Arranged and edited by William Michael Rossetti. New York, 1899.

Saint-Simon, Comte Henri de. *Oeuvres choisies de Comte Henri de Saint-Simon.* 3 vols. Brussels, 1859.

————. *Oeuvres de Saint-Simon publieés par les membres du conseil institué par Enfantin.* Vols. I and III. Paris, 1868–1869.

Saintsbury, George. "The Young England Movement," in *Miscellaneous Essays.* New York, 1892.

Salomon, Gottfried. *Das Mittelalter als Ideal in der Romantik.* Munich: Drei Masken Verlag, 1922.

Samuels, Ernest. *Henry Adams: The Major Phase.* Cambridge, Mass.: Havard University Press, Belknap Press, 1964.

————. *Henry Adams: The Middle Years.* Cambridge, Mass.: Harvard University Press, Belknap Press, 1958.

————. *The Young Henry Adams.* Cambridge, Mass.: Harvard University Press, 1948.

Schlegel, Frederick von. *The Philosophy of History.* 3 vols. Vol. II. Translated by James Burton Robertson. London, 1835.

Scott, Sir Walter. *The Letters of Sir Walter Scott.* Edited by H. J. C. Grierson. 12 vols. London: Constable & Co., 1932–1937.

————. *The Miscellaneous Prose Works of Sir Walter Scott.* Vol. VI. Boston, 1829.

————. *Poetical Works.* 12 vols. Edinburgh, 1833–1834.

————. *Waverley Novels.* 48 vols. Edinburgh, 1829–1833.

Shaw, George Bernard. *William Morris As I Knew Him.* New York: Dodd Mead, 1936.

Shine, Hill. *Carlyle and the Saint-Simonians. The Concept of Historical Periodicity.* Baltimore, Md.: Johns Hopkins Press, 1941.

————. *Carlyle's Early Reading, to 1834, with an Introductory Essay on his Intellectual Development*. Occasional Contribution, no. 57. Lexington, Ky.: University of Kentucky Libraries, 1953.

Sir Walter Scott Lectures, 1940–1948. Edited by Sir Herbert Grierson, Edwin Muir, G. M. Young, S. C. Roberts. Edinburgh: Edinburgh University Press, 1950.

Smart, William. *Economic Annals of the Nineteenth Century, 1801–1820*. 2 vols. London: Macmillan, 1910–1917.

Smith, Paul. *Disraelian Conservatism and Social Reform*. London and Toronto: Routledge and Kegan Paul and University of Toronto Press, 1967.

―――. "The Young England Movement." Ph.D. dissertation, Columbia University, 1951.

Somervell, D. C. *Disraeli and Gladstone: A Duo-Biographical Sketch*. New York: George H. Doran, 1926.

Southey, Robert. *The Book of the Church*. 2 vols. London, 1825.

―――. *The Complete Poetical Works*. Collected by himself. New York, 1850.

―――. *Essays*. Collected by J. M. B. 3 vols. Tunbridge Wells, 1853.

―――. *Essays, Moral and Political*. 2 vols. London, 1832.

―――. *Joan of Arc: An Epic Poem*. Bristol, 1796.

―――. *Selections from the Letters*. Edited by John Wood Warter. 4 vols. London, 1856.

―――. *Sir Thomas More; or Colloquies on the Progress and Prospects of Society*. 2 vols. London, 1829.

―――, and Southey, Caroline. *Robin Hood: A Fragment*. Edinburgh, 1847.

Spacks, Patricia Meyer. *The Insistence of Horror: Aspects of the Supernatural in Eighteenth-Century Poetry*. Cambridge, Mass.: Harvard University Press, 1962.

Stevenson, Elizabeth. *Henry Adams: A Biography*. New York: Macmillan, 1955.

Stuart, Gilbert. *View of Society in Europe*. 2nd ed. London, 1782.

Summers, Montague. *The Gothic Quest: A History of the Gothic Novel*. New York: Russell and Russell, 1964.

Thackeray, William Makepeace. *The Works of William Makepeace Thackeray*. Vol. XX. London: Smith, 1911.

Thompson, E. P. *William Morris: Romantic to Revolutionary*. London: Lawrence and Wishart, 1955.

Thompson, James Westfall. *A History of Historical Writings*. New York: Macmillan, 1942.

Thompson, Paul. *The Work of William Morris*. New York: Viking, 1967.

Thomson, James. *The Complete Poetical Works of James Thomson*. Edited by J. Logie Robertson. Oxford: Oxford University Press, 1908.

Traill, Henry Duff, ed. *Social England*. Vol. V. New York, 1896.

Trappes-Lomax, Michael. *Pugin: A Mediaeval Victorian*. London: Sheed and Ward, 1933.

Turner, Sharon. *The History of the Anglo-Saxons from the Earliest Period to the Norman Conquest*. 5th ed. 3 vols. London, 1828.

Walzel, Oskar. *German Romanticism*. Translated by Alma Elise Lussky. New York: G. P. Putnam's Sons, 1932.

Warton, Thomas. *The History of English Poetry*. London, 1870.

Welland, D. S. R. *The Pre-Raphaelites in Literature and Art*. New York: Barnes and Noble, 1953.

Wellek, René. *The Rise of English Literary History*. Chapel Hill, N. C.: University of North Carolina Press, 1941.

Welsh, Alexander. *The Hero of the Waverley Novels*. Yale Studies in English. Vol. 154. New Haven: Yale University Press, 1963.

Whibley, Charles. *Lord John Manners and His Friends*. 2 vols. Edinburgh and London: Blackwoods, 1925.

Wilenski, R. H. *John Ruskin: An Introduction to Further Study of His Life and Work*. New York: Frederick A. Stokes, 1933.

Wilson, David Alec. *Carlyle at His Zenith* (1848–1853). London: Paul, 1927.

——, and MacArthur, David Wilson. *Carlyle in Old Age*. London: Kegan Paul, 1934.

——. *Carlyle on Cromwell and Others* (1837–1848). London: Kegan Paul, Trench, Trubner, 1925.

————. *Carlyle till Marriage* (1795–1826). London: Kegan Paul, Trench, Trubner, 1923.

————. *Carlyle to "The French Revolution"* (1826–1837). London: Kegan Paul, Trench, Trubner, 1924.

————. *Carlyle to Threescore and Ten* (1853–1865). London: Kegan Paul, Trench, Trubner, 1929.

Wood, Esther. *Dante Gabriel Rossetti and the Pre-Raphaelite Movement.* London, 1894.

Wordsworth, William. *The Poetical Works of Wordsworth.* New ed. Revised by Ernest de Selincourt. London: Oxford University Press, 1950.

————. *The Prose Works of William Wordsworth.* Edited by Alexander B. Grosart. 3 vols. London, 1876.

————, and Wordsworth, Dorothy. *The Early Letters of William and Dorothy Wordsworth (1787–1805).* Arranged and edited by Ernest de Selincourt. Oxford: The Clarendon Press, 1935.

————. *The Letters of William and Dorothy Wordsworth: the Later Years (1820–1850).* Arranged and edited by Ernest de Selincourt. 3 vols. Oxford: The Clarendon Press, 1939.

————. *The Letters of William and Dorothy Wordsworth: the Middle Years (1806–1820).* Arranged and edited by Ernest de Selincourt. 2 vols. Oxford: The Clarendon Press, 1937.

Young, Arthur. *An Inquiry into the Propriety of Applying Wastes to the Better Maintenance and Support of the Poor.* Bury, 1801.

Young, Arthur B. *The Life and Novels of Thomas Love Peacock.* Norwich: A. H. Goose, 1904.

Yvon, Paul. *Le Gothique et la renaissance gothique en Angleterre (1750–1880).* Caen: Jouan et Bigot, 1931.

Index

Abbot, The (Scott), 45, 48

Abbotsford, 50, 186

Abelard, Peter, 246

Adams, Brooks, 242 and *n.*, 243 and *n.*

Adams, Henry, 183, 195, 233, 234–248; on anarchism, "vehicles of," 244, 245, 246, 247; on Aquinas, 242, 246, 247; on degradation as law of history, 243; in Germany, 237; Lowell's influence on, 235; pessimism of, 248; and Ruskin, 236–237; Scott's influence on, 234; as teacher at Harvard, 239–240; on Virgin Mary, 244, 245, 246, 247

Adams, Marian Hooper, 238 and *n.*

Aelfric, 14

Agincourt, Battle of, 72

Agrarian Age (MacLean), 58 *n.*

Agrarianism, 77, 78, 79, 82 *n.*, 112, 183

Aidan, Francis, 66 *n.*

Akenside, Mark, 19 and *n.*, 23, 24 *n.;* quoted, 19, 22, 23–24

Alfred, King, 25, 69, 75, 85, 87, 88, 101

Allen, B. Sprague, 16 *n.*, 185 *n.;* quoted, 186

American Revolution, 73

Anarchism, "vehicles of" (Adams), 244, 245, 246, 247

Anatomy of Melancholy (Burton), 155

Ancient English Metrical Romances (Ritson), 27

Anderson, Thornton, 243 *n.*

Anglican church, 13, 14, 64, 154

Anglo-Catholic revival, 158, 160, 161, 215

Anglo-Saxon chronicles, 14

Anglo-Saxon law, 240

Anglo-Saxon psalter, 14

Anne of Geierstein (Scott), 31, 34, 42, 43

Antiquarian societies, 135

Antiquary, The (Scott), 210

Antiquities of Warwickshire (Dugdale), 16

Anti-Scrape (SPAB), 218, 219

Apologia Pro Vita Sua (Newman), 155 *n.*

Apology for the Revival of Christian Architecture in England, An (Pugin), 189 and *n.*

Apprentice system, 57, 79

Aquinas, St. Thomas, 96, 98, 155, 242, 246, 247

Arkwright, Richard, 122, 148

Arnold, Matthew, 163, 232, 233 and *n.*

Arthur of the English Poets, The (Maynadier), 232 and *n.*

Artisans' Dwelling Bill, 181

Asser, 14

Assize of Bread, 57

Attlee, Clement, 229

Aubrey de Vere (Reilly), 157 *n.*

265

Austen, Jane, 116
Autobiography (Mill), 114 *n.*
Awakened Conscience, The (Hunt), 194

Baillie-Cochrane, Alexander, 159 and
   n., 166, 169; quoted, 159
Baker, Joseph Ellis, 158 *n.*
Ball, John, 80, 103, 225, 226, 227, 228
Ballads, Scott's interest in, 27
Bannatyne society, 15, 27
Barbauld, Anna Letitia, 82 *n.*
Barbour, John, 27
Barchester Towers (Trollope), 163
Barnes, William, 232
Baym, Max, 240
Beattie, James, 19 and *n.*, 22 *n.*, 24 *n.;*
   quoted, 19
Becket (Tennyson), 232
Becket, Thomas à, 153
Beckford, Henry, 186
Berlin-Jena group, 127
Betrothed, The (Scott), 48
Bevis of Hampton, 13
Bible of Amiens, The (Ruskin), 207
Black Death, 223
Blackstone, William, 81
Blackwood's Magazine, 49, 159 *n.*
Blair, Robert, 19
Blake, Robert, 167 and *n.*, 181 and *n.*
Blake, William, 19, 80
Bonald, Louis de, 132, 155
Book of the Church (Southey), 103 *n.*
Boon work, 122
Bopp, Franz, 126
Borthwick, Peter, 159
Bowles, William Lisle, 114 and *n.*
Brinton, Crane, 49 *n.*
British Labour party, 229
Broad Stone of Honour, The (Digby),
   155 and *n.*, 160 and *n.*
Brooke, Stopford, 238

Brooks Adams (Anderson), 243 *n.*
Brown, Ford Madox, 192, 194
Browning, Robert, 214, 232
Bruce (Barbour), 27
Buckle, George Earl, 168 *n.*
Buller, Charles, 135
Burdett, Francis, 87
Burke, Edmund, 29 and *n.*, 39, 46 and
   n., 47, 48, 94, 134, 152, 160, 168, 199,
   205
Burne-Jones, Edward, 211, 212, 213
Burne-Jones, Georgiana, 211 *n.*
Burns, Robert, 19, 144
Burton, Robert, 155
Butterfield, William, 190

Cade, Jack, 30
Caedmon, 14
Calder, Grace J., 136 and *n.*
Calidore (Peacock), 117
Cambridge, 14, 160
Camden, William, 14
Camden antiquarian society, 135, 136,
   190
Canterbury Tales (Chaucer), 27
Capitalism, 219, 220, 221, 226; paternalistic, 133
Captain Swing, 80, 121
Carlyle, Thomas, 12, 43, 51, 62, 81, 109,
   110, 122–131, 132, 133–151, 152,
   160, 174, 178, 182, 187, 194, 195, 196,
   236; Cobbett's influence on, 134–135;
   faith as key to medievalism of, 144–
   145; and German idealism, 123, 124,
   125, 126, 127, 131; on hero worship,
   126, 127, 128, 141, 142, 144, 146, 152,
   233; materialism opposed by, 124;
   and new feudalism, 147; order
   sought by, 128, 130; quoted, 130–
   131, 134, 137, 139, 141, 143, 146, 217;
   on work, 217

Carlyle (Cazamian), 125 *n.*
Carlyle (Neff), 124 *n.*
Carnall, Geoffrey, 105 *n.*
Cartwright, John, 87
Casaubon, Isaac, 14
Castle Dangerous (Scott), 42, 48
Castle of Otranto, The (Walpole), 20, 186
"Cathedral, The" (Lowell), 235
Catholic Emancipation, 64, 95, 99, 100, 108
Catholicism, Roman, 19, 65, 72, 84, 96, 100–101, 128, 132, 155, 157, 165, 178, 192
Cazamian, Louis, 125 *n.*
Cervantes, Miguel de, 229
Champeaux, William of, 246
Chartism (Carlyle), 174
Chartist movement, 174, 224
Chatterton, Thomas, 18
Chaucer, Geoffrey, 13, 27
"Childe Rolande" (Browning), 232
Chivalry: and medievalism, 195; Ruskin's conception of, 195, 206; Scott's attitude toward, 38–39, 48, 233
"Christabel" (Coleridge), 91
Christenheit oder Europa, Die (Novalis), 127, 129
Chronica Jocelini de Brakelonda, 136
Chronicles, Anglo-Saxon, 14
Chronicles (Froissart), 27
Church Building Act (1818), 187
Church of England, 99, 160, 165, 189
Churchill, Randolph, 158
Cimabue, Giovanni, 192, 193, 197
Clapham, J. H., 54 *n.*, 56, 57 *n.*
Clark, Kenneth, 184 and *n.*, 190 *n.*
Cobbett, James P., 62 *n.*, 64 *n.*, 65 *n.*
Cobbett, John M., 62 *n.*, 64 *n.*, 65 *n.*
Cobbett, William, 59–82, 83, 94, 95, 99,

109, 110 *n.*, 112, 119, 122, 123, 145, 152, 160, 166, 177, 178 and *n.*, 180, 182, 196, 224; Carlyle influenced by, 134–135; militarism opposed by, 74; paternalistic views of, 78–79, 82; pro-Catholic medievalism of, 64, 65, 67 *ff.*, 71–73, 74; quoted, 60–61, 63–64, 66–67, 71, 77, 165, 179; as Radical, 61, 70–71, 78; as Tory, 61, 78
Coincy, Gaultier de, 241
Cole, G. D. H., 62 *n.*, 65 and *n.*, 75 *n.*, 82 *n.*, 135 *n.*
Cole, Margaret, 62 *n.*, 75 *n.*, 135 *n.*
Coleridge, Samuel Taylor, 30 and *n.*, 58, 85 and *n.*, 87, 91–98, 98 *n.*, 99, 100, 104 *n.*, 110, 116, 134, 160, 161, 202, 233; quoted, 30, 92, 93, 96, 97
Collection of Old Ballads (Philips), 16
Collinson, James, 193
Colloquies (Southey), 108 and *n.*, 110, 112, 113, 114, 118, 195, 223
Commines, Philippe de, 27
Communist Manifesto, The, 199
Comte, Auguste, 240
Coningsby (Disraeli), 163, 169, 171, 173, 174, 176, 180
Consolidations Act (1878), 181
Constitution of Church and State (Coleridge), 100, 134
Contractualism, and Hallam, 88
Contrasts (Pugin), 187–188
Co-operatives, 112
Corn Laws, 158, 166, 171
Cornelius, Peter von, 191, 192
Correspondence of Thomas Carlyle and Ralph Waldo Emerson 138 *n.*
Cottage Economy (Cobbett), 224
Cottage system, 77
Cottle, Joseph, 85
Cotton, Robert, 14
Coulton, G. G., 80 and *n.*

Count Robert of Paris (Scott), 31, 34
Cowper, William, 19
Crécy, Battle of, 72
Critical and Historical Essays (Macaulay), 113 *n.*
Croker, John Wilson, 170
Cromwell, Oliver, 15, 73, 138, 147 *n.*
Crotchet Castle (Peacock), 119, 121
Cullum, John, 90 and *n.*, 114
Culture and Anarchy (Arnold), 163

Dante Alighieri, 98, 238
Darwinism, 234
De Laudibus Legum Angliae (Fortescue), 67
De Lisle, Ambrose Phillipps, 157, 169, 171
De Vere, Aubrey, 157
"Defense of Guenevere, The" (Morris), 214
Defoe, Daniel, 185
"Deserted Village, The" (Goldsmith), 94
Determinism, 233, 247
Diaries of John Ruskin, 195 *n.*, 197 *n.*, 201 *n.*
Dickens, Charles, 163, 164, 231 and *n.*
Digby, Kenelm, 155 and *n.*, 156, 157, 160 and *n.*, 161, 211; quoted, 156
Disraeli, Benjamin, 47, 48, 150, 158, 159, 163, 165, 166, 167–183, 196, 219; as prime minister, 181–183; quoted, 167, 171, 172, 174–175, 177, 178, 179, 180; Tory-Radicalism of, 180
Disraeli (Blake) 167 *n.*, 181 *n.*
Dissenters, 84
Doctors of Philosophy and Doctors of Science of Harvard University, 240 *n.*
Dream of John Ball, A (Morris), 214, 219, 224, 227
Dugdale, William, 16
Dyce, William, 192

Early Kings of Norway, The (Carlyle), 147
Early Letters of Thomas Carlyle, 137 *n.*
Earthly Paradise, The (Morris), 228
Eastern Question Association, 219
Eastlake, Charles, 190 and *n.*, 191 and *n.*
Ecclefechan, Scotland, 122, 136
Ecclesiastical Sonnets (Wordsworth), 99
Economic History of England, The (Lipson), 55 *n.*, 57 *n.*
Economic History of Modern Britain, An (Clapham), 54, 57 *n.*
Eden, Frederick Morton, 56 and *n.*, 90 and *n.;* quoted, 91
Edinburgh, 122, 123, 136
Edinburgh Review, 113
Education of Henry Adams, The, 234 *n.*
Edward the Confessor, 241
Edward III, 57, 89
Edwin, King, conversion of, 99
Eggar, J. Alfred, 55 *n.*
Eliot, Charles, 239
Eliot, George, 56
Elizabethan era, 12, 66
Ellis, George, 27
Elton, Oliver, 138 *n.*
Emerson, Ralph Waldo, 138
Employers and Workmen Bill, 181
Enclosure acts, 13, 54, 93, 94 *n.*
England in Transition (George), 54 *n.*, 61 *n.*
England's Trust (Manners), 161 and *n.*, 162
English Utilitarians, The (Stephen), 46 *n.*
Enlightenment, 191
Erastianism, 153, 156
Essays (Macaulay), 113 *n.*
Essays (Southey), 107 *n.*
Essays in Anglo-Saxon Law (Adams), 240, 241 *n.*

Esther (Racine), 239

Evan, Evan, 16

Evergreen (Ramsay), 16

Faber, Frederick, 160, 161

Fabianism, 229

Fair Maid of Perth, The (Scott), 28, 42, 43, 48

"Farewell to Feudalism" (Froude), 154, 157

Farnham Castle, 59

Farnham Common, 60

Faust (Goethe), 126

Ferrand, William Busfield, 159, 166

Feudalism, 28, 33, 39, 51, 88, 92, 106, 115, 119, 149, 164, 167, 207, 208, 222; as aspect of medievalism, 195; and capitalism, dividing point between, 220; and democracy, conflict between, 108; vs. liberal-utilitarian ethic, 154

Fichte, Johann Gottlieb, 125, 127, 131, 133, 140

"Fine Arts in Florence" (Palgrave), 135 *n.*, 238

"First Gothic Revival and the Return to Nature, The" (Lovejoy), 23 *n.*

Flores Historiarum (Roger of Wendover), 21

Foedera (Rymer), 14

Fonthill, Beckford's, 186

Ford, Worthington C., 234 *n.*, 236 *n.*, 237 *n.*, 241 *n.*, 244 *n.*

Fors Clavigera (Ruskin), 205, 207, 208, 209

Fortescue, 67, 69

Foxe, John, 13

Frederick the Great, 147 *n.*

Freeman, Edward, 221, 240

French Revolution, 41, 50 and *n.*, 73, 102, 103, 112, 128, 224

Friedrich, Caspar David, 191

Froissart, Jean, 27

Froude, Hurrell, 153, 155, 157; quoted, 154

Froude, James Anthony, 134 *n.*

Galileo, 98 *n.*

Gandhi, Mahatma, 230

Gaskell, Charles Milnes, 238

Gaskell, Elizabeth, 163

Gasquet, Francis Aidan, 80 *n.*

Gemälde beschreibungen aus Paris und den Niederlanden (Schlegel), 191

General View of the Agriculture of the County of Surrey (James and Malcolm), 59 *n.*

Gent, Thomas, 16 and *n.*, 185

George, M. Dorothy, 54 *n.*, 61 *n.*

George IV, 49, 67

German Romance (Carlyle), 127

Germania (Tacitus), 43

Geschlossene Handelsstaat (Fichte), 125, 133

Giorgione, 204

Giotto, 192, 193, 197

Glorious Revolution (1688), 85, 88

God, views on, 123, 124, 125, 196, 201, 202, 205, 208, 244, 245, 246, 247

Goethe, Johann Wolfgang von, 28, 29, 30, 39, 40, 125, 126, 131, 140, 205, 235; quoted, 29

Golden Treasury, The, 238

Goldsmith, Oliver, 19, 94

"Goody Blake and Harry Gill" (Wordsworth), 98 and *n.*

Gothic architecture, 13, 18, 23, 116, 185, 186, 187, 190, 202, 203, 231, 235

Gothic novel, 20–21, 23, 26, 116, 133, 231

Gothic Revival, 184, 186, 191, 212, 231, 238

Gothic Revival, The (Clark), 184 and *n.*, 190 *n.*

"Goths" (Coleridge), 92

Götz von Berlichingen (Goethe), 28, 29, 39, 48, 127

Grant, Ulysses Simpson, 241

Graveyard Poetry, 18–19, 20, 33, 184, 200

Gray, Thomas, 14, 19, 235

Great Expectations (Dickens), 231

Greeks, 92

Green, John Richard, 221

Grimm, Jacob, 126

Guild system, 57, 220, 221, 222

Guy of Warwick, 13

Halévy, Elie, 53 *n.*, 54

Hall, Edward, 13

Hallam, Henry, 88 and *n.*, 89, 90 and *n.*, 92, 93, 114, 160

Hammond, J. L. and Barbara, 54 *n.*

Hansard's *Parliamentary Debates*, 67, 165 and *n.*

Hard Times (Dickens), 163, 231

Hardy, Thomas, 56, 232

Harleian Miscellany, 14

Harley, Robert, 14

Harold (Southey), 103

Harold (Tennyson), 232

Harold the Dauntless (Scott), 34

Harrison, Frederic, 207

Hart, Francis R., 38 *n.*

Harvard Magazine, 236

Hauréau, Bartelemy, 242

"Haystack in the Flood" (Morris), 228

Headlong Hall (Peacock), 115

Heart of Midlothian, The (Scott), 32

Heir of Redclyffe, The (Yonge), 211

Henderson, Philip, 212 *n.*, 215 and *n.*, 219 *n.*

Henry, Robert, 15, 28

Henry II, 154

Henry VI, 67, 89

Henry VI (Shakespeare), 30

Henry VII, 185

Henry VIII, 14, 60, 66, 73, 96, 174

Henry Adams (Stevenson), 244 *n.*

Henry Adams and His Friends, 239 *n.*

Herder, Johann Gottfried, 27, 125, 126 and *n.*, 129

Hereward the Wake (Kingsley), 232

Heroes and Hero Worship (Carlyle), 146

Herzergiessungen eines Kunstliebenden Klosterbruder (Wackenroder), 191

Hickes, George, 14

Historical novel, 21, 231

History and Antiquities (Cullum), 90 and *n.*

History of England (Lingard), 65

History of England (Macaulay), 24–25, 113, 114 *n.*

History of England (Rapin-Thayras), 21

History of England (Turner), 67

History of English Poetry (Warton), 17 and *n.*

History of German Literature (Carlyle), 125, 130 *n.*, 140

History of Parliament (Cobbett), 67

History of the Anglo-Saxons (Turner), 28, 85 and *n.*, 87

History of the English People in the Nineteenth Century (Halévy), 53 *n.*

History of the Gothic Revival (Eastlake), 190, 191 and *n.*

History of the Poor (Ruggles), 90 and *n.*

History of the Protestant Reformation in England and Ireland (Cobbett), 66 and *n.*, 67, 68, 70, 75, 79, 80 *n.*, 134–135, 178 *n.*, 179 and *n.*

Homer, 17

Houghton, Walter E., 153 *n.*

House of the Wolfings, The (Morris), 228

Howitt, William, 55 and *n.*, 56 *n.*
Hundred Years' War, 104
Hungry Forties, 161, 174
Hunt, Henry, 87
Hunt, William Holman, 192 and *n.*, 193, 194
Hurd, Richard, 17 and *n.*, 22, 160

Idealism, German, 123, 124, 125
Idylls of the King (Tennyson), 232
Industrial Revolution, 51, 87, 112, 123, 176
Inquiry into the Propriety of Applying Wastes to the Better Maintenance and Support of the Poor (Young), 60 *n.*
Insistence of Horror, The (Spacks), 20 *n.*
Ivanhoe (Scott), 28, 31, 34, 37, 38, 39, 41, 43, 47, 48, 145

Jacobinism, 116, 128, 152, 187
Jacqueries, 108, 111, 121
James, William, and Jacob Malcolm, 59 *n.*
James I, 15
Joan of Arc (Southey), 104 and *n.*, 105 and *n.*, 112
John, King, and Magna Carta, 88
Joy Forever, A (Ruskin), 204

Kapital, Das (Marx), 166 *n.*, 199, 219
Keats, John, 194
Kelmscott Press, 211, 229
King Lear (Shakespeare), 35
King of the Golden River, The (Ruskin), 204
King's Lesson, A (Morris), 228
Kingsley, Charles, 232
Kirkstall Abbey, 16, 185

Lady of the Lake, The (Scott), 27, 32, 33, 34, 48

Laissez faire, 81, 113, 133, 138, 150, 196, 204, 236
Lake Poets, 85, 91–113, 123, 152
Langley, Batty, 185
Laslett, Peter, 54 *n.*, 57 *n.*
"Last of the Flock, The" (Wordsworth), 98
Law of Civilization and Decay, The (Adams), 242 and *n.*, 243 *n.*
Lay of the Last Minstrel, The (Scott), 27, 32, 33
Lay Sermon Addressed to the Higher and Middle Classes (Coleridge), 93, 116
Learned Societies and English Literary Scholarship (Steeves), 83 *n.*
Legacy to Labourers (Cobbett), 79, 81 *n.*
Legacy to Parsons (Cobbett), 79
Leland, John, 14
Leland, Thomas, 21, 22
"Letter to Lord John Russell" (Cobbett), 68 *n.*
Letters of Henry Adams, 234 *n.*, 236 *n.*, 237 *n.*, 241 *n.*, 244 *n.*
Letters of Mrs. Henry Adams, 238 *n.*
Letters of Thomas Carlyle, 124 *n.*, 136 *n.*
Letters of William and Dorothy Wordsworth, 99 *n.*, 100 *n.*
Letters on Chivalry and Romance (Hurd), 17 and *n.*
Letters to His Wife (Carlyle), 138 *n.*
Lewes, John Frederick, 192
Liberalism, 153, 158, 181, 207
Liberty (Thomson), 24
Life of Alfred (Asser), 14
Life of Benjamin Disraeli (Monypenny and Buckle), 168 *n.*, 177 *n.*
Life of William Cobbett (Cole), 65 *n.*, 82 *n.*
Life of William Morris (Mackaill), 210 *n.*, 211 *n.*
Lindsay, Lord, 193, 198

Lingard, John, 65, 66, 80

Linguarum Veterum Septentrionalium Thesaurus Grammatico-Criticus et Archaeologicus (Hickes), 14

Lipson, E., 55 *n.*, 57 *n.*

Lockhart, John Gibson, 26 *n.*, 28 and *n.*, 48, 49 *n.*

London, 62, 110 *n.*, 136, 204

London Society of Antiquaries, 15

London Spy (Ward), 185

Longfellow, Henry Wadsworth, 235

Longsword, Earl of Salisbury (Leland), 21

Lord John Manners and His Friends (Whibley), 160 *n.*, 161 *n.*, 164 *n.*

Lovejoy, Arthur O., 23 *n*

Lowell, James Russell, 235 and *n.;* quoted, 235

"Lowther" (Wordsworth), 102

Lutheranism, 128

Lyra Apostolica, 154 and *n.*

Lyrical Ballads (Coleridge and Wordsworth), 98

Mabinogion, 118

Macauley, Catherine, 24, 86

Macauley, Thomas Babington, 89, 113 and *n.*, 114 *n.*, 115; quoted, 113–114

Mackail, J. W., 209, 210 *n.*, 211 *n.*

MacLean, Kenneth, 58 *n.*

Maclise, Daniel, 192

Macpherson, James, 18

Madoc (Southey), 107

Magna Charta, 88, 89

Maid Marian (Peacock), 117, 118

Maistre, Joseph de, 132, 155

Malcolm, Jacob, 59 *n.*

Mallet, David, quoted, 20

Malthus, Thomas R., 70, 86 *n.*

Manchester school, 205

Manners, Lord John, 42, 158–169 *passim*, 171, 172, 182, 212, 225; quoted, 161, 162, 164, 165

Marx, Karl, 166 *n.*, 199, 219, 220, 221 and *n.*, 222, 228, 234

Massachusetts Historical Society, 236, 242

Materialism, 124, 152, 155, 160, 183, 223, 233, 237

Maumus, Eli, 242 and *n.*

Maurice, Frederick Denison, 194

Maynadier, Howard, 232 and *n.*

Mead, George Herbert, 18

Medievalism, 195–196, 232, 233, 239, 248; in arts, 191, 192; and chivalry, 195; and Christian unity, 128; Cobbett's pro-Catholic, 64, 65, 67 *ff.*, 71–73, 74; emotion and tradition central to, 153; faith as key to Carlyle's, 144–145; and feudalism, 195; and Gothic Revival, 184; as ground for pessimism, 248; and naturalism, 195; as philosophy, 12; and primitivism, 23, 24, 25, 196; as program of resistance, 152; as transitional philosophy, 183; utilitarianism opposed to, 196; and utopianism, 102

Melincourt (Peacock), 116

Memoirs (Commines), 27

Memoirs of the Life of Sir Walter Scott (Lockhart), 26 *n.*, 28 *n.*, 49 *n.*

"Michael" (Wordsworth), 98 and *n.*

Michelet, Jules, 240

Mill, John Stuart, 91, 109, 114 and *n.*, 115, 129, 153, 236

Millais, John Everett, 193

Milnes, Richard Monckton, 159

Minstrelsy of the Scottish Border (Scott), 27

Misfortunes of Elphin (Peacock), 118

Mittelalter als Ideal in der Romantik, Das (Salomon), 131 *n.*

Modern Painters (Ruskin), 196, 198, 204, 211

Monastery, The (Scott), 45

Monasticism, 108 *n.*, 154, 212

Mont-Saint-Michel and Chartres (Adams), 183, 233, 234, 235, 236 237 and *n.*, 241, 242, 244, 247, 248

Monypenny, William Flavelle, 168 *n.*, 177 and *n.*

More, Thomas, 94 *n.*, 110, 223; in Southey's *Colloquies*, 108, 109

Morris, May, 224

Morris, William, 42, 112, 183, 195, 209–230; as artisan, 216, 217; in Iceland, 217; on nature, 210; at Oxford, 211; quoted, 213, 214, 220, 222–223, 225–226; revolution advocated by, 223, 227, 228; as socialist, 210, 217, 218, 219, 223, 233; as utopian, 227–228; on work, 217, 227

Morris and Company, 215, 216

Morte d'Arthur (Malory), 211

Munera Pulveris (Ruskin), 195

Mysteries of Udolpho, The (Radcliffe), 20, 21 and *n.*

Napoleonic Wars, 62, 128

Nationality (Coleridge), 96, 97

Natural History and Antiquities of Selborne (White), 67

Nazarene Brotherhood, 191–192, 193, 212

Neff, Emery, 124 *n.*

New Letters of Thomas Carlyle, 137 *n.*

New Oxford Illustrated Dickens, The, 231 *n.*

Newman, John Henry, 110, 155 and *n.*, 160

News from Nowhere (Morris), 219, 227

Nicholas Nickleby (Dickens), 164

Nightmare Abbey (Peacock), 116, 117

Northanger Abbey (Austen), 116, 239

Novalis, 125, 126, 127, 128, 129; quoted, 127–128

Novel and the Oxford Movement, The (Baker), 158 *n.*

Oastler, Richard, 180

O'Connell, Daniel, 68

Ode (Thomson), 25

"Ode to the Country Gentlemen of England" (Akenside), 23

Oeuvres choisies de Comte Henri de Saint-Simon, 132 *n.*

Old English Baron, The (Reeve), 21

Oldfield, T. H. B., 25

On the Constitution of the Church and State (Coleridge), 95

Open-field system, of English villages, 54, 221

Opinions of William Cobbett, The, 62 *n.*

Ossian poems (Macpherson), 18

Outlines of a Philosophy of the History of Man (Herder), 126 *n.*

Overbeck, Johann Friedrich, 191, 192, 193

Owen, Robert, 112

Oxford, 13, 14, 15, 16, 211

Oxford and Cambridge Magazine, 213

Oxford movement, 153, 155, 157, 160, 165

Palgrave, Francis, 135 and *n.*, 238 and *n.*

Palgrave, Francis Turner, 238

Pantisocracy, 106

Paris, Gaston, 241

Paris Commune, 224

Parker, Matthew, 14

Parliamentary Debates (Hansard), 67, 165 and *n.*

Parochial History of Bremhill (Bowles), 114 *n.*

Past and Present (Carlyle), 43, 51, 126, 129, 134, 135, 136, 137 and *n*., 138–140, 146, 147, 163, 164, 169, 174, 187, 211, 236 and *n*.

Patriot King, The, 84

Peacock, Thomas Love, 115–121; quoted, 116–117, 119, 120

Peardon, Thomas Preston, 25 *n*., 83 *n*.

Peel, Robert, 142, 158, 166, 170, 181

Percy, Thomas, 16, 17 and *n*., 22, 26, 103 *n*., 126; quoted, 17

Peterloo massacre, 224

Phantasien über Kunst (Wackenroder), 191

Philips, Ambrose, 16

Philosophy of History, The (Schlegel), 130 *n*.

Piers Plowman, 149

Pitt, William, 63, 74

Plantagenet, House of, 84

Plea for National Holy-Days, A (Manners), 42, 162, 163 *n*., 166, 225

Pleasures of England, The (Ruskin), 207

"Pleasures of Imagination, The" (Akenside), 19

Plough Monday, 56

Political Ideas of the English Romantics, The (Brinton), 49 *n*.

Poetical Works (Akenside and Beattie), 19 *n*., 22 *n*., 24 *n*.

Poetical Works (Arnold), 233 *n*.

Poetical Works (Lowell), 235 *n*.

Poetical Works (Scott), 29 *n*., 32 *n*.

Poetical Works (Southey), 103 *n*.

Poetical Works (Thomson), 24 *n*.

Poetical Works (Wordsworth), 98 *n*., 100 *n*., 101 *n*.

"Poor, The" (Southey), 107 *n*.

Poor Law, 101, 137, 165, 170, 171, 172, 188

Pope, Alexander, 19

Positivism, 234

"Prayer to the Virgin of Chartres" (Adams), 239, 247

Preface to *Lyrical Ballads* (Wordsworth), 98

Pre-Raphaelite Brotherhood, 191, 192, 193, 194, 238; second, 212, 213

Pre-Raphaelitism (Hunt), 192 *n*.

Primitivism: hard, 130, 232; and medievalism, 23, 24, 25, 196

Primrose League, The (Robb), 158 *n*.

Progress, analysis of doctrine of, 115, 116

Progress of Romance and the History of Charoba, The (Reeve), 22 *n*.

Progressivism, cyclic, 131

Prose Works (Wordsworth), 100 *n*.

Psalter, Anglo-Saxon, 14

Public Health Act (1875), 181

Pugin, Augustus Welby, 187, 188–189, 189 *n*., 190, 194, 218; quoted, 189

Puritanism, 84

Pusey, Edward, 154

Pye, Henry, 85

Quarterly Review, 103 *n*., 107 *n*.

Quentin Durward (Scott), 28, 31, 32, 34, 39, 40, 42, 43

Radcliffe, Ann, 21 and *n*., 33, 35

Ragnarok, 218, 228

Ramsay, Allan, 16, 26

Ranke, Leopold von, 240

Raphael, 193, 198

Rapin-Thayras, Paul de, 21

Rationalism, 123, 125, 128, 129, 153, 191

Reeve, Clara, 21, 22 and *n*., 33

Reflections on the Revolution in France (Burke), 29, 39, 47

Reform Bill (1832), 85, 100, 101, 142, 170

Reformation, 65, 66, 68, 69, 73, 74, 76, 79, 155, 165, 166, 178, 221
Reilly, S. M. Paraclita, 157 *n.*
Reiss, H. S., 128 *n.*
Reitzel, William, 60 *n.*, 62 *n.*
Religion: as basis for medieval greatness (Schlegel), 129–130; and cyclic progressivism, 131; Erastianism in, 153; essential in government (Carlyle), 145
Reliques of Ancient English Poetry (Percy), 16, 17 *n.*, 26, 27
Remains (Froude), 153
Remembrances of Life and Customs . . . (Eggar), 55 *n.*
Reminiscences by Thomas Carlyle, 134 *n.*
Renaissance, 203, 204
Rethel, Alfred, 191
Revolutionary Epick, The (Disraeli), 169
Richardson, Henry Hobson, 238
Rights of Man, The (Paine), 103
"Rime of the Ancient Mariner, The" (Coleridge), 91
Rio, Alexis François, 198
Rise of English Literary History, The (Wellek), 13 *n.*
Ritson, Joseph, 27
Rivers Pollution Act (1876), 181
Rob Roy (Scott), 28
Robb, Janet Henderson, 158 *n.*
Robert Southey and His Age (Carnall), 105 *n.*
Robin Hood (Ritson), 27, 117
Robin Hood (Robert and Caroline Southey), 106 and *n.*
Robin Hood's Garland, 117
Rochdale movement, 112
Roderick, Last of the Goths (Southey), 107
Roger of Wendover, 21

Rogers, Samuel, 19
Rogers, Thorold, 222
Roman Catholicism, 19, 65, 72, 84, 96, 100–101, 128, 132, 155, 157, 165, 178, 192
Romanticism, 23, 51, 80, 81, 83, 98, 101, 124, 125, 129, 159, 183, 191, 193, 230
Roots of the Mountains, The (Morris), 228, 229
Rossetti, Dante Gabriel, 192, 193, 194, 212
Rossetti, William Michael, 193 and *n.*, 194 *n.*
Rossetti (Ruskin), 194 *n.*
Rousseau, Jean Jacques, 178
Rowley poems (Chatterton), 18
Roxburghe society, 15, 27
Ruggles, Thomas, 90 and *n.*
"Ruined Cottage, The" (Wordsworth), 98
Runge, Philipp Otto, 191
Rural Life of England, The (Howitt), 55 and *n.*, 56 *n.*
Rural Rides (Cobbett), 75 and *n.*, 79, 135 and *n.*, 224
Ruskin, John, 12, 42, 49, 110, 135 *n.*, 159, 183, 188 and *n.*, 192, 193, 194 and *n.*, 195–209, 215–218 *passim*, 229, 230, 233, 236, 238; on largesse, 195, 206; on nature, 196, 197, 198, 199; on obedience, 199, 201, 207, 208, 209; on order of universe, 208, 209; on paternalism, 205, 209, 224; quoted, 198, 199, 200, 201, 203, 205–206; on sacrifice, 199, 203, 206
Rymer, Thomas, 14

Sabbatarianism, 166
Sacred History of the World, The (Turner), 88 *n.*

Sadler, Michael, 180

St. George's Guild, 206, 207, 208

St. Ronan's Well (Scott), 31

Saint-Simon, Claude Henri de, 132 and *n.*, 133, 139, 148, 240

Sale of Food and Drugs Act (1875), 181

Salomon, Gottfried, 131 *n.*

Samuels, Ernest, 237

Sartor Resartus (Carlyle), 51, 129

Saxon England, 84, 86 *n.*, 87, 88

Schlegel, Friedrich von, 125, 126, 127, 129, 130 *n.*, 155, 191

Scholasticism, 246

Scotland, 58, 122, 123

Scott, Gilbert, 190, 218

Scott, Walter, 12, 13, 15, 22, 25–28, 29 and *n.*, 30–51, 58, 85, 88, 94, 107, 111, 118, 122, 133, 134, 146, 152, 160, 204, 231, 240; attitude of, toward chivalry, 38–39, 48, 233; and concept of order, 31, 34, 41–42, 43; concern of, for freedom, 31, 37, 43; conservatism of, 46 *ff.;* quoted, 26, 32, 33, 35–36, 38–39, 40, 44, 45

Scott's Novels (Hart), 38 *n.*

Selected Speeches (Disraeli), 167 *n.*

Selections from Cobbett's Political Works, 62 *n.*, 64 *n.*, 65 *n.*

Seven Lamps of Architecture, The (Ruskin), 199, 206, 208

Shaftesbury, Lord, 64

Shakespeare, William, 104, 180

Shaw, George Bernard, 150, 229 and *n.*

Shenstone, William, 19, 22

Shrewsbury, Lord, 157, 172

Sigurd the Volsung, 218

"Sir Galahad" (Tennyson), 211

Sismondi, Jean Charles, 133

Six Centuries of Work and Wages (Rogers), 222

Sketches of the History of Christian Art (Lindsay), 193

Smart, Christopher, 19

Smart, William, 54 *n.*

Smith, Adam, 124, 156

Smythe, George, 159, 160, 163, 165, 166, 169, 172

Socialism, 133, 183, 217, 218

Society of Antiquarians, 14

Some Specimens of the Poetry of the Ancient Welsh Bards (Evan), 16

Southey, Robert, 12, 58, 77, 85 and *n.*, 102–113, 118, 134, 145, 146, 160, 166, 182, 187, 195, 223; order advocated by, 106; quoted, 103, 105, 106, 107, 109

SPAB (Anti-Scrape), 218, 219

Spacks, Patricia Meyer, 20 *n.*

Specimens of Early English Poets (Ellis), 27

Specimens of Early English Romances in Meter (Ellis), 27

Spirit of the Age, The (Mill), 114 *n.*

Spirit of Whiggism, The (Disraeli), 169

Staatslehre, Die (Fichte), 125

Stanton, George, 32

State of the Poor, The (Eden), 90 and *n.*, 91 and *n.*

Steeves, Harrison Ross, 83 *n.*

Stephen, Leslie, 46 and *n.*

Stephens, Frederick George, 193

Stevenson, Elizabeth, 244 and *n.*

Stones of Venice, The (Ruskin), 135 *n.*, 201–202, 203, 211, 224

"Story of an Unknown Church, The" (Morris), 213

Strawberry Hill, 186

Street, George Edmund, 190, 212

Strutt, Joseph, 15, 28

Stuart, Gilbert, 25

Stuarts, 84

Stubbs, William, 221, 240
Survey of English Literature, A (Elton), 138 n.
"Svend and His Brethren" (Morris), 213
Swinburne, Algernon Charles, 232, 237
Swing, Captain, 80, 121
Sybil (Disraeli), 169, 173, 174, 176, 179, 180, 181

Tacitus, Cornelius, 43, 130
Talisman, The (Scott), 31, 32, 48
"Tamworth Manifesto," 158
Ten Hours Bill, 180
Ten Medieval Studies (Coulton), 80 n.
Tennyson, Alfred, 157, 193, 211, 232, 235
Tennyson-D'Eyncourt, Charles, mansion of, 187 and n.
Thackeray, William Makepeace, 169; quoted, 52
Thirlage, 122
Thomas Aquinas, St., 96, 98, 155, 242, 246, 247
Thompson, Paul, 218 n.
Thomson, James, 19, 24 and n., 86, 221; quoted, 24
Tides in English Taste (Allen), 16 n., 185 n.
Tieck, Johann Ludwig, 127
"To the British Catholic Association" (Cobbett), 66 n., 67 n.
Tocqueville, Alexis de, 236
Tories, 83, 84, 87, 88; New, 157, 158
Tory democracy, 158, 180, 181
Tractarians, 154, 155
Tracts for the Times, 211
Transcendentalism, 234
Transition in English Historical Writing, The (Peardon), 25 n., 83 n.
Tristram and Iseult (Arnold), 232

Tristram of Lyonesse (Swinburne), 232
True Principles of Pointed or Christian Architecture (Pugin), 188, 189 n.
Tudor period, 13, 15, 16, 22
Tull, Jethro, 55
Turner, Joseph Mallord William, 204
Turner, Sharon, 15, 28, 67, 85 and n., 86, 87, 88 and n., 89, 160; quoted, 86
Tyler, Wat, 111, 224, 225

Unto This Last (Ruskin), 205, 230
Ussher, James, 14
Utilitarianism, 114, 152, 196, 199
Utopia (More), 94 n., 110, 223
Utopianism, 227–228; and medievalism, 102

Victorian Frame of Mind, The (Houghton), 153 n.
Victorian age, 12, 126, 151, 159, 162, 163, 169
View of the Middle Ages (Hallam), 88 and n., 92
Village Labourer, The (J. L. and Barbara Hammond), 54
Vindication of the English Constitution, The (Disraeli), 169
Viollet-le-Duc, Eugène, 218, 238
Virgin Mary, as "vehicle of anarchism" (Adams), 244, 245, 247
Vision of Judgment, A (Southey), 104

Wackenroder, Wilhelm, 127, 191
Wales, 68
Walpole, Horace, 20, 33, 186
Walters, John, 159, 169
Ward, Ned, 185
Wars of the Roses, 110
Warton, Thomas, 17 and n.
Wat Tyler (Southey), 103, 112

Waverley (Scott), 28, 32
Waverley Abbey, 16, 59
Waverley Novels (Scott), 31, 36 *n.*, 210
Welfare state, 233
Wellek, René, 13 *n.*
Wenlock Abbey, 238
Whibley, Charles, 160 *n.*, 161 *n.*, 164 *n.*
Whigs, 83, 84, 86, 88, 89, 114, 141
White, Gilbert, 67

William Morris (Henderson), 212 *n.*, 215 *n.*, 219 *n.*
William Morris (Shaw), 229 *n.*
William of Champeaux, 246
William of Wykham, 73
Witenagemot, 86, 87, 88
Wood, Anthony à, 15, 16
Woodford Hall, 209, 210
Woolner, Thomas, 193, 238
Wordsworth, Dorothy, 99 *n.*
Wordsworth, William, 25, 85 and *n.*, 98–102, 108, 111, 122, 160, 187; democracy feared by, 99; quoted, 101, 102

Works (Burke), 29 *n.*, 46 *n.*
Works (Carlyle), 123 *n.*, 129 *n.*, 135 *n.*, 147 *n.*, 217 *n.*
Works (Coleridge), 85 *n.*
Works (Disraeli), 168 *n.*, 179 *n.*
Works (Morris), 213 *n.*
Works (Palgrave), 238 *n.*
Works (Peacock), 115 *n.*
Works (Ruskin), 188 *n.*, 195 *n.*
World We Have Lost, The (Laslett), 54 *n.*, 57 *n.*
Writings of James Russell Lowell, The, 235 *n.*
Wycliffe, John, 99

Yarrow Revisited (Wordsworth), 100 *n.*
Yeomen, 59, 63, 67, 162, 223
Yonge, Charlotte, 211
Young, Arthur, 60 *n.*, 77
Young, Edward, 19
Young, G. M., quoted, 50 *n.*
Young England, 47, 48, 81, 158, 159, 160, 163, 165, 166, 167, 169, 173, 175, 180, 181, 182